BAUDELAIRE AND
THE POETICS OF CRAFT

BAUDELAIRE AND
THE POETICS OF CRAFT

GRAHAM CHESTERS

Senior Lecturer in French
University of Hull

The right of the
University of Cambridge
to print and sell
all manner of books
was granted by
Henry VIII in 1534.
The University has printed
and published continuously
since 1584.

CAMBRIDGE UNIVERSITY PRESS

Cambridge
New York   New Rochelle   Melbourne   Sydney

Published by the Press Syndicate of the University of Cambridge
The Pitt Building, Trumpington Street, Cambridge CB2 1RP
32 East 57th Street, New York, NY 10022, USA
10 Stamford Road, Oakleigh, Melbourne 3166, Australia

© Cambridge University Press 1988

First published 1988

Printed in Great Britain at the University Press, Cambridge

British Library cataloguing in publication data
Chesters, Graham
Baudelaire and the poetics of craft.
1. Baudelaire, Charles – Criticism and
interpretation
I. Title
841'.8   PQ2191.Z5

Library of Congress cataloging in publication data
Chesters, Graham.
Baudelaire and the poetics of craft.
Bibliography.
Includes index.
1. Baudelaire, Charles, 1821–1867 – Technique.
2. French language – Versification. I. Title.
PQ2191.Z5C45   1988   841'.8   87-15164

ISBN 0 521 22536 1

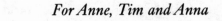

For Anne, Tim and Anna

'Il n'y a pas de hasard dans l'art, non plus qu'en mécanique.'

Baudelaire (II, 432)

'Il importe fort peu que la ruse et l'artifice soient connus de tous, si le succès en est certain et l'effet toujours irrésistible.'

Baudelaire (II, 717)

'. . . et il serait bien possible aussi, après tout, que les plus belles expressions du génie, ailleurs que dans le ciel pur, c'est-à-dire sur cette pauvre terre, où la perfection elle-même est imparfaite, ne pussent être obtenues qu'au prix d'un inévitable sacrifice.'

Baudelaire (II, 744)

'[Le dandysme] est avant tout le besoin ardent de se faire une originalité, contenu dans les limites extérieures des convenances.'

Baudelaire (II, 710)

CONTENTS

PREFACE

The aim of this book is to bring to awareness the principles underlying the skill with which Baudelaire satisfies and manipulates the demands of French versification and the skill with which he orchestrates the raw material of the French language within a formal framework: in short *la science du métier*. Chapter 1 looks at Baudelaire's view of the act of composition, through an analysis of his remarks on Poe's *Philosophy of Composition* and an examination of the multiple images of the poet at work that find their way into Baudelairean texts of all kinds. Chapters 2 and 3 attempt to demonstrate that sound repetition in Baudelaire has to be seen (or heard) in its convergence with other patterning forces, namely conventional verse-form and sense-structures. When the inessential (the sound pattern, other than rhyme) combines with the essential (verse-rules and sense) in a drive towards Order, then there is a formidable alliance against the threat of randomness. Chapter 4 attempts, through an investigation of some of Baudelaire's variants, to glimpse the craftsman at his bench, to share the critical moment of choice between different possible versions, and – most importantly – to weigh the shifts in effect. The focus complements that of Chapters 2 and 3 and falls on the manipulation of sound patterns in the process of composition. Chapter 5 changes direction in two ways: it moves from inessential sound patterns to the mandatory presence of rhyme (mandatory, that is, until the advent of the *vers libre*) and it largely abandons the analysis of poetic segments torn from their context in favour of an examination of whole poems. These two switches are related. Since rhyme is mandatory, the question is not so much why Baudelaire used it as how he used it, to what particular effect in what particular context. Unlike inessential sound patterns, which emerge and disappear unpredictably throughout a poem and are likely to have a specifically local effect, rhyme is intricated in a scheme which pervades the whole poem at every moment. Local effects exist, of course, but they need to be seen in relation to the effects of rhyme in neighbouring lines, stanzas or larger developments (including the complete poem). Rhyme as a necessary formal requirement contributes enormously to the sense of order and harmony that dominates French verse; some would say that without it French verse has never been the same. But that is to speak of rhyme almost as an abstraction. What I wish to look at is the function of rhymes, and to do that, one has to examine them in context. Whether talking of Rhyme or rhymes, no one will doubt their role in establishing pattern as a defining principle of French verse. The sound-repetitions analysed in the preceding chapters all participate in this search for Order. Chapter 6 considers the principle in theory, including patterns of syntax and structure and going beyond verse into the problematic domain of the prose-poem. The argument here stresses the critical fact that the dynamics of pattern must include the fracturing of pattern. Tension between form and formlessness permeates Baudelaire's work and is exploited to marvellous effect, giving body to an ironically lucid awareness of a (necessary?) imperfection. The perverse fracturing of pattern, and the search for the unexpected and the formally bizarre, have been judged harshly by some critics. Chapter 7 seeks to recuperate what others might deem to be lapses in poetic excellence but what I prefer to consider as evidence of an experimental poetics (born perhaps of a genuine creative difficulty experienced by Baudelaire). A similar spirit of experimentation imbues the material examined in the final two chapters, where I consider Baudelaire's response to the acute problem of marrying the traditional French verse-form with the pulsating newness, difference and energy of modern Paris.

Blocked in one paragraph, the above summary does not promise much of a 'plot'. If one were to press for the definition of a general principle underlying the book, then I would say that the tensions between harmony and dissonance, form and formlessness, pattern and fracture inform most of the arguments presented and can be seen as central to Baudelairean poetics. They are investigated in various lights (for example, the atomistic analysis of Chapters 2 and 3, the compositional angle of Chapter 4 or the diachronic approach in Chapters 8 and 9) and at various levels (the phonetic, the syntactical, the structural, the metrical). It is partly on account of this variety that the chapters (sometimes pairs of chapters) can be read as separate essays. But my hope is that the whole will convince as an appreciation of a poet's craft and the principles that sustain that craft.

ACKNOWLEDGEMENTS

Among the many people who have played a part in making the writing of this book possible, I should like particularly to thank the following: Dennis Plackett, Roy Lewis, Lloyd Austin, Felix Leakey and Alison Fairlie. My gratitude is also due to Michael Black of Cambridge University Press, whose encouragement has been invaluable; to the British Academy for funding some of the necessary research; to the Editorial Board of *French Studies* and to Cambridge University Press for permission to rework material already published (Chapters 8 and 9 respectively); and to the General Editor of the University of Hull Occasional Papers in Modern Languages for similar permission (Chapters 2 and 3). Finally, I should like to record my appreciation of the help given and kindnesses shown throughout the maturation of this book by Garnet Rees, whose no-nonsense love of poetry has been an inspiration to all those he taught and to all who were fortunate enough to be his colleagues.

NOTE ON THE TEXT

For references to all Baudelaire's texts (unless otherwise stated), I have used *Baudelaire, Œuvres complètes*, edited by Claude Pichois, Bibliothèque de la Pléiade, 2 vols (Paris: NRF, Gallimard), 1975–6, henceforth designated simply by I or II, followed by the page number. For his correspondence, references are made to *Baudelaire: Correspondance*, edited by Claude Pichois, Bibliothèque de la Pléiade, 2 vols (Paris: NRF, Gallimard), 1973, henceforth designated *Corres.*, followed by volume and page number.

1

THE POETICS OF CRAFT

Inspiration, work, chance

In a *Tel Quel* essay, Paul Valéry depicts a poet who, at one point in the midst of composition, lists his needs:

> Je cherche un mot (dit le poète) qui soit féminin,
> de deux syllabes,
> contenant P ou F
> terminé par une muette
> et synonyme de brisure, désagrégation,
> et pas savant, pas rare,
> Six conditions – au moins!   (1957–60, II, 676)

Whether poets do indeed search in this way for a particular word ('rupture' is generally held to be the solution here) is of course open to doubt, and Valéry himself stresses that the poetic act is not so much a search as a wait for the right expression:

Ainsi le poète en fonction est une attente . . . Nous attendons le mot inattendu –
et qui ne peut être prévu, mais attendu   (1957–60, I, 1448)

But the notion of *a priori* conditions governing poetic choice held a powerful fascination for many French poets in the last century, even though its most provocative articulation came from America in Poe's *Philosophy of Composition*, Baudelaire's translation of which, *La Genèse d'un poème*, was first published in 1859. Poe's essay purports to explain how he came to write his poem, 'The Raven', and is based on the premise that compositional imperatives (theme, scenario, protagonists, metre, refrain, phonetic dominants) can be established in advance through a process of supposedly rigorous reasoning. His aim, as rendered by Baudelaire in a vocabulary that recurs in his own writings, is to

démontrer qu'aucun point de la composition ne peut être attribué au hasard ou
à l'intuition, et que l'ouvrage a marché pas à pas, vers sa solution, avec la
précision et la rigoureuse logique d'un problème mathématique

1

Baudelaire and the poetics of craft

(Poe, 1951, 986; I shall use Baudelaire's translation for all quotations from *The Philosophy of Composition*)

The fact that few (if any) are prepared to believe that 'The Raven' was actually composed according to this process is not important (Baudelaire himself recognizes in the essay 'une légère impertinence', II, 335 and 'un peu de charlatanerie', II, 344); the essay is best seen as a piece of theoretical polemic which, like most polemic, has in its sights a particular contradictory view. That contradictory view is already implied in the statement of intent cited above and belongs to those who believe in the role of chance and intuition in the process of composition. Their allies in this misconception are in many cases, according to Poe, writers themselves:

Beaucoup d'écrivains, particulièrement les poètes, aiment mieux laisser entendre qu'ils composent grâce à une espèce de frénésie subtile ou d'intuition extatique.　　　　　　　　　　　　　　　　　　　　　(Poe, 1951, 985)

Reading these words for the first time, Baudelaire must have been struck yet again by the extraordinary affinity between himself and the American writer. For, several years earlier, in his *Conseils aux jeunes littérateurs* (1846), he had proclaimed with a youthful confidence:

L'orgie n'est plus la sœur de l'inspiration: nous avons cassé cette parenté adultère . . . L'inspiration est décidément la sœur du travail journalier. (II, 18)

The common ground is, in broad terms, clear: a mistrust of any emotional, effusive, Dionysian concept of poetic creativity and a promotion of a wilful, methodical act of craftsmanship. Baudelaire's impatience with the Dionysian view becomes more and more evident in his *Notes nouvelles sur Edgar Poe* (1857). Here he refers disparagingly to 'les partisans de l'inspiration', 'les fatalistes de l'inspiration' and 'les amateurs de hasard' (all II, 335), and assumes that it was for this group that *The Philosophy of Composition* had been written. In the preamble to his translation of Poe's poem and essay, Baudelaire again identifies their common adversaries, this time as 'les amateurs du *délire*' (II, 343, Baudelaire's italics). So both writers are advocating against a dominant, pseudo-Romantic perception of poetic creation, a perception sustained by the connivance of other writers who parade their intuitive power and receptivity to the products of chance.

The first paragraph of Baudelaire's preamble to *La Genèse d'un poème* raises questions that are central to his view of poetic composition, as well as offering some carefully phrased distancing from Poe's amusing disingenuousness. He begins by stressing the originality of Poe's *a priori* poetics:

2

The poetics of craft

La poétique est faite, nous disait-on, et modelée d'après les poèmes. Voici un poète qui prétend que son poème a été composé d'après sa poétique.

(II, 343)

The phrase 'qui prétend que' reveals immediately Baudelaire's suspicion that the 'genèse' is in a strict sense a fabrication. Out of anxiety lest his sentence should imply that Poe composes according to some kind of poetic recipe that excludes inspiration (a word that Poe largely avoids in his essay), Baudelaire insists on claiming for Poe both genius and inspiration, although he is careful to define the latter in his own terms:

Il avait certes un grand génie et plus d'inspiration que qui que ce soit, si par inspiration on entend l'énergie, l'enthousiasme intellectuel et la faculté de tenir ses facultés en éveil. (II, 343)

This definition is more Apollonian than Dionysian, suggesting cerebral excitement, a central mastery of the creative drama and an alertness which evokes waiting rather than searching. Baudelaire is (rightly) reluctant to exclude inspiration and, in this, is entirely consistent with the early *Conseils aux jeunes littérateurs* cited above: 'l'inspiration est . . . la sœur du travail journalier' (II, 18). If the third sentence of the preamble leaves the reader in no doubt as to Baudelaire's view of Poe and inspiration, the fourth sentence sings the companion virtues of work:

Mais il aimait aussi le travail plus qu'aucun autre; il répétait volontiers, lui, un original achevé, que l'originalité est chose d'apprentissage, ce qui ne veut pas dire une chose qui peut être transmise par l'enseignement. (II, 343)

Originality is not a matter of chance, nor is it the gift of destiny (as the 'fatalistes de l'inspiration' might have held). It is rather something that can be learnt (but not taught) – and the learning demands work. Work – as exemplified, one is meant to understand, in the composition of 'The Raven' – combines with inspiration not just in order to create but also to put to flight Poe's 'grands ennemis': 'le hasard et l'incompréhensible' (II, 343). Nothing must challenge the poet's mastery of means to achieve the desired effect: the deliberateness of craft allows no place for chance nor for any kind of random obscurity. The aleatory and the obscure may, at times, appear to be metaphysically ascendant, but not in the poet's universe.

Baudelaire's opening sentences portray Poe as the incarnation of his youthful *conseils*, but the imbalance of Poe's polemic with its eclipsing of inspiration still prompts Baudelaire to insist further on the American poet's genius:

3

S'est-il fait, par une vanité étrange et amusante, beaucoup moins inspiré qu'il ne l'était naturellement? A-t-il diminué la faculté gratuite qui était en lui pour faire la part plus belle à la volonté? Je serais assez porté à le croire; quoique cependant il faille ne pas oublier que son génie, si ardent et si agile qu'il fût, était passionnément épris d'analyse, de combinaisons et de calculs.   (II, 343)

The final qualification ('quoique cependant . . . ') ventures a reconciliation of natural inspiration and the methodical application of will by suggesting that a part of Poe's genius was precisely his love of method and calculation. The alliance between inspiration and work is all the more fruitful if inspiration *contains* the passion for work.

The paragraph closes with an indication of the essay's usefulness: it will show the 'amateurs du *délire*' the benefits of 'délibération' and to the reading public in general it will reveal 'quel labeur exige cet objet de luxe qu'on nomme Poésie'. 'Travail' has become the more arduous 'labeur' and the product of inspiration and work is finally named through the periphrastic 'objet de luxe qu'on nomme Poésie', highlighting its status as commodity and, by extension, hinting at the artist's role as worker–craftsman enmeshed in the cycles of supply and demand.

The use of the word 'travail' in Baudelaire's preamble betrays both a confusion and an obsession. The confusion arises in the equation of work with analysis and calculation; it is not obvious from the major part of *The Philosophy of Composition* that Poe's creative method involves the 'labeur' of which Baudelaire speaks. On the contrary, the impression that Poe deliberately creates is of a masterly scientific brain pursuing a series of reasonings in order to arrive with as little hindrance as possible at the desired outcome: the poem 'a marché pas à pas, vers sa solution, avec la précision et la rigoureuse logique d'un problème mathématique'. But the confusion is not entirely of Baudelaire's making, for in the early pages of his essay Poe presents a picture of poetic creation which sits ill with the dominant image of smooth achievement. Writers have good reason not to let the public take a glimpse backstage:

ils auraient positivement le frisson s'il leur fallait autoriser le public à jeter un coup d'œil derrière la scène, et à contempler les laborieux et indécis embryons de pensée, la vraie décision prise au dernier moment, l'idée si souvent entrevue comme dans un éclair et refusant si longtemps de se laisser voir en pleine lumière, la pensée pleinement mûrie et rejetée de désespoir comme étant d'une nature intraitable, le choix prudent et les rebuts, les douloureuses ratures et les interpolations – en un mot, les rouages et les chaînes, les trucs pour les changements de décor, les échelles et les trappes, – les plumes de coq, le rouge, les mouches et tout le maquillage qui, dans quatre-vingt-dix-neuf

4

cas sur cent, constituent l'apanage et le naturel de l'*histrion littéraire*.

(Poe, 1951, 985)

This evocative passage has been seen by Michael Black as a vital corrective to the whole notion of prior insight, chosen effect and swift access to available means; the suggestion here is rather that 'intentions are realized only in their working out and this is a laborious matter in which formulation is the end result, not a prior insight' (Black, 1975, 479). Baudelaire's use of the words 'travail', 'apprentissage' and 'labeur' is justified by this passage alone, the whole of which inspired a section of one of Baudelaire's *projets de préface* (to which I shall return).

Baudelaire's emphasis on work betrays an obsession too, touching on several levels: literary, social, personal and metaphysical. The notion of work as a necessary ingredient in producing the conditions for inspiration offers a direct refutation of the 'fine frenzy' myth of literary creation, but it also offers to the poet a chance to assimilate his activity with the socially acceptable activity of the worker. When Baudelaire designates poetry as an 'objet de luxe', he is talking the language of commerce, acknowledging his role as a lyric poet in an era of high capitalism.[1] By proclaiming the poet's need to toil at his task, he is marking out a place for him in the world of labour. One has, however, only to look into the *Journaux intimes* to realise how crucially important the concept of work became to Baudelaire's personal equilibrium, at once a torment and a panacea:

qu'il est *grandement temps* d'agir ... de faire ma *perpétuelle volupté* de mon tourment ordinaire, c'est-à-dire du Travail! (I, 668)

or again:

A chaque minute nous sommes écrasés par l'idée et la sensation du temps. Et il n'y a que deux moyens pour échapper à ce cauchemar, – pour l'oublier: le Plaisir et le Travail. Le Plaisir nous use. Le Travail nous fortifie. Choisissons.

(I, 669)

The poignant exhortations to the self show how close work comes to being synonymous with Good or the Ideal, a life-sustaining means of escaping Ennui. Work, as an exercise of the will, repairs the psyche, but, as a weapon to be used against 'le hasard et l'incompréhensible', it can be seen as an instrument of metaphysical as well as psychological importance.

The obsession with work relates to the metaphysical and aesthetic doctrine of eliminating randomness, a doctrine that was to attain its most profound literary expression in the writings of Mallarmé. What I have called Baudelaire's confusion is in fact a practical insight into the application of the doctrine in the domain of literary creativity: in most

5

poets (Poe suggests 99 per cent), randomness is eliminated from language through struggle (if at all). That struggle – and, amongst the equivocations of Baudelaire's preamble, this is the critical point – includes 'analyse', 'combinaisons', 'calculs', the 'admirable méthode' which consists of knowing one's conclusion before putting pen to paper, and the search for 'la rigoureuse logique d'un problème mathématique'. Poe's hyperbolically rational poet is simply one more role taken by the *histrion littéraire*: the slick show of reason hides the creative battles that fill the spaces between premise and realization. The fight against chance is waged with an armoury of inspiration ('énergie', 'enthousiasme intellectuel', 'la faculté de tenir ses facultés en éveil') and work ('méthode', 'analyse', 'combinaisons', 'labeur'). Together these two companions can exploit what Baudelaire calls, in a marvellous phrase from his *Conseils aux jeunes littérateurs*, the 'mécanique céleste' (II, 18) of the human mind. This concept marries the mechanistic view of poetic creation put forward polemically in *La Genèse d'un poème* with the more inspirational view which would see the poet as an apprehender of some necessary metaphysical pattern. It suggests ultimately a link between the pattern-making properties of the human brain and the divine order of the universe. Inspiration and work, by exploiting the 'mécanique céleste', will produce a poetry that seems as free from chance, as necessary as – say – the arrangement of seeds in a sunflower head or the workings of a machine. 'Il n'y a pas de hasard dans l'art, non plus qu'en mécanique,' argued Baudelaire in his *Salon de 1846* (II, 432), defending Delacroix against the charge that 'le hasard, honnête et complaisant serviteur du génie, joue un grand rôle dans ses plus heureuses compositions' (II, 430). This dismissal of chance predates Baudelaire's reading of Poe, and the whole passage anticipates remarkably *The Philosophy of Composition*, especially the precept that 'une chose heureusement trouvée est la simple conséquence d'un bon raisonnement', qualified in order to allow room for genius by 'dont on a quelquefois sauté les déductions intermédiaires' (II, 432).

An example of such a genius, for whom 'raisonnement' was not a matter of work, the one poet out of a hundred, was in Baudelaire's eyes Théophile Gautier. The Gautier whom Baudelaire portrays in his 1859 article (and whose method of composition may or may not correspond to that of the real Gautier) has such unparalleled linguistic resources that creative obstacles are brushed aside: he possesses a 'connaissance de la langue qui n'est jamais en défaut', an inner 'dictionnaire dont les feuillets, remués par un souffle divin, s'ouvrent tout juste pour laisser jaillir le mot propre, le mot unique' and a 'sentiment de l'ordre qui met chaque trait et chaque touche à sa place naturelle' (II, 117). The 'mécanique céleste' of Gautier's mind is made immediately accessible through the power of language – indeed it may consist of language. It is significant that Baudelaire conjoins linguistic knowledge and a sense of order, as if one were a consequence or a corollary of the other. He goes on to say that this sense of order presupposes 'une immense intelligence innée de la *correspondance* et du symbolisme universels' (II, 117). The poetic harmony of a word slotted into its proper place is, one infers, a simulacrum of a metaphysical pattern, a facsimile of a sacred harmony to which the great poet will attain with the ease of a *savant*–magician, and with a 'justesse qui ravit, qui étonne, et qui fait songer à ces miracles produits dans le jeu par une profonde science mathématique' (II, 118). Gautier's work partakes of the same mathematical precision as the creative process behind 'The Raven'. But, whereas Poe remains on the level of pure 'mathematical' reasoning, Baudelaire insists upon the link between linguistic, 'mathematical' skill and the apprehension of a metaphysical truth: 'il y a dans le mot, dans le *verbe*, quelque chose de *sacré* qui nous défend d'en faire un jeu de hasard' (II, 117–8). It is the *sacredness* of language that demands the elimination of chance and the cultivation of a mathematical 'justesse'.

This view of language implies – at least for most poets – a poetry born of deliberation and achieving its effect with deliberateness. While I do not presume, in the chapters that follow, to discover what Baudelaire intended or to claim that he intended every effect discussed, it is none the less broadly true that Baudelaire's poetry is a poetry of intention, 'où tout a sa raison d'être' (II, 432). To argue otherwise is to allow chance to reconquer lost ground. Even his less happy effects can be allowed to ignore the excuse of chance; it was Gautier himself who argued of Baudelaire: 'là même où il déplaît, il l'a voulu ainsi, d'après une esthétique particulière et un raisonnement longtemps débattu' (cited in Noyer-Weidner, 1976, 27).

The discussion of methods of composition has relied almost entirely on what Baudelaire and Poe said about the poetic task. Both are theorists, fascinated by their own poetics but not necessarily capable of realizing the theory they themselves expound. Poe's reconstruction of the way in which he supposedly composed 'The Raven' is no doubt fictitious and belongs to a world of provocation and wishful thinking; Baudelaire, while elevating 'Travail' to a principle of creativity, was all too often unable to find the will to carry out his programme. The discrepancy between theory and practice (examined in sections of Chapter 7), far from invalidating the theory or belittling the practice, actually enhances the interest of both. The reading of theory and practice through each other, as it were, offers an enticement. I find it tempting to view Baudelaire's entire writings as a single text, so that what he says about poetry and the poetic task is part of the same text as the poems themselves. The individual poem will naturally display a unity, a formal integrity that the entire work cannot possess; but that is to say no more than that the poem will give one kind of aesthetic experience (relating, for example, to an impression of order and necessity) and that the whole work will give another (relating, for example, to an impression of diversity, contradiction, affinity or even potential order and unity). Baudelaire's comments on poetry are to be found not just in his literary or art criticism but everywhere: his correspondence, his essays on intoxicants, and – perhaps most significantly – in the poems themselves (whether in prose or verse). Claude Pichois is right to stress that 'cette poésie est réflexive. Elle est réflexion du poète sur la nature et la fonction de la poésie ... la poésie devient à elle-même son objet' (I, 803). For Baudelaire, poetry is not a mere instrument but a theme in itself. So, in order to gain access to thematic understanding it becomes a necessity rather than an indulgence for the reader to explore the poet's view of his own activity. For Baudelaire, this activity was, to say the least, problematic. The images he uses to describe it and the roles adopted by the *histrion littéraire* are one particular form of theoretical reflection: they tend to focus our attention on a central idea, the concept of the working poet as an apprentice or skilled practitioner of a craft.

Images of the poet

In a late essay (1861), Baudelaire tells the story of a visit he had paid many years before to a poet friend, Gustave Le Vavasseur. He had found Le Vavasseur, half-naked, balancing precariously on a carefully stacked pile of chairs, trying to imitate the professional acrobats that he and Baudelaire had seen the evening before. The attempt, however manic, does not surprise Baudelaire, who recognises the affinity between the skill and performance of the *saltimbanque* and the verbal dexterity and *tours de force* of a virtuoso poet such as Le Vavasseur. As an 'amateur du subtil, du contourné', Le Vavasseur loves the intricate music of 'la rime triplée, quadruplée, multipliée', the 'jeu de mots ... la pointe faisant résumé et éclatant comme une fleur pyrotechnique' (II, 180). Such feats of verbal manipulation are indeed acrobatic, or perhaps have something in common with the horticulturalist (the *pointe* is cultivated like a flower), the firework-master ('fleur pyrotechnique') or even the brilliant swordsman (Baudelaire says later that they remind him of 'les ruses compliquées de l'escrime', II, 180). I shall come back to Baudelaire's tendency to sow his texts with multiple analogues of the poet-figure.

In another critical piece written the same year as his essay on Le Vavasseur, Baudelaire, attacking what he saw as the spontaneous banalities of 'la jeunesse réaliste', complains that 'elle [la jeunesse réaliste] ignore que le génie . . . doit, comme le saltimbanque apprenti, risquer de se rompre mille fois les os en secret avant de danser devant le public; que l'inspiration, en un mot, n'est que la récompense de l'exercice quotidien' (II, 183). (This final maxim is a close rewording, at fifteen years' distance, of 'L'inspiration est décidément la sœur du travail journalier.') Both the Le Vavasseur anecdote and the complaint against the careless writings of young Realist authors illustrate a double analogy: that of poet as performer and that of poet as seeker of skills (with the ambition of moving from apprentice to expert). The first involves the relationship between artist and public and leads into arenas of discussion largely explored already in fascinating essays by Jean Starobinski (1970), Walter Benjamin (1973) and Ross Chambers (1971a; 1971b). The second part of the analogy, the poet–creator engaged in dangerous apprenticeship (like Le Vavasseur balancing on his chairs), takes us back one step into the privacy of composition: the acrobat's practice, his perfection of a routine, are analogous to the poet's battles with his material before he finally arrives at a version which he can offer to his audience. 'L'originalité est chose d'apprentissage' (II, 343).

The figure of the poet–performer implies a dependence on an audience, bringing the possibility of triumphs comparable to those of the bullfighter or actor, who 'faisant de leur personne une glorieuse pâture publique, soulèvent l'enthousiasme du cirque et du théâtre' (yet more poet-images from the same essay on Le Vavasseur, II, 180). But reliance on the fickleness of public taste is not always seen in such glamorous terms by Baudelaire. His poem 'La Muse vénale' bemoans the commercial self-display of the hungry poet in front of the crowd, his parading of feigned emotions and his concealment of true ones:

> Il te faut, pour gagner ton pain de chaque soir,
> Comme un enfant de chœur, jouer de l'encensoir,
> Chanter des *Te Deum* auxquels tu ne crois guère,
>
> Ou, saltimbanque à jeun, étaler tes appas
> Et ton rire trempé de pleurs qu'on ne voit pas,
> Pour faire épanouir la rate du vulgaire.

9

The need to eat is inseparable from the need to please one's public; the poet's vulnerability to market forces is not only honestly acknowledged but is courageously admitted as the major theme of a sonnet (courageous because such a confession of insincerity was hardly likely to appeal to those who viewed the artist as the conveyor of spiritual or emotional truths). Another victim of the fairground crowd is the 'vieux saltimbanque' of the prose-poem of that title, who is portrayed as 'l'image ... du vieux poète sans amis, sans famille, sans enfants, dégradé par sa misère et par l'ingratitude publique' (I, 297). The triumphant bullfighter and the abject showman are both images of the poet.

The instability of the poet–performer role, now representing success, now total failure, might be thought to be absent from its partner, the poet–skilled-worker analogy, since for the poet, at least, the creator and the judge of his creation are one and the same person. In the quiet of his gymnasium, the acrobat may work at and savour the mastering of a routine in much the same way as a craftsman eyes the process of his workmanship, caressing an inner pleasure which is independent of public reception. Even the difficulties of the craft can be a source of delight – of Le Vavasseur, Baudelaire says 'Une difficulté a pour lui toutes les séductions d'une nymphe. L'obstacle le ravit' (II, 180). Elsewhere, he proudly confesses his own 'goût passionné de l'obstacle' (I, 181). The images of poet as accomplished expert or aspiring apprentice are pervasive in Baudelaire, alluring confirmations of the creator's ability to solve all problems through skill and intelligence (or so it might seem). But not all difficulties are seductive, nor resolved with neat precision. The rags lying on the wardrobe-mistress's floor, the discarded make-up in an actress's dressing-room, the ungainly block and tackle holding up a stage-set, the scribbled alterations on a writer's drafts – all these, 'toutes les horreurs qui composent le sanctuaire de l'art' (I, 185), are evidence, not of cool, confident artistic control, but of a toilsome, creative struggle, by no means a simple, polished process which the concept of an acquired craft might suggest. In other words, the poet–skilled-worker images have their own instability, occasionally offering the promise of deft verbal manipulation, and at other times evoking the sweat, toil and debris of an untidy *atelier*.

The theatrical allusions just cited come from a famous passage in one of Baudelaire's projected prefaces to *Les Fleurs du Mal*, a passage certainly inspired by Poe's 'coup d'œil derrière la scène' cited earlier. His publisher has asked him to explain to his public the why and how of his book; the poet replies:

10

Mène-t-on la foule dans les ateliers de l'habilleuse et du décorateur, dans la loge de la comédienne? Montre-t-on au public affolé aujourd'hui, indifférent demain, le mécanisme des trucs? (I, 185)

Apart from the recurrent suspicion of public fickleness and the refusal to lay bare the 'mécanisme des trucs' (although at least we know they exist), what interests here is the conjoining of the preparation and performance. The wardrobe-mistress, the scene painter and the actress are all evoked as analogues of the poet, since they all play a part in the creation of illusion and artifice. But the most artisanal view of the poet does not here exclude instinct and sincerity, the yardsticks of the sentimental audience; it is simply that these two Romantic guarantors are reduced to ingredients in a formula:

Lui [au public] explique-t-on . . . jusqu'à quelle dose l'instinct et la sincérité sont mêlés aux rubriques et au charlatanisme indispensable dans l'amalgame de l'œuvre? (I, 185)

The fairground charlatan and the studious alchemist (both 'amalgame' and 'œuvre' are alchemical terms) step into the text as further doubles of the artist. Each of these identifications deserves its own discussion, no doubt, provoking as it does rich suggestions on the level of creative method, theme and poetic effect. The alchemical allusion, for example, draws an image of the patient sage working his occult way through the long hours with a 'volonté infatigable' (II, 449) in order to find the secret formula which will convert base matter into gold; the poet–alchemist seeks out with equal rigour the form and formulation which will mysteriously transmute the most unpromising material into poetic riches. The process is a central notion in Baudelaire's aesthetics: addressing Paris, he proclaims 'Tu m'as donné ta boue et j'en ai fait de l'or' (I, 192). The multiple analogues surfacing in the projected preface are fascinating, however, precisely because they are multiple. There are other examples. Introducing his translation of *The Philosophy of Composition*, Baudelaire invites his readers to see it as 'la coulisse, l'atelier, le laboratoire, le mécanisme intérieur' (II, 345) of the creative act, allowing them a choice of analogues: poet as performer, poet as worker, poet as craftsman/artist, poet as scientist, poet as machine. Baudelaire's refusal to settle on a single equation does not betray uncertainty but rather reveals the protean conception he has of the poet's creative act. At one moment he may be a skilled manual worker handling stage-sets, at another the performer preparing in the dressing-room, at another the solitary *savant* in secret experiment. The plurality demystifies the idea of the poet as fulfilling a unique and perhaps divinely appointed task, but at the same time it introduces a more complex mystification. Can we accept such shifting images of the self? Is there not something unsettling and histrionic in the proliferation of these roles, even though there is nothing essentially contradictory about them?

It seems as if charlatanism is a part of the poet's projection of his own activity; he mystifies in engaging in his poetic act and mystifies in discussing it. One further example will illustrate this tendency. In the detailed notes towards a letter which Baudelaire intended to send to Jules Janin, a contemporary writer and critic, he launches a provocative question:

> Pourquoi le poète ne serait-il pas un broyeur de poisons aussi bien qu'un confiseur, un éleveur de serpents pour miracles et spectacles, un psylle amoureux de ses reptiles, et jouissant des caresses glacées de leurs anneaux en même temps que des terreurs de la foule? (II, 238)

The first images suggest melodramatically the poet's purveying of dangerous themes (grinding poisons or preparing drugs for the reader like a diabolic herbalist), as well as offering the sweetmeats of 'acceptable' literature. But what has this to do with the snake-breeder who suddenly slips into the list? There is no obvious link and we must suppose that here again we have a complex mystification, a deliberate use of the explorable analogue, a juxtaposition of the disparate which challenges the normal contiguity of lists. The brutal shift from confectionery to exotic reptiles is followed by a much more subtle change, this time from snake-breeding to snake-charming. The poet can be the patient trainer who prepares for the 'miracles et spectacles' (the rhyme is an ironic echo of the showman's crowd-gathering cry) and he can also be the snake-charmer himself (the 'psylle') – both stage-hand and actor, to revert to an earlier metaphor. Snakes and poetry are associates in Baudelaire's universe. The snake is all sinuosity and rhythm, elasticity and undulation, words used by Baudelaire to describe the verse of Théophile Gautier; it represents a poetry which is both alluring and dangerous. Its serpentine grace also evokes the poetry of female motion (one needs to look at 'Le Serpent qui danse' and 'Avec ses vêtements . . .'). But here the poet–'psylle' is master, savouring the rhythmic sensuality of his verse/snake as well as the successful terrorizing of the audience. One part of his pleasure is a refined aesthetic enjoyment independent of the disturbing effect his art creates in others (the impressionable crowd). This separation of aesthetic seduction and emotional recoil reappears in other guises in Baudelaire: 'c'est un des privilèges prodigieux de l'Art que l'horrible, artistement exprimé, devienne beauté' (II, 123). The poetic sensitivity of the 'psylle' relishes the beauty of the snake's movement and touch while the crowd is repelled by the horror. A true appreciation of the showman would suppress the reaction of horror and promote the assessment of the artistry with which he manipulates the arabesques of the snakes. Similarly, students of poetry, it might be argued, should centre their gaze on the artistic expression if they are to see how the horrible is beautified, rather than be the simple victim of the theme (Baudelaire's 'Une charogne' provides the best material for an experiment seeking to test this argument).

The proliferation of analogues could continue: poet as juggler, poet as obstetrician, poet as fencer, poet as mathematician, poet as musician, poet as cook, etc.,[2] but it would require a book to do justice to all these guises. My less ambitious aim in the scope of this liminal section has been to stress Baudelaire's view of the poetic craft as the acquisition and practice of special skills, akin to the particular knowledge needed by practitioners of other *métiers*. The following chapters will attempt to lead the reader of his poetry to an enhanced appreciation of his craft and the general poetics attached to it, and to persuade the same reader that an examination of Baudelaire's handling of language and the demands of versification can only enrich the imagination's grasp of the poetry as a whole. Talking of Théodore de Banville's brilliance as a versifier, Baudelaire draws attention to the 'mille gymnastiques que les vrais amoureux de la Muse peuvent seuls apprécier à leur juste valeur' (II, 163). Is it rash to hope that the essays that follow will increase the number of those who enjoy the 'gymnastiques' and see in poetic craft something more than the execution of technique?

2

A SINGULAR CLARITY OF TIMBRE, I: SOUND REPETITION AND CONVENTIONAL FORM

It would be traditional to begin a study such as this by investigating how Baudelaire satisfied the demands of versification, that is, the essential prerequisites which define French verse: rules governing metre, rules governing rhyme, rules governing fixed stanzaic forms. (I am relieved of the task of outlining the most basic of these rules by Clive Scott's *French Verse-Art: A Study*, which goes beyond the fundamentals of technique and gives an excellent general introduction to the ways in which poets have exploited the impositions of versification.) What I prefer to do, however, is to look first at Baudelaire's handling of the inessential. By this, I mean, for example, his use of alliteration – a strictly unnecessary feature of French verse, indeed a feature which some theoreticians of French poetry have positively discouraged. It seems to me more persuasive (at least initially) to illustrate the promotion of craftsmanship by examining areas where technique is less conspicuously present. There is, for instance, less opportunity for the sceptic to argue that what I claim as craft is no more than a necessary obedience to preordained rules. In this and the next chapter, I hope to show through an analysis of Baudelaire's orchestration of that smallest of units, the phoneme, that a poet's craft deserves the magnifying glass.[1]

Baudelaire refers in a projected preface, as we have seen, to 'le mécanisme des trucs' to be found in verse. What might he have meant by this? The most mechanical feature of poetry is versification in its strictest sense; yet versification can hardly be called a trick of poetry. If one were to expand Baudelaire's theatrical metaphor (the context of the phrase, 'le mécanisme'), one might say that versification corresponded to the stage-set, the more or less rigid mould in which the action takes place, and that to find the stage-effects of his verse, one must look to the more informal devices of poetry. Amongst these one can include alliteration, assonance and internal rhyme, that is to say those elements in the sound-structure of a poem which are inessential from the point of view of theory. Baudelaire is justly celebrated for his mastery of these extraneous features; Valéry alludes indirectly to them when, in an introduction to an edition of *Les Fleurs du Mal*, he attributes the fame and power of Baudelaire's poetry 'à la plénitude et à la netteté singulière de son timbre' (Valéry, 1957–60, I, 611).

In the pages that follow, I have avoided as far as possible the terms 'alliteration' and 'assonance' on the grounds that they have been much abused in the past and are clumsy tools even when properly defined. The terms that replace them (and which I shall define as they occur) are largely those suggested by R.A. Lewis, firstly in an important article on 'The Rhythmical Creation of Beauty' (1970) and then in a major book, *On Reading French Verse* (1982). They are intended either to situate patterns of repetition[2] with respect to the metrical line or to specify the richness, frequency and order of repetition. It is hoped that their use will both highlight and disentangle the complexities of sound-patterning in Baudelaire and show that the distribution of extraneous phonetic patterns is scarcely ever as random as it might appear. The rest of this chapter considers their distribution within the conventional form of verse (*e.g.* how they enrich rhymes or interact with metrical stress). The next chapter examines their relationship with units of sense and more specifically with the structure of metaphor and simile.

Rhyme

Baudelaire's use of rhyme as a conventional feature of French versification will be the subject of Chapter 5. Under the present heading, I shall look at other aspects of rhyme which are extrinsic to the strict theories of versification but which nevertheless play a role in evoking the atmosphere of formal necessity which emanates from a carefully crafted poem. These aspects involve the enrichment of the phonetic texture of a poem's rhymes by the addition of informal, inessential, sound-repetition: as in what can be called reinforced[3] rhymes (see pp. 16–17), *e.g.* 'litige'/'la tige', where the phonetic identity of the terminal syllable is supported by a repeated [l] which does not theoretically form part of the rhyme; or as in similar rhymes, which display to a greater or lesser degree a phonetic equivalence between adjacent sets of rhymes (see pp. 17–20), *e.g.* 'braises'/'bruns'/'punaises'/'parfums'. A third method of enrichment is through the use of internal rhyme (see pp. 21–7). Both reinforced rhymes and similar rhymes bolster the sense of symmetry which is characteristic of French verse, since both enhance the phonetic privilege which resides in the terminal syllables; to that extent, although inessential, they cooperate with the regular ambitions of conventional form. Internal rhymes, on the other hand, subvert the anticipated regularity by their randomness and their tendency to deflect attention away from end-rhyme. The role of regular pattern, expectation and surprise is crucial to the way in which the reader reacts to intrusions of the irregular; although the discussion here will obviously take account of these concepts, a more developed consideration will occupy Chapter 6.

Reinforced rhymes

Albert Cassagne, in the first and only book devoted entirely to Baudelaire's versification, makes the following comment on the poet's rhyme:

> Des rimes faibles ou médiocres, comme *couteau* et *troupeau*, – *repos*, *rideaux*, – *debout*, *dégoût* . . . *perdus*, *vertus* . . . se trouvent, mais sont rares chez Baudelaire.
>
> (Cassagne, 1906, 8-9)

These rhymes are indeed all theoretically weak in that the strict rhyme involves a single vowel with no consonantal support; but what is striking about this list is that in each case the weak rhyme is reinforced by equivalences which lurk further back in the line – the [u] in the first example, the [r] in the second, the [d] in the third and the [ɛr] in the fourth. Baudelaire rescues his theoretically weak rhymes through the trick of reinforcement. This trick is found throughout his verses and is not simply reserved as a device for fattening up enfeebled rhymes. On a small and obvious scale, it helps to produce a banal rhyme such as 'sommeil'/'soleil' ('Tristesses de la lune') and similarly constructed rhyme-pairs such as 'poli'/'pâli' ('Confession'), 'vivace'/'vorace' ('Le Voyage') and 'volupté'/'volonté' ('Paysage'). Some examples involve more than one element, as in 'solitaire'/'sur la terre' ('Le Vin de l'assassin'), 'sous les cieux'/'silencieux' ('Le Cygne'), 'luisants'/'les ans' ('L'Invitation au voyage'). These rhymes display the extensibility and compressibility of a concertina. Even richer examples can be found:

> Elles tournent leurs yeux vers l'horizon des mers,
>   ri(z)ɔ̃

> . . . Ont de douces langueurs et des frissons amers.
>   ri(s)ɔ̃
>   ('Femmes damnées: Comme un bétail pensif . . .')

> Et les voleurs, qui n'ont ni trêve ni merci,
>   tr v

> Vont bientôt commencer leur travail, eux aussi,
>   tr v   ('Le Crépuscule du soir')

The equivalence can be extended to cover almost all of the second hemistich of an Alexandrine:

> Pour l'enfant, amoureux de cartes et d'estampes,
> kart   e d ɛ

> . . . Ah! que le monde est grand à la clarté des lampes!
> k arte de   ('Le Voyage')

or even a whole line:

> Quand viendra le matin livide,
> v   ra   ma

> Tu trouveras ma place vide,
> v ra ma   ('Le Revenant')

> A te voir marcher en cadence,
> ã k

> Belle d'abandon,
> b   d b (d)

> On dirait un serpent qui danse
> ã k

> Au bout d'un bâton.
> b   d   b (t)
> ('Le Serpent qui danse')

What can be said about the function of this principle of reinforcement? It clearly relates to the function of rhyme itself, about which a later chapter has more to say. It may indeed be Baudelaire's answer to the problem of using a very rich rhyme without its becoming frivolous. But one could go further. Whereas normal alliteration tends to enhance what might be called a horizontal musicality (*i.e.* along and within the line), the reinforcing equivalences cited above seek to enrich the vertical musicality and the visual effect of rhyme. The device suggests a poet working, not along a chain of language (as the prose-writer might move from clause to clause, sentence to sentence, paragraph to paragraph), but between segments of language which relate to each other according to quite different, seemingly arbitrary, rules; it suggests a poet seeking further methods of imposing regular form. I propose that the reader should follow the poet into this domain where even the humblest phoneme can participate in the cultivation of poetic artifice.

Similar rhymes

The received wisdom at the time Baudelaire was writing (and for a long time before) was that a poet should avoid a succession of rhymes which assonate with each other; the theory was that a blurring of the distinctiveness between adjacent rhyme-pairs would act against the neat harmonics of a rhyme-scheme. Cassagne examines the question with respect to Baudelaire, finds several examples, defends three cases on the grounds of their expressiveness, but dismisses the rest ('pâture'/'mur'/'impur'/'pourriture' from 'Un voyage à Cythère'; 'fleuve'/'soucieux'/'abreuve'/'yeux' from 'Le Masque'; 'tranquille'/ 'voici'/'ville'/'merci'/'servile'/'ici' from 'Recueillement') as 'de simples négligences' (Cassagne, 1906, 11). The answer is not so simple. The binding of the A and B rhymes (*i.e.* adjacent rhyme-pairs) by phonetic equivalences can be classed as an extension of the desire for form. The positional equivalence at the ends of lines ensures that the form suggested to the reader, although abnormal, is still symmetrical. And Cassagne is wrong, in my view, to limit his examples to vocalic echoes. The bond is also achieved by consonants (as in the first of Cassagne's examples above where 'impur' is linked to 'pâture' and 'pourriture' by the [p] and [r] as well as by the assonance in [y]). The consonant pattern in the rhyme-words of a stanza from 'Le Serpent qui danse' ('profonde'/'parfums'/'vagabonde'/'bruns') constitutes an altogether different scheme from that of the rhyme proper; the pretonic consonant scheme can be represented as AABB ([pr-f-d/p-rf/b-d/b]) as opposed to the ABAB of the true rhymes. Another variation is the contrast of an ABBA pretonic consonant scheme with an ABAB rhyme-scheme, as in a stanza from 'Le Voyage' with the rhymes 'histoire'/'mers'/'mémoires'/'éthers' giving [t-r/m-r/m-r/t-r] for the consonants and [(w)a/ɛ/(w)a/ɛ] for the vowels. The opening rhymes of 'Le Guignon' provide a more complex example: in 'lourd'/ 'courage'/'l'ouvrage'/'court', the [u] and [r] link all the rhymes, the [l] and [k] alternate ABAB, while the [aʒ] provides the true B-rhyme. A stanza from 'Le Flacon' offers a *tour de force*, a rich interweaving of common elements: in the rhyme-words 'séculaire'/'suaire'/'spectral'/ 'sépulcral', [s] and [r] occur in all four, [k, y, l], [ɛ] in three, and [e] and [p] in two. There are some sequences of rhymes which seem to reach towards a cumulative climax: for example, the 'lutin'/'urnes'/ 'mutin'/'Minturnes' of 'La Muse malade', where the final rhyme-word manages to capture anagrammatically the previous two rhyme-words. The word 'portrait' achieves a similar climax in 'colore'/ 'attrait'/'aurore'/'portrait' from 'L'Amour du mensonge'; and 's'établiront' in 'tiendront'/'mélancolique'/'oblique'/'s'établiront' from 'Les Hiboux'.

For Cassagne, the insistence on symmetry and artifice is evidently not sufficient justification for similar rhymes. He prefers to

18

recuperate these 'négligences' by arguing, in certain cases, for their expressiveness:

Ainsi, dans la courte pièce, intitulée 'Spleen' 'J'ai plus de souvenirs . . .', qui ne compte que 12 rimes, les 2 premières ('ans'/'bilans'; 'romances'/'quittances') et les 5e, 6e, 7e, 8e, 9e ('vers'/'chers'; 'fanées'/'surannées'; 'Boucher'/ 'débouché'; 'journées'/'années'; 'incuriosité'/'immortalité') assonnent entre elles. L'effet produit est une forte impression de monotonie en rapport avec le sujet de la pièce.   (Cassagne, 1906, 10)

While I would prefer to say that the suggestion of form is always a sufficient reason for similar rhymes, I would not deny that sometimes the formal unity enhanced by such rhymes can underpin the semantic unity of the lines. For example, in the final two stanzas of the first section of 'Le Voyage', the narrator reaches the climax of a lengthy development and offers a description of 'les vrais voyageurs'; the eight lines hold together as a single thematic unit:

> Mais les vrais voyageurs sont ceux-là seuls qui partent
> Pour partir; cœurs légers, semblables aux ballons,
> $\tilde{\mathrm{o}}$
>
> De leur fatalité jamais ils ne s'écartent,
> Et, sans savoir pourquoi, disent toujours: Allons!
> $\tilde{\mathrm{o}}$
>
> Ceux-là dont les désirs ont la forme des nues,
> n
>
> Et qui rêvent, ainsi qu'un conscrit le canon,
> k nõ
>
> De vastes voluptés, changeantes, inconnues,
> k n
>
> Et dont l'esprit humain n'a jamais su le nom!
> nõ

The continuation of the [õ] in the rhymes of the two quatrains parallels the continuation of the description of 'les vrais voyageurs'; the unusual rhyme-scheme which this produces (allowing for the assonance) makes the form and, in this case, the content distinctive. The second stanza adds to this distinctiveness through the similar rhymes based on pretonic [n]'s and reinforced in the rhyme-words 'canon' and 'inconnues' by the presence of [k]. The structural function of the extra phonetic equivalences in these stanzas is to help to define the lines as a unit.

The structural use of similar rhymes is taken to its extreme in the tercets of 'Parfum exotique':

19

Guidé par ton odeur vers de charmants climats,
ma

Je vois un port rempli de voiles et de mâts
ma

Encor tout fatigués par la vague marine,
marin

Pendant que le parfum des verts tamariniers,
marinje

Qui circule dans l'air et m'enfle la narine,
arin

Se mêle dans mon âme au chant des mariniers.
marinje

This luxuriant rhyming demands comment, partly because of the swelling richness ('climats'/'mâts' consists of two repeated phonemes, 'marine'/'narine' of four, 'tamariniers'/'mariniers' of seven), partly because of their similarity (as if one rhyme has grown out of its predecessor). Maurice Schaettel says of these rhymes:

De tels effets, rares chez Baudelaire, pourront paraître trop recherchés, et confinent aux jeux des Grands Rhétoriqueurs – ou à ceux d'un Banville . . . Ces effets, selon nous, doivent se fondre dans la mélodie et concourir au charme musical du dernier mouvement. Une lecture juste et sensible doit les atténuer, non les souligner, et jouer simplement des modulations. (Schaettel, 1976, 99)

A reciter of the poem might well be content with the enhanced 'charme musical', but the *reader* of literature has no need anxiously to smooth over the artifice in the speed and emotion of a recital. He can savour the full functionality of the *jeu*, noting the remarkable parallel between the progressively richer, interlocking rhymes and the progression of the poet towards a state in which the senses combine climactically in a 'vision of abundant richness and harmony' (Killick, 1980, 30): sight ('je vois . . .'), scent ('le parfum . . . m'enfle la narine') and sound ('au chant des mariniers') merge to produce a spiritual euphoria ('Se mêle dans mon âme'). Form and content match beautifully.

Although similar rhymes can no doubt be expressive and structural in function, their most consistent function is to suggest and stress the idea of poetic form; the rhymes provide variation without dislocation. The positional equivalence is important in that it preserves the symmetry of the verse.

Internal rhymes

Unlike similar rhymes, internal rhymes do not, by definition, display any narrow positional equivalence in the metrical scheme. The absence of positional equivalence (that is, in relation to the rhyme-scheme) in two words that rhyme has traditionally been condemned by theory; internal rhymes, it is argued, confuse the expectation of regularity and disrupt the balanced harmony of the rhyming system. Quicherat, for example, in his comprehensive *Traité de versification française* (1850, 128), states with legislative force:

Le poète pèche contre l'harmonie, quand il fait rimer la césure avec la fin du vers:

> Sortons; qu'en sûreté j'examine avec vous,
> Pour en venir à bout, les moyens les plus doux   (Corneille)

and then on the next page:

Les hémistiches de deux vers ne doivent pas rimer entre eux. Cette consonnance trompe l'oreille, et lui fait croire qu'elle entend quatre vers de six syllabes, au lieu de deux alexandrins:

> Damon, tes sens tromp*eurs*, et qui t'ont gouverné,
> T'ont promis un bonh*eur* qu'ils ne t'ont pas donné   (Voltaire)

This latter type of internal rhyme, far from being proscribed, was in the sixteenth century, at least, a recognized form and the defining characteristic of the *vers léonin*. Baudelaire significantly praises Poe for using 'un genre de rime qui introduit dans la poésie moderne, mais avec plus de précision et d'intention, les surprises du vers léonin' (II, 336). The phrasing here deserves close analysis. The surprise of the *vers léonin* lies in its challenge to the end-rhyme; the reader has to modify his expectation that rhyme accompanies line-ends only. But Poe's internal rhymes are not identical with those which characterize the *vers léonin*; the American poet uses 'un genre de rime' which resembles it in its effect of surprise. And, rather than being a codified formal device which might risk becoming more conventional than functional, Poe's internal rhyming is inserted into the text 'avec plus de précision et d'intention'. One can expect to find the same deliberateness in Baudelaire's exploitation of the internal rhyme and the same appreciation of its disruptive, surprise effect. Once again, what theory perceives as transgression, Baudelaire sees as an opportunity to play with the expectations of the reader.

A comparison of two stanzas, one from 'Le Cygne' and the other from 'Chant d'automne', will illustrate the functionality of Baudelaire's internal rhymes:

21

Je pense . . .

A quiconque a perdu ce qui ne se retrouve
Jamais, jamais! à ceux qui s'abreuvent de pleurs
Et tètent la Douleur comme une bonne louve!
Aux maigres orphelins séchant comme des fleurs!   ('Le Cygne')

Il me semble, bercé par ce choc monotone,
Qu'on cloue en grande hâte un cercueil quelque part.
Pour qui? – C'était hier l'été; voici l'automne!
Ce bruit mystérieux sonne comme un départ.

('Chant d'automne')

In the first of these examples, the capitalized 'Douleur' on the caesura is given further emphasis by its rich echoing of the 'pleurs'/'fleurs' rhyme; the phonetic rubrication confirms it as a key-word in the metaphorical weave of these lines and in the thematic development of the whole poem. As the penultimate stanza of the poem, these lines recall the opening syntax ('Andromaque, je pense à vous!') but also major phonetic elements of lines three and four of the first stanza: 'L'immense majesté de vos douleurs de veuve,/Ce Simoïs menteur qui par vos pleurs grandit', which contain the triple internal rhyme, 'douleurs'/'menteur'/'pleurs', as well as 'veuve' (echoed by the later 's'abreuvent'). The highlighting of 'Douleur' is thus part of a wider recapitulative movement that largely governs the closing section.

In the second example, the internal rhyming of 'sonne' with 'monotone'/'automne' functions in the general auditory drama of the stanza. The sound referred to (that of falling logs) is problematic ('bruit mystérieux'): it has the paradoxical ability to be violent and monotonous at the same time ('choc monotone' – a splendid description of rhyme, by the way), to be sinister ('on cloue . . . un cercueil') and lulling ('bercé'). But the doubts surrounding the sound ('Il me semble . . ./Qu'. . .' and 'Pour qui?') are dispelled somewhat in a much more decisive movement ('C'était . . . départ') which will turn the sense of imminent disintegration into a determination in Part II of the poem to 'Goûter, en regrettant l'été blanc et torride,/De l'arrière-saison le rayon jaune et doux'. Central to this realization is the key-word 'sonne', which transforms the raw 'bruit', into an interpretable, purposeful *son*. Partly by virtue of the internal rhyme, the prosodic stress can be moved from its normal place on the sixth syllable to the seventh, where it helps to express the transformation of mood. The self-confidence of the usurping 'sonne' emblematizes the idea of sound as theme. The associations caused by the sound are, after all, the way the poem proceeds, indeed, the way it means. Phonic substance and poetic substance are in analogical connection.

In the stanza from 'Le Cygne', the internal rhyme was superimposed on the word before the caesura, with the result that 'Douleur' was (at least) doubly stressed. In 'Chant d'automne', one sees the ability of internal rhyme to play a part in over-riding the regular pattern of emphasis in the Alexandrine line. Here the surprise of the intrusive rhyme produces an effect of syncopation.

The rhyme-echo will always draw attention to itself. However there is discernible difference of effect between an internal rhyme which precedes its proper rhyming partner, as in

> Il est amer et doux, pendant les nuits d'hiver
>
> ('La Cloche fêlée')

and one which succeeds the rhyme proper, as in the stanza from 'Chant d'automne'. While both suggest irregularity, the echo rather than the pre-echo attracts the greater stress, since it can be said that stress accompanies the words or phonemes which cause the surprise and fulfil the irregular pattern rather than those which initiate it. The difference means that a pre-echo can produce an irregularity but not an effect of syncopation, whereas an echo proper can do both. Here the irregularity draws attention to the conjunction of 'amer' and 'hiver', a powerfully negative alliance, overwhelming the 'doux' and foreshadowing the anguish of the tercets.

The ability of an internal rhyme to exploit its surprise value as a means of shifting stress may serve to emphasize an important word or to achieve some elaborate variation of rhythm for what seems to be its own sake:

> Des meubles luisants,
> Polis par les ans,
> Décoreraient notre chambre;
> Les plus rares fleurs
> Mêlant leurs odeurs
> Aux vagues senteurs de l'ambre
>
> ('L'Invitation au voyage')

Here the end-rhymes 'fleurs'/'odeurs' find an echo in the 'senteurs' of the next line. What is more, the internal rhyme falls on the fifth syllable and could easily mislead the ear into thinking that it had heard three five-syllable lines – momentarily, of course. If one accepts a reading based on this deception, it is possible to treat 'de l'ambre' as an unusual sort of *rejet*, an unexpected addition when completion seemed to have been achieved. In any reading, the internal rhyme must cause a certain confusion of the rhythm (by which one does not mean jerkiness but rather a deviation from the expected). Paradoxically, the theoretical blemish provokes in the reader an awareness of the very form that has been violated; the irregularity foregrounds the regularity and *vice versa*.

A characteristic of the internal rhyme is that it does allow unusual readings of lines, as, for instance, in this passage taken from 'Le Guignon':

> Loin des sépultures célèbres,
> εbr
>
> Vers un cimetière isolé,
> Mon cœur, comme un tambour voilé,
> Va battant des marches funèbres.
> nεbr
>
> – Maint joyau dort enseveli
> Dans les ténèbres et l'oubli,
> nεbr
> Bien loin des pioches et des sondes.

The phonetic equivalence of 'ténèbres' is strong enough, even at a line's distance, to recall the rhymes ('célèbres', 'funèbres') and create an effect of irregularity; a slight lengthening of the pause after 'ténèbres' would not only emphasize this effect but also, by the consequent suspension of 'et l'oubli', give added force to the syllepsis (the yoking to the same preposition, 'dans', of the physical darkness and the mental space of oblivion). The sound-link has a structural effect too. It binds together the quatrains and tercets of a sonnet, the octet of which is largely an adaptation of a verse from Longfellow's 'Psalm of Life' and the sestet an adaptation of a verse from Gray's 'Elegy Written in a Country Churchyard'; by providing a phonetic bridge, Baudelaire's rich internal rhyme blurs the hybridization of the plagiarism.[4]

Any rhythm generated by sound-repetition is to some extent proportionate to the richness of the equivalence; end-rhyme and internal rhyme can thus be said to constitute part of a strong rhythmic pattern. Internal rhymes can also give an impression, not just of surprise, but of abundance and rhythmic plenitude. As such, they can provide the conclusion of a poem with a rare flourish and an effect of incantation. The tercets of 'La Mort des pauvres' read:

> C'est un Ange qui tient dans ses doigts magnétiques
> tik
>
> Le sommeil et le don des rêves extatiques,
> tik
>
> Et qui refait le lit des gens pauvres et nus;

24

C'est la gloire des dieux, c'est le grenier mystique,
                                               tik

C'est la bourse du pauvre et sa patrie antique,
                              p-tri   tik

C'est le portique ouvert sur les Cieux inconnus!
       p-rtik

Here the internal rhyme is rich ('magnétiques'/'extatiques'/'mystique'/ 'antique', all echoed by 'portique') and the equivalence between 'portique' and 'patrie antique' is reinforced by the [p, t, r] repetition. The duplication of rhymes in [-tik], admittedly plural and singular, within the confines of the tercets of a sonnet, is already unusual (one normally expects three distinct sets of rhymes); to add a further internal rhyme which gains prominence too by being syntactically different (a noun as opposed to the adjectives of the line-ends) is the certain indication of a phonetic hyperbole designed to match the intense, incantatory power of the concluding hymn to death.

A further example of a conclusion which uses the energizing potential of internal rhymes comes from 'Ciel brouillé':

O femme dangereuse, ô séduisants climats!
Adorerai-je aussi ta neige et vos frimas,
        re 3   ε3

Et saurai-je tirer de l'implacable hiver
       re 3

Des plaisirs plus aigus que la glace et le fer?

The stress-carrying sequence [re3-ε3-re3] is independent of the main rhymes. It makes possible the shift of principal stress from 'aussi' (occupying the conventional place of medial stress) to 'neige', emphasizing by the pause after the eighth syllable the opposition between 'ta neige' (addressed to the woman) and 'vos frimas' (addressed to the 'séduisants climats').

This example leads us on to discussion of cases in which the internal rhyme is independent of the end-rhymes and seems to set up an entirely separate counter-system. Clearly, with independent internal rhymes, there can be no question of that expectation which accompanies end-rhyme; their effect lies not in the fulfilment of an expectation but in the intrusion made upon regularity. It is normally the second element of the internal rhyme-pair that benefits from the surprise created by the device; placed more often than not on the secondary caesura of the final hemistich, it can steal some of the stress which conventionally falls on

25

the main caesura and the rhyme. This transference of stress can emphasize a semantic device such as metonymy in

> Qui font se fondre en pleurs les cœurs ensorcelés,
>
> œ r   œ r   ('Ciel brouillé')

or a particularly important word:

> Amante ou sœur, soyez la douceur éphémère
> (t) u sœ r   (d)u sœ r

'douceur' being the quality sought by the poet in the second part of 'Chant d'automne'. Its rich phonetic link with 'Amante ou sœur' fuses quality and its embodiment.

In 'Le Voyage', a variant reading gives adequate proof that Baudelaire must have been aware of the power of internal rhyme. In its early form, the second stanza of the fourth section read:

> La gloire du soleil sur la mer violette,
> La gloire des cités dans le soleil couchant,
> Allumaient dans nos cœurs une envie inquiète
> De plonger dans un ciel au reflet alléchant.

but was altered by a variant in the third line which became:

> Allumaient dans nos cœurs une ardeur inquiète.
>
> œ r   œ r

Admittedly there is a good semantic reason for the change; the literal sense of 'ardeur' is nicely appropriate to its verb 'Allumaient' and to the sun-images of the first two lines. The new word identifies the literal heat of the sun with the metaphorical fire in the men's hearts. This interpretation makes 'ardeur' a far more important word than 'cœurs', which would conventionally take the màin stress. The internal rhyme allows transference of the principal stress to 'ardeur', the phonetic irregularity drawing attention to the more suggestive word. In Chapter 4 we shall look at further examples of variants apparently made for both semantic and phonetic reasons.

There are of course many more internal rhymes in Baudelaire than those briefly examined above. Each rhyme will produce its own particular effect, but the sample given is intended to suggest ways in which this especially subversive device can work. Let me stress, however, that such subversions are rare and never succeed in permanently overthrowing the regime of strict poetic form; but what they can do is to remind the reader, through their very dislocation, of the regular artifice within which the poem operates.

26

End-rhyme is an obvious theatre for the skilled poet. What we have looked at so far has shown Baudelaire going beyond the requirements of the rules of versification to enhance the purely technical aspects of rhyme with a freer exploitation of sound. He elaborates and experiments, as any craftsman will do once the manual is left behind.

Rhythm

When one talks of rhythm in poetry, one is normally talking about an effect of sound. What are the constituents of sound (or, if one prefers, voice) which rhythm exploits? It can be said to consist of four elements: intensity, duration, pitch and character. The first three are all more or less measurable; a particular sound can be more or less loud, more or less long, more or less high-pitched. The fourth element, that of character, by which I mean the phoneme, is, contrary to the other three, qualitative; roughly speaking, to the normal ear, an individual sound (*e.g.* [d]) cannot be more or less than what it is.

It follows from this that phonetic patterns are essentially a qualitative phenomenon; and a study of them is primarily concerned with sounds of the same character rather than those with the same intensity, duration or pitch. But rhythm is usually defined in terms of quantitative aspects. La Drière (1965, 670) defines the rhythm of speech as

a structure of ordered variation in the quantitative aspects of the flow of sound in which contrast is balanced by a cyclic recurrence of some identity.

A characteristic of the rhythm of poetry is that it possesses a structure of ordered variation in the quantitative *and* qualitative aspects of sound.

Poetic rhythm is a complex amalgam of speech rhythm (quantitative aspects) and phonetic rhythm (qualitative aspect). The primary factor in the creation of poetic rhythm in most systems of versification is contained in either the intensity or duration of sound or both: the verse relies on patterns of stress or structured line-lengths or both. With these quantitative structures there may exist qualitative structures which include rhyme, alliteration and more complex phonetic patterns. Such figurations are secondary rhythmic elements which can be integrated into primary rhythms. What Baudelaire inherited was a system of French versification which operated on the triple principles of stress-patterning (the metrical units within a line), isosyllabism (equal line-lengths) and rhyme. Other qualitative structures were optional (or, as I have said, inessential).

27

Sound-patterns and the metrical line

Since phonetic patterns are secondary structures superimposed on the primary structures of a line of verse (the measured lengths of sound, the distribution of stress), they are bound to exist in some sort of relationship with primary structures; for example, any phoneme will either bear stress or not. A consonant can be either pre-tonic, post-tonic or atonic; a vowel can be either tonic or atonic. Already it should be possible to see the potential for convergent patterns, the dovetailing of a pattern of stress and a pattern of repeated phonemes. A line from Baudelaire's 'Le Voyage' will show the poet achieving just such a coincidence:

> Tel le vieux vagabond, piétinant dans la boue,
>   b   b

and, again, in this line from 'Harmonie du soir':

> Valse mélancolique et langoureux vertige!
>   i   i

In both lines, there is a phonetic linking of the precaesural syllable with the rhyme. Such a linking I shall call a terminal echo. The stronger forms of terminal echoes suggest symmetry; weaker forms tend to be less blatant and blend more subtly into the texture of the line. The [t] doublet in

> Voici venir les temps où vibrant sur sa tige
>   t   t
>   ('Harmonie du soir')

is cushioned by an asymmetric triplet of initial [v]'s, a doublet of stressed [õ]'s and a series of [i]'s, two of which are stressed. (A *simple doublet* consists of one repetition of a single sound; an *asymmetric triplet* consists of two repetitions of a single sound, giving an asymmetric distribution with respect to the central caesura of an Alexandrine.) The symmetry is only part of the general phonetic unity achieved in the line.

A form of terminal echo which may not directly involve metrical stress is that which links words on the caesura and rhyme (as opposed to the single stressed vowel or consonant); this may rely on initial stress:

> Dit celle dont jadis nous baisions les genoux.
>   3   3   ('Le Voyage')

or the very richness of the equivalence:

> Comme des chariots ou des socs déchirants;
>   d   ʃ rj   de ʃ ir
>   ('Femmes damnées: Delphine et Hippolyte')

Terminal echoes, by their position at the end of adjacent hemistichs, produce to varying degrees the symmetry of the *vers léonin*, but, unlike the latter, cannot be accused of misleading the ear. They also throw into relief the phonetic importance of the rhyme, which, in these cases, not only fulfils its normal vertical pattern but also completes a secondary horizontal pattern; it suggests a double symmetry.

The examples chosen to illustrate the superimposition of a secondary qualitative rhythm on a primary quantitative rhythm of a single line of verse have all displayed a very neat coincidence of stress and sound equivalence. The rich intricacy of sound-patterning in Baudelaire is such that neat coincidences are rarely found in isolation. One line may contain several patterns all of which can have a different relationship with the primary rhythm:

> Fruits purs de tout outrage et vierges de gerçures,
> yr   yr
>   tut ut
>   r 3   εr3   3εr
>   ('J'aime le souvenir . . .')

The compound [yr/yr] accompanies stress; the pattern in [tu] is off-beat; the mixed [εr3/3εr] with a pre-echo [r-3] is at once on- and off-beat.

Similarly complex lines will always display such variation. Confronted with a seemingly unattached pattern (*e.g.* the [εr3/3εr] pattern), or indeed any pattern, one ought not to relate it solely to the stresses of the line but also to consider its position in the linear movement. The [εr3/3εr] doublet, for example, superimposes its qualitative rhythm on the second hemistich which it divides into two ('et vierges ‖ de gerçures'). Equivalences that enrich the rhythm of a line by virtue of their position rather than their neat coincidence with the stress can be described as defining, liminal, medial, prevailing and terminal clusters. The phonemes of a *defining* cluster stress the form of a line or hemistich by establishing a phonetic equivalence between the beginning and the end of those units:

> Vient tendre ses filets au fond de nos cerveaux,
> v   v   ('Spleen')

> Ma jeunesse ne fut qu'un ténébreux orage,
> a 3   a3   ('L'Ennemi')

> Dans ce noir océan où l'autre est enfermé;
> ɑ̃   ɑ̃   ('La Chevelure')

The *liminal* cluster involves the first words of a line or hemistich:

29

Pénétré dans ton flanc plus avant que la lance?
e e e   ('Le Reniement de saint Pierre')

The *medial* cluster involves words which are situated in close proximity but divided by the medial caesura:

Je croyais respirer le parfum de ton sang.
p r   p r   ('Le Balcon')

The *prevailing* cluster is characterized by the frequent repetition of phonemes which dominate the line or hemistich:

Mes baisers sont légers comme ces éphémères
e ɛ e   e e   e e e ɛ
('Femmes damnées: Delphine et Hippolyte')

La Curiosité nous tourmente et nous roule
u   u   u   u   ('Le Voyage')

The *terminal* cluster involves the last words of a line or hemistich:

Bouche ouverte, dormaient de leur sommeil stupide;
s   s
('Le Crépuscule du matin')

Nos péchés sont têtus, nos repentirs sont lâches;
t t   ('Au Lecteur')

The use of the medial cluster in Baudelaire is of interest because the ternary structure which, in conjunction with a defining cluster, it can impose on a line resembles the metrical grouping of a Romantic Alexandrine (4+4+4). The strength of a phonetic pattern which straddles the medial caesura militates against the traditional symmetry of the Classical Alexandrine:

Je fermerai partout portières et volets
ɛr re/p rt   p rt/ɛr e   ɛ   ('Paysage')

Voilà le souvenir enivrant qui voltige
v l ℣   v nir nivr /   v l   ('Le Flacon')

La rue assourdissante autour de moi hurlait.
l ry /   u rd   t   tu r d /   yrl
('A une passante')

Michel-Ange, lieu vague où l'on voit des Hercules
k ɛl   / l va   l   va / e   ɛ k l
('Les Phares')

30

The secondary phonetic rhythm is not strong enough to usurp the primary stress rhythm, but it does complicate the reader's perception of symmetry, blurring the sharpness of any simple division. In the last three examples above, the slight disorientation of the rhythm corresponds to moments of thematic disorientation: the intoxication of memory in 'Le Flacon', the bewildering hubbub of a street scene in 'A une passante' and the uncertain visual background in 'Les Phares'. Whereas the medial cluster seems to refuse to acknowledge the divisiveness of the caesura, prevailing clusters – particularly when superimposed upon adjacent hemistichs – can have the opposite effect, emphasizing the differentiation wrought by the caesura, as in

> La véritable tête, et la sincère face
>   t   t t ‖   s   s   s   ('Le Masque')

Both hemistichs are made distinctive by their own phonetic rhythm; this difference is played against their overwhelming sameness: metrical (4+2 ‖ 4+2), grammatical (definite article+adjective+noun), semantic ('véritable'='sincère', 'tête'='face'). Similar examples are

> O fangeuse grandeur! sublime ignominie!
>   ã   ø   ã   œ ‖   im   i   mi   i
>   ('Tu mettrais l'univers entier . . .')

> De terribles plaisirs et d'affreuses douceurs.
>   εr ibl   plε ir ‖   r ø z   s œr
>   ('Les Deux Bonnes Sœurs')

In the first, the phonetic differentiation accompanies a complex amalgam of chiasmus, oxymoron and syntactic parallelism: the nouns ('grandeur', 'ignominie') contradict each other and are themselves contradicted by adjectives ('fangeuse' and 'sublime') which seem to have strayed into the wrong half of the line. The result is, on the thematic level, a collapse of moral opposites, a paradoxical subversion of obvious values – whereas, on the formal level, the authority of the symmetrical Alexandrine, supported by prevailing clusters, reigns unchallenged. Such a clash between form and content is typical of Baudelaire. In the second example, the phonetic differentiation accompanies a rhetorical structure which combines oxymoron with syntactic (article+adjective+noun/article+adjective+noun), metrical (3+3 ‖ 3+3) and thematic ('terribles'='affreuses', 'plaisirs' ='douceurs') parallelism. In all three examples, it could be said that the phonetic difference sets in relief the general sameness – and *vice versa*.

There is the glow of a highly polished object radiating from such lines. Even where the syntactic symmetry is absent, adjacent prevailing clusters nearly always add profile to a line, and particularly to the individuality of those syntactic units which they characterize:

> A travers les déserts courez comme les loups;
> r ɛr ɛ   ɛr ‖k u   k   l   l u
>
>   ('Femmes damnées: Delphine et Hippolyte')

> Cueilli quelques croquis pour votre album vorace,
> k   ik   k   k k i‖   r vɔ r   a   ɔ   vɔra
>
>   ('Le Voyage')

> Dis donc à ces danseurs qui font les offusqués:
> d   d   s   d   s   ‖k   f   f   k
>
>   ('Danse macabre')

And other examples could be cited, from 'A une Malabaraise' (line 18), 'Les Deux Bonnes Sœurs' (line 6), 'Le Cygne' (line 3), 'Le Voyage' (line 140), 'Le Squelette laboureur' (line 21).

In Classical Alexandrines such as those cited above, the convergence of metrical, syntactical and phonetic divisions on the caesura suggests powerfully the idea of symmetrical form; readers are left in no doubt that they are treading a path through a sculptured artefact. The fact that the phonetic differentiation is an inessential supplement to symmetry simply indicates a craftsman's refinement of accepted technique.

Medial and prevailing clusters are figurations of the qualitative aspect of sound, the function of which is defined in terms of their position within the poetic line; it has been shown that they can coincide with, or contradict, primary figurations. But the most common rhythmic effects produced by phonetic patterns have yet to be examined; of these the most important are the binary and ternary rhythms.

The basis of the binary rhythm is the simple doublet; the most intricate form is akin to the Welsh *cynghanedd*, which places the consonants of one half of the line in the same order in the other. The nearest that Baudelaire comes to this is in the following three lines:

> Comme de longs échos qui de loin se confondent
> k   də l ɔ̃ z k ‖k   də l   s k ɔ̃   ɔ̃ d
>
>   ('Correspondances')

> Ainsi qu'un vieux soldat qui veille sous la tente!
> s k   vj   s l a‖k   v j   s   la
>
>   ('La Cloche fêlée')

> Tes baisers sont un philtre et ta bouche une amphore
> t   b   f   r ‖ t   b   f   r
>
>   ('Hymne à la Beauté')

The first example and its following line in the sonnet – 'Dans une ténébreuse et profonde unité' – deserve further comment, for the richness and rigour of the phonetic patterning (the internal rhyme 'confondent'/'profonde' and the ingenious echo 'une té . . .'/'unité' can be added to the prolific patterns already identified) seem themselves to exemplify the harmonious mingling of distant echoes of which the lines speak. The sound-repetition mimes the content.

The exactness in the order of repeated phonemes in the three examples above is naturally rare in Baudelaire. But the mixed doublet (*i.e.* a repetition of two or more sounds in random order) can display an equal precision in an almost anagrammatical way:

> La froide majesté de la femme stérile.
> l a fr a də ma ste‖ də la fam ə ster
> ('Avec ses vêtements . . .')

> Une femme passa, d'une main fastueuse
> y nə fam ə as a‖ y nə m   fas   ('A une passante')

> Valse mélancolique et langoureux vertige!
> v l   el ã k lik ‖e l ã g   v i
> ('Harmonie du soir')

> Va te purifier dans l'air supérieur,
> pyri je ‖   r yperj r   ('Elévation')

> Les fruits miraculeux dont votre cœur a faim;
> fr   r k ø ‖   r kœ r f   ('Le Voyage')

All these lines are convincing proof of an effort towards the binarism displayed by *cynghanedd*. This effort to make the two hemistichs rich in phonetic equivalence is the very opposite to that which produces adjacent prevailing clusters such as those examined above; and yet, because they both emphasize the central division of the line, they can both be said to support the binary nature of the Classical Alexandrine.

On the other hand, the ternary rhythm of a triplet demands, by definition, an unequal division of its elements in relation to the break of the Classical Alexandrine. Unless all three elements occur in one hemistich, the spacing will fall under one of two schemes, exemplified in the final lines of 'La servante au grand cœur . . .':

> Que pourrais-je répondre à cette âme pieuse,
> p   p   ‖   p

> Voyant tomber des pleurs de sa paupière creuse?
> p   ‖   p p

Rather than stressing any particular division, asymmetric triplets of this type tend to strengthen the unity of the whole line. The cumulative effect of a triplet also tends to highlight the final element, especially when the latter accompanies metrical stress – as in the case of rhyme:

> Le poison du pouvoir énervant le despote,
>   p   p   p   ('Le Voyage')

> Par la griffe et la dent féroce de la femme.
>   f   f   f   ('Causerie')

> Avec le cœur joyeux d'un jeune passager.
>   3   3   3   ('Le Voyage')

> Et cognent en volant les volets et l'auvent.
>   ã v ã   v   v ã
>   ('Le Crépuscule du soir')

(the line also contains a triplet in [ɔ], four [e]'s and four [l]'s)

> Les hommes vont à pied sous leurs armes luisantes
> l z   l z   l z
>   ('Bohémiens en voyage')

Since, in French verse, stress is naturally directed towards the end of the line, this use of the triplet to herald the rhyme is particularly striking.

So far the analysis has been limited (with the exception of the lines from 'Correspondances') to the rhythm of phonetic patterns within the unit of a single line. Given the structure of French verse, the single line with its rigorously defined boundaries (signalled graphically by the capital letter at its beginning and phonically by the rhyme at its end) and internal patterns of stress is no doubt a privileged unit, and it can be seen as a kind of display case, an isolated advertisement of its own integrity as unit. But the single line belongs also of course to the larger units of stanza and poem and reverberates dynamically within those larger structures. Phonetic patterns radiate beyond the display case.

Sound patterns beyond the metrical line

Phonetic copula

The first of such patterns is the phonetic copula which serves as a link between lines by connecting in sound the end of one line with the beginning of the next. The phonetic copula will always direct extra stress on to the second element of the pattern which is an echo of the previous rhyme; the unexpectedness of a phonetic equivalence to the rhyme which occurs so prematurely draws the reader's attention to the beginning of the line. The copula can be used for expressive purposes; the sudden surprising dislocation of the rhythm echoes the abrupt action of breaking-open in:

> Des Cieux Spirituels l'inaccessible azur,
> Pour l'homme terrassé qui rêve encore et souffre,
>   s u f r
>
> S'ouvre et s'enfonce avec l'attirance du gouffre.
> s   u vr   ('L'Aube spirituelle')

and of diving-into in:

> Laissez, laissez mon cœur s'enivrer d'un *mensonge*,
>   ɔ̃ ʒ
>
> Plonger dans vos beaux yeux comme dans un beau songe,
> ɔ̃ ʒ   ('Semper eadem')

Almost by definition, the phonetic copula seems destined to be used in conjunction with that other rhythmic device which runs from one line to the next, enjambement; in Baudelaire, this is often the case. The following examples are limited to the richer equivalences:

> Nul ne vous reconnaît! un ivrogne incivil
>   ɛ̃ s v l
>
> Vous insulte en passant d'un amour dérisoire;
> v   ɛ̃ s l   ('Les Petites Vieilles')
>
> Et l'Esprit qui le suit dans son pèlerinage
>   p l r
>
> Pleure de le voir gai comme un oiseau des bois.
> pl   r   ('Bénédiction')
>
> Où tu fus maître enfin? Le remords n'a-t-il pas
>   n   t   p
>
> Pénétré dans ton flanc plus avant que la lance?
> p n t   ('Le Reniement de saint Pierre')

(In passing, it is worth pointing out that 'Pénétré' is stressed by other phonetic means besides the phonetic copula, namely a concentrated liminal triplet in [e] and its phonetic isolation from the rest of the line, which is dominated by patterns in [ɑ̃] and [l].)

> Par les fentes des murs des miasmes fiévreux
>   fj   r
> Filtrent en s'enflammant ainsi que des lanternes
> fi   r   ('Femmes damnées: Delphine et Hippolyte')

Si ses balances d'or n'ont pesé le déluge
d l

De larmes qu'à la mer ont versé tes ruisseaux?
d   l

('Lesbos')

It is possible that in the last three examples the enjambement and the accompanying copula perform some expressive function, the intrusion into the regular rhythm suggesting the idea of breaking-in or hurried flow (in the last example).

The expressive potential is more clearly illustrated in these lines from 'A celle qui est trop gaie':

Les retentissantes couleurs
Dont tu parsèmes tes toilettes
ɛt

Jettent dans l'esprit des poètes
ɛt
L'image d'un ballet de fleurs

where 'Jettent' forces itself upon the attention of the reader by its phonetic equivalence and position, just as the 'retentissantes couleurs' capture the eye of the poet. The striking sound effect imitates the striking visual effect.

Other types of enjambement can be reinforced by the phonetic copula. Stanzaic enjambement, a rare feature in any French poetry, is used sparingly in Baudelaire. Two of the most noticeable examples are supported by a qualitative sound pattern:

Ils trottent, tout pareils à des marionnettes;
Se traînent, comme font les animaux blessés,
Ou dansent, sans vouloir danser, pauvres sonnettes
Où se pend un Démon sans pitié! Tout cassés
k s

Qu'ils sont, ils ont des yeux perçants comme une vrille,
k   s

('Les Petites Vieilles')

and

Un cygne qui s'était évadé de sa cage,
Et, de ses pieds palmés frottant le pavé sec,
Sur le sol raboteux traînait son blanc plumage.
Près d'un ruisseau sans eau la bête ouvrant le bec
bɛ   bɛ

Baignait nerveusement ses ailes dans la poudre,
bɛ

('Le Cygne')

36

The effect of the dislocation caused by stanzaic enjambement will be commented upon later; the phonetic copula insists on the conjoining of what is normally kept apart, that is, the syntactic units of adjacent stanzas. It collaborates in the transgression.

Stanza patterns

Patterns, then, need not be restricted to the line-unit. Beyond the phonetic copula, one can venture even further and consider the looser patterns which are to be found in the stanza-unit. Apart from the formal bond of the rhyme-scheme, there can exist a basic dominant sound or group of sounds around which the internal phonetic unity of the stanza is built. Such patterns are much freer and more difficult to categorize than those contained within the single line. A brief analysis of a stanza from 'Le Voyage' will illustrate the phenomenon and the special problems encountered in discussing stanza-patterns:

> Pour ne pas oublier la chose capitale,
> Nous avons vu partout, et sans l'avoir cherché,
> Du haut jusques en bas de l'échelle fatale,
> Le spectacle ennuyeux de l'immortel péché.

One can distinguish two intricate phonetic schemes (apart from the rhyme-scheme) which dominate these four lines: the first and richer pattern is that based on 'capitale' and 'spectacle', which gives a five-element mixed doublet [kap-tal/p-ktakl] the phonemes of which recur with more or less effect in the central two lines; the second pattern is that dominated by the phonemes [ʃe]. The latter scheme follows a neat symmetry in the placing of [ʃ] on the penultimate and then the ultimate word in alternating lines; the support given by [ɛ] emphasizes this symmetry in the last three lines, producing a series:

> cherché/échelle/immortel péché
> ʃɛ   ʃe   eʃɛ   ɛl eʃe

Nobody would deny the existence of these equivalences; but it is perfectly reasonable to ask whether, at such a distance, even rich echoes will be heard by the reader. Stanza-patterns will necessarily be obscured to some degree by the more conspicuous recurrences of the primary rhythm and indeed by the strong qualitative echo of the rhyme. This fact puts into doubt the rhythmical value of widely spaced patterns, since rhythm depends upon the perception of repetition; if patterns cannot be heard, how can they be rhythmical? One answer would be to accept that distant patterns are not rhythmical in effect but that they fulfil, once perceived at a studied re-reading, a ludic function, persuading the reader of the manipulative skill of the poet and his general exploitation of verbal tricks. The rhythmical function should not be so easily dismissed, however. Clearly a great deal depends on the auditive memory of the reader/listener. Without the expectation which accompanies rhyme, the ear must be exceptionally acute or well-trained to respond to distant echoes. There are, however, certain circumstances under which the stanza-pattern may assert itself sufficiently to be heard.

(i) *Coincidence of stress*
When the stanza-pattern has the support of metrical stress, it naturally becomes more conspicuous. Consider the last tercet of 'Les Chats':

> Leurs reins féconds sont pleins d'étincelles magiques,
> ɛ̃   ɛ̃   ɛ̃ sɛl
>
> Et des parcelles d'or, ainsi qu'un sable fin,
> p rsɛl   ɛ̃   ɛ̃
>
> Etoilent vaguement leurs prunelles mystiques.
> pr ɛl

The repetition of the suffix *-elles* is accompanied by metrical stress in all its occurrences; this fact may highlight the subtler phonetic progression in the three words: the consonants of the second member of the sequence 'parcelles' recall 'étincelles' ([s] doublet) and announce 'prunelles' ([pr] compound doublet). (A *compound* doublet consists of a repetition of two or more sounds in the same order.) An analysis of the sequence in [ɛ̃] could have shown another method by which a pattern might assert itself, but this deserves a separate heading.

(ii) *Frequency of the repeated element*
If the phoneme is repeated several times, even without the consistent accompaniment of stress, then, not surprisingly, the pattern will draw attention to itself. Take the simple [ɑ̃] sequence in this stanza from 'L'Amour du mensonge':

> Quand je te vois passer, ô ma chère indolente,
> ɑ̃   ɑ̃
>
> Au chant des instruments qui se brise au plafond
> ɑ̃   ɑ̃
>
> Suspendant ton allure harmonieuse et lente,
> ɑ̃ ɑ̃   ɑ̃

    Et promenant l'ennui de ton regard profond;
      ã   ã

or the more complex [vɛr] pattern in:

    Homme, vers toi je pousse, ô cher déshérité,
      vɛr   ɛr

    Sous ma prison de verre et mes cires vermeilles,
           vɛr   vɛr

    Un chant plein de lumière et de fraternité!
              ɛr   ɛr   ('L'Ame du vin')

(iii) *Influence of the rhyme*
The rhyme is the most important type of distant echo; its phonetic strength can influence the internal sound of a line and produce a freer, more informal pattern. The resulting widely-spaced pattern takes on some of the phonetic importance of the rhyme and becomes more conspicuous thereby. The influence of the rhyme is apparent in:

    Antinoüs flétris, dandys à face glabre,
               as g ɑbr

    Cadavres vernissés, lovelaces chenus,
    ka ɑvr v r   as

    Le branle universel de la danse macabre
    br   v r   akɑbr

    Vous entraîne en des lieux qui ne sont pas connus!
                      ('Danse macabre')

and in this quatrain from 'Le Voyage':

    O le pauvre amoureux des pays chimériques!
      m   r   m r

    Faut-il le mettre aux fers, le jeter à la mer,
      m   r   m r

    Ce matelot ivrogne, inventeur d'Amériques
    m   r   m r

    Dont le mirage rend le gouffre plus amer?
      m r   m r

For an example of a very persistent and recurrent pattern over four stanzas, we should turn to lines 11–30 of 'Lesbos', where repetition of [t, i, r] dominates both the rhymes and the internal sonority, creating a quite remarkable effect of incantation.

(iv) *Symmetry in the position of the elements*
The effect of symmetrical placing of equivalences has been described in
earlier comments on the *vers léonin*, which concerned words occupying
positions at the end of adjacent hemistichs. Symmetry can also occur at
the beginning of the line:

> Pour n'être pas changés en bêtes, ils s'enivrent
> D'espace et de lumière et de cieux embrasés;
>   as
>
> La glace qui les mord, les soleils qui les cuivrent,
>   as
>
> Effacent lentement la marque des baisers.
>   as   ('Le Voyage')

> Qu'ils sont, ils ont des yeux perçants comme une vrille,
> k il s   il z
>
> Luisants comme ces trous où l'eau dort dans la nuit;
> l iz
>
> Ils ont les yeux divins de la petite fille
> il z
>
> Qui s'étonne et qui rit à tout ce qui reluit.
> k i s   ('Les Petites Vieilles')

Symmetry is one of the most effective methods of producing a
rhythmical distant echo, since it is more easily perceived than the more
random patterns.

(v) *Phonetic energy*
Phonetic energy may be said to occur when there is an outburst of
complex sound-patterning which, by its very richness, almost defies
analysis and draws attention to itself as being a phonetic *tour de force*. I
shall take as an example a stanza from 'L'Amour du mensonge':

> Je me dis: Qu'elle est belle! et bizarrement fraîche!
> Le souvenir massif, royale et lourde tour,
> La couronne, et son cœur, meurtri comme une pêche,
> Est mûr, comme son corps, pour le savant amour.

The complexity is such that one can only trace themes: the [ur]
sequence in 'souvenir'/'lourde tour'/'couronne'/'pour . . . amour'; the
[k-r] sequence in 'couronne'/'cœur'/'corps'; the [m-r] sequence in
'meurtri'/'mûr'/'amour'; the [k-m] doublet in 'comme'/'comme' which

forms a link between the last two sequences, as does the rich echo 'cœur'/'meurtri' ([kœr/mœr]). Outbursts such as this highlight stanza patterns as much as patterns within the separate lines.

In the above sections I have been concerned with the relationships between qualitative and quantitative aspects of sound. We have seen how phonetic patterns (qualitative figurations) can be grafted upon primary rhythmic structures; how they can emphasize, or militate against, the symmetry of the Classical Alexandrine by their position in the line (medial, prevailing clusters) or by their structure (binary or ternary); how they can support the rhythmical device of enjambement (phonetic copula); and, finally, how they can contribute to the sound-structure of the quantitative stanza-unit. Whereas this chapter has been devoted to the interplay between inessential sound-patterning and the conventional matrix of verse, the mould of rhyme and metre, the next will analyse the relationship between phonetic patterns and some syntactical structures.

3

A SINGULAR CLARITY OF TIMBRE, II: SOUND REPETITION AND UNITS OF SENSE

Syntax

In several of its characteristics, poetry can usefully be described as anti-prose. Yet clearly the opposition between poetry and prose is very far from absolute; for example, with the exception of a very small amount of twentieth-century verse, poetry has always carefully preserved the normal syntactical structure of prose. Inversion and ellipsis may modify the order and length of certain structures but basically they refer back to their prosaic equivalent. Classical versification recognized the vital function of syntax when it insisted on the coincidence of metrical and syntactical break. The caesura is frequently accompanied by a comma, indicating a syntactical pause, and the lines are nearly always end-stopped by punctuation. This rule is based on the assumption that the reader is always aware of syntactical patterns and that, without the support of these patterns, the metrical structure to which he is not by experience conditioned would collapse. Later poets (beginning in earnest with the Romantics) realized that by modifying the syntax/metre parallel they could obtain various unusual rhythmic effects; hence the cultivation of enjambement as a respectable device. Enjambement occurs when the syntax blatantly refuses to be restrained by the mould of the metre. What is important is the tension between syntactical rhythm ('natural') and metrical rhythm ('artifice'). Without syntax, all the subtlety of poetic rhythm is lost.

However it would be an error to suppose that Baudelaire, or any poet, leaves syntactical structures in their raw state, as it were. The relationship of syntax and metre does not only benefit metre. By trimming syntax to fit nicely into the metrical mould, the Classical poet was already drawing attention to the size, structure and rhythm of the syntactical unit as well as to its actual meaning. The effect is an example of what has become known as foregrounding, a primary characteristic of poetry. The concept of foregrounding refers to the contrast between the automatic utilitarian function of linguistic elements in normal

42

communication (words serve simply as instruments of communication) and the deautomatized linguistic elements in poetry which draw attention to themselves as language. So, in the expression 'saveur souveraine', linguistic elements (*e.g.* the phonemes [s-v-r] and the noun–adjective unit) are foregrounded by sound-repetition. In a typical hemistich from Racine, the syntactical unit is foregrounded by the recurrent matrix of stressed and unstressed syllables that forms the metre. The frequent parallelism of syntax and metre is another device for suggesting positively the idea of form (while enjambement would be a negative suggestion of form).

I wish to examine the way in which Baudelaire uses sound-patterns in order to foreground syntactical units. This foregrounding exists when a phonetic equivalence is superimposed upon the units of a syntactic chain (a syntagm) to a greater or lesser degree. Two types of the phenomenon can be distinguished:

(a) when the phonetic equivalence exists between words which belong to the same grammatical class (paradigm) and to the same total syntagm, for example when two adjectives qualify the same noun,

> Comme après un nocturne et terrible repas.
>   t r   t r
> ('Femmes damnées: Delphine et Hippolyte')

(b) when the phonetic equivalence exists between words which are syntagmatically related but do not belong to the same grammatical paradigm, for example when a noun and the adjective that qualifies it are phonetically related,

> Semblait lui réclamer un suprême sourire
>   s   r   s rr
> ('Don Juan aux Enfers')

These superimposed patterns do not fulfil a merely rhythmical function, although this will always be present; their primary function is structural. They unite in sound elements which are already united by syntax.

Type (a) foregrounding

Type (a) will be recognized as the definition of such stylized idioms as *sain et sauf, bel et bon, fort et ferme, gros et gras* and *frais et froid.* One could add: *il va et vient, à cor et à cri, de but en blanc, comme chien et chat, par le fer et par le feu, pleurs et plaintes, de long en large.* In popular speech such alliterative pairs are used emphatically to strengthen the idea expressed.

They have four characteristics: (1) initial alliteration; (2) equivalence of consonants rather than vowels; (3) monosyllabic structure; and (4) semantic equivalence of the two elements. Given these characteristics, one can judge how far Baudelaire's cultivation of the device takes it away from popular speech. The poet, seeking a refined language, must try to eliminate the banality from the device and extract only its potential as a phonetic means of supporting a syntactical structure. The effort to avoid the banal leads Baudelaire to use very few pairings which rely solely on initial alliteration. Rare examples would be:

> Rêvais-tu de ces jours si brillants et si beaux
>   b   b
> ('Le Reniement de saint Pierre')

> Montant comme la mer sur le roc noir et nu?
>   n   n ('Semper eadem')

The second example is rarer still in that it couples monosyllabic adjectives, a characteristic of idiomatic pairs. Baudelaire tends to couple polysyllabic adjectives (not surprisingly, since they are more numerous in the language), either by simple doublets:

> D'un air vague et rêveur elle essayait des poses,
>   v   v   ('Les Bijoux')

> Sont heureux, dispos et repus;
>   p   p   ('Les Plaintes d'un Icare')

or by compound doublets:

> Reine du doux empire, aimable et noble terre,
>   abl   bl   ('Lesbos')

> Dans le réseau mobile et bleu
>   b l   bl   ('La Pipe')

> Malade et morfondu, l'esprit fiévreux et trouble,
> m   d   m   d   ('Les Sept Vieillards')

Another characteristic of idiomatic pairs, and one which the above examples also display, is that they rely heavily upon the repetition of consonants rather than vowels. This is not always the case in Baudelaire:

> Une senteur montait, sauvage et fauve,
>   o v   o v   ('Un fantôme')

> Semblables à des nains cruels et curieux.
>   kry   kyr   ('La Béatrice')

Semantically, the words of the idiomatic pairs are very close, almost to the point of becoming synonymous, *e.g. gros et gras*. Baudelaire does not couple phonetically related synonyms in this way; but he accurately adopts the idiomatic formula to couple antitheses. All the character-istics of the idioms (initial alliteration, consonant equivalence, mono-syllables, semantic equivalence) are present in the lines:

<pre>
          De sa fourrure blonde et brune
                      b   b
                            ('Le Chat: Dans ma cervelle . . .')

          Je poserai sur lui ma frêle et forte main;
                               fr   f r   ('Bénédiction')

          De la danseuse folle et froide qui se pâme
                           f   f   ('Confession')
</pre>

The antithesis of the last example becomes clearer in its context, in which Baudelaire contrasts the mood of the dancer as dancer ('folle') with the mood of the dancer as woman ('froide'). The phonetic equivalence renders the surprising juxtaposition of antithetical adjec-tives more acceptable. Baudelaire uses the idiomatic formula to induce in the reader a sense of *déjà entendu*, while at the same time he preserves the semantic surprise of the antithesis. He contrasts the banality of the form with the novelty of the content.

The discussion of type (a) has so far been restricted to pairs of adjectives, mainly because this form of conjoining is the most frequent in Baudelaire. But nouns can be linked phonetically too. Examples of noun-pairs can be found in ordinary discourse; compare the expression *ni rime ni raison* with the line from 'Le Voyage':

<pre>
          A qui rien ne suffit, ni wagon ni vaisseau,
                                    v   v
</pre>

This line serves as a model for other occurrences of the device in Baudelaire, since it possesses three features which are characteristic: (1) the syntagm which contains the phonetically related words occupies a hemistich; (2) the words are stress-containing; and (3) the alliteration is initial. These features are of course only characteristic and are far from indispensable. The structure of noun-pairs of this type can be described as a convergence, in two words, of conventional poetic equivalence (metrical stress), syntactical equivalence (two nouns in comparable positions) and phonetic equivalence (repetition of pho-nemes). This convergence may be observed in

<pre>
          La Maladie et la Mort font des cendres
               m   m   ('Un fantôme')
</pre>

45

Je suis l'Ange gardien, la Muse et la Madone.'

      m   m

                  ('Que diras-tu ce soir . . .')

Car je cherche le vide, et le noir, et le nu!

          n   n   ('Obsession')

Et charmer les loisirs d'un pontife ou d'un prince.

          p   p   ('Le Masque')

Nous voulons voyager sans vapeur et sans voile!

         va   v a   ('Le Voyage')

The noun-pair, it can be seen, fits naturally into the hemistich of the Alexandrine with the metrical stresses falling on both nouns. Placed elsewhere in the line, the pair, by its strong syntactical rhythm and phonetic support, can affect the regular pattern of the Alexandrine. It could be argued that the main stress on the rhyme is weakened by the multiple equivalences of the noun-pair in

Me sauvant de tout piège et de tout péché grave,

        də t u p ɛ ʒ   də t u pe ʃe

                           ('Le Flambeau vivant')

En échangeant maint signe et maint clignement d'yeux:

        m ɛ̃   i ɲ   m ɛ̃   i ɲ   ('La Béatrice')

Type (a) phenomena (*i.e.* convergences of phonetic and grammatical equivalences in two words which belong to the same total syntagm) are important to the study of Baudelaire's poetry because of the way in which his obsessive dualism leads him to cultivate parallelisms of all sorts; phonetic patterns can support such a structure. Equally important is the observation that type (a) phenomena in Baudelaire differ from their idiomatic counterpart; poetry takes, expands and refines a feature of popular discourse.

Type (b) foregrounding

Type (b) foregrounding (the convergence of phonetic equivalence and syntactical relationship in words which do not belong to the same grammatical paradigm) is pervasive in Baudelaire, indeed so common that it almost becomes systematic. Two straightforward examples would be:

Exhale le vertige, et les danseurs prudents

                   d ɑ̃   r   r d ɑ̃ ('Danse macabre')

Et qui n'est pas saisi d'un frisson fraternel,
                                fr   fr   ('Les Sept Vieillards')

Both examples display the phonetic bonding of an adjective to its noun. Foregrounding of this particular syntagm is the most frequent, relying on simple initial alliteration (*e.g.* 'rayon rose' from 'Un Fantôme', 'sommeil stupide' from 'De profundis clamavi'), reinforced initial alliteration (*e.g.* 'vastes voluptés' from 'Le Voyage', 'mouvantes merveilles' from 'Rêve parisien') or more complex clusters (*e.g.* 'pâture suprême' from 'Lesbos', 'salutaire instrument' from 'Tu mettrais l'univers entier . . .', 'hypocrite lecteur' from 'Au Lecteur'). All these categories could be illustrated much more amply and the reader is referred to the lists in Chesters 1975, 58–63. How does one explain the frequency of the adjective–noun coupling? A linguist's explanation would point to the fact that in a phrase such as 'frisson fraternel' one finds a minimal syntagm in its simplest binary form: the qualified ('frisson') is bound to its qualifier ('fraternel'). The intimacy of this relationship is of course acknowledged in French by the need to make noun and adjective agree in number and gender. The close interdependence which is part of the language is foregrounded by the sense of phonetic interdependence given by the repeated phonemes. One could go further: the bonding may affect the semantic acceptability of the unit; the adjective may appear somehow suitable to the noun and therefore rhetorically persuasive. The persuasiveness may simply reinforce the apparent naturalness of the meaning, as in 'fleur flétrie' ('Le Léthé'), 'nuit noire' ('Le Possédé') or 'noirs ennuis' ('La Muse vénale'); or even go so far as to validate a more daring juxtaposition, such as 'fantôme frileux' ('Spleen'), 'maussade hôtesse' ('Un fantôme'), 'printemps trempés' ('Brumes et pluies'), 'cadavre adoré' ('Lesbos') or 'enfer polaire' ('Chant d'automne'). But most commonly the bonding serves an uncomplicated but important poetic purpose: it draws the attention to the syntactical form and parades the poet's ability to seek order and pattern wherever it may occur.

Baudelaire gives other syntagms similar phonetic support, but never with the same frequency as the adjective–noun group. The next most favoured groups are subject–verb and verb–object (see Chesters 1975, 64–7). Examples of the first might be:

Deviner si son cœur couve une sombre flamme
              k   k   ('La Géante')

Un vieux Souvenir sonne à plein souffle du cor!
          s   n   s n   ('Le Cygne')

47

– La jouissance ajoute au désir de la force.

a ʒu   aʒu   ('Le Voyage')

The verb–object bondings are characterized by rich equivalences:

Pour engloutir mes sanglots apaisés
ã gl   ã gl   ('Le Léthé')

Son œil ensorcelé découvre une Capoue
k u   k   u   ('Le Voyage')

Je découvre un cadavre cher,
d k   vr   k d vr   ('Alchimie de la douleur')

Pour châtier ta chair joyeuse,
ʃ ɑtj   ta ʃ   ʒ aj   ('A celle qui est trop gaie')

Both type (a) and type (b) foregrounding display what one can only call the logic of poetry; they superimpose a phonetic relationship upon words that are syntactically related. Attention is drawn to the words as words and away from the words as concepts; and the syntactical relationship between words is also emphasized. Herein lies the importance of the device; Baudelaire makes us aware of the form of words, and, more especially, of the form of syntagms, and, in so doing, leads us back to the sentence and away from the normal referential function of language. Unlike prose, poetic language draws attention to itself and refuses to be discarded once the surface meaning has been skimmed off. It claims for itself the ability to achieve memorability and a formal permanence which Valéry describes:

Mais au contraire, le poème ne meurt pas pour avoir servi; il est fait expressément pour renaître de ses cendres et redevenir indéfiniment ce qu'il vient d'être.
La poésie se reconnaît à cet effet remarquable par quoi on pourrait bien la définir: qu'elle tend à se reproduire dans sa forme, qu'elle provoque nos esprits à la reconstituer telle quelle.   (Valéry 1957–60, I, 1373)

Metaphor and simile

Imagery and sound repetition both represent the tendency towards equivalence which has been seen as characteristic of poetry. Phonetic patterns can link words which have no obvious bond on the level of meaning. Metaphor and simile likewise establish a relationship of similarity between two concepts which often belong logically to different areas of meaning. Of these two concepts I shall call the original idea or principal subject the *tenor* and the other half of the image, the borrowed idea, the *vehicle*. A third term is often present which limits the comparison; 'profond et doux' serves this function in

> A mon amour profond et doux comme la mer,   ('Les Bijoux')

This limiting factor is called the *ground*. (The terminology is that proposed by I. A. Richards, 1936, 96.) In all images which contain a ground, the tenor and vehicle are drawn into a meaning-based paradigm of which the ground is the key: thus, in the above example, 'amour' and 'mer' are drawn into a paradigm of words to which 'profond et doux' could be applied. They are also drawn together by their common consonants [m, r].

Accepting as an initial premise that, on different levels, sound patterns and imagery fulfil approximately similar functions, that of encouraging a sense of order and unity, one can examine the ways in which the two phenomena interact to produce an even greater sense of oneness within the poem. There are two principal ways in which phonetic patterns can affect an image: by phonetic logic, and by foregrounding.

Phonetic logic

To illustrate what is meant by phonetic logic it is merely necessary to take the simplest form of image, the direct comparison:

A is like B

and then take the simplest form of phonetic pattern:

phoneme A is the same as phoneme B

and then combine these two facts:

A (containing phoneme A) is like B (containing phoneme B)

and we obtain a parallel structure, an example of which is:

> Le Poète est semblable au prince des nuées
> p   p   ('L'Albatros')

Even though one might object that on the phonemic level there is identity and on the metaphorical level similarity, the convergence of two analogous structures can only help to strengthen in the reader's mind the idea of a fusion between what are very often, from the strictly logical point of view, different things. Here there need be no question of the expressiveness of sound or onomatopœia; the phonetic patterns are integrated into another poetic device as a means of emphasis. On the

49

one hand, the gratuitousness of the phonetic resemblance between tenor and vehicle is reduced by their metaphorical equivalence; on the other, the image itself gains in acceptability precisely because it has, behind it, that certain aura of logical necessity created by an indisputable sound-link.

The most obvious structural use of the phonetic pattern integrated into the simile is when the phonetic equivalence supports the metaphorical equivalence of tenor and vehicle. The most basic form of support is that given by the simple doublet:

> L'homme est aveugle, sourd, fragile, comme un mur
> m   m ('L'Imprévu')

> La musique souvent me prend comme une mer!
> m   m   ('La Musique')

The richer the patterns become, the more the parallel is strengthened:

> Aux maigres orphelins séchant comme des fleurs!
> r   r f l   fl   r
> ('Le Cygne')

> Les mystères partout coulent comme des sèves
> s ɛ   sɛ
> ('Les Sept Vieillards')

> Son fantôme dans l'air danse comme un flambeau
> f ã o   f ã   o
> ('Que diras-tu ce soir . . .')

One also needs to take into account the adjectives and their equivalents which qualify either tenor or vehicle. The first example below will illustrate what I mean:

> Le navire roulait sous un ciel sans nuages,
> n vir

> Comme un ange enivré d'un soleil radieux.
>   nivr   ('Un voyage à Cythère')

Here is a case where the ground ('roulait sous un ciel sans nuage') applies literally to the tenor ('le navire'), whereas it would be clearly less applicable to an unqualified vehicle ('un ange'). Angels do not roll but sun-drunk angels do; the qualification is essential in order to make the ground–vehicle relationship acceptable. Thus 'navire' is compared to a specific type of angel, one who is 'enivré d'un soleil radieux'; and the phonetic structure parallels this important link in that 'navire'/'enivré' gives a four-element mixed doublet, [n-vir/nivr].

50

A very similar example illustrates again a phonetic equivalence which gives support to a necessary qualification:

> La Curiosité nous tourmente et nous roule,
> k y r
>
> Comme un Ange cruel qui fouette des soleils.
> kry   ('Le Voyage')

An adjective which modifies the tenor can also form part of the supporting mechanism:

> Et bois, comme une pure et divine liqueur,
> l k   r
>
> Le feu clair qui remplit les espaces limpides.
> kl r   ('Elévation')
>
> Avec tes yeux de feu, brillants comme des fêtes,
>   d f   d f   ('Causerie')
>
> Le Destin charmé suit tes jupons comme un chien;
> ɛ̃ ʃ   ʃ ɛ̃
>   ('Hymne à la Beauté')

The phonetic similarity may extend to cover even larger units than the modifying adjective, as, for example, when the tenor and vehicle include verb parallels:

> Comme un navire qui s'éveille
>   v r   ɛj
>
> Au vent du matin,
> Mon âme rêveuse appareille
>   r v   ɛj
>
> Pour un ciel lointain.   ('Le Serpent qui danse')

A chiastic doublet [v-r/r-v] links 'navire' and 'âme rêveuse'; the verb constituents of tenor and vehicle are joined by the homophony of rhyme, [ɛj/ɛj]. No such formal device unites the verbs of

> Delphine la couvait avec des yeux ardents,
> Comme un animal fort qui surveille une proie,
>   ('Femmes damnées: Delphine et Hippolyte')

but the symmetry of the patterns plus metrical stress suffice to establish the parallel: [lf/lf] in 'Delphine'/'animal fort'; [vɛ-vɛ/vɛ] in 'couvait avec'/'surveille'.

So far, all the examples have illustrated phonetic logic in the service of simile. Most metaphors do not lend themselves to this device since very often the tenor-word is explicitly absent; when Baudelaire refers to a woman's hair as 'forêt aromatique' he has no need to use the word 'cheveux' or 'chevelure' in the immediate context. But there are metaphors where both tenor and vehicle are present. These can take the form of literal assertion (A is B) or, by abbreviation, a phrase in which the vehicle is in apposition to the tenor. Examples of phonetic logic in the service of literal assertion would be:

La Nature est un temple où de vivants piliers
        t   t   ('Correspondances')

Mais les ténèbres sont elles-mêmes des toiles
        t   t   ('Obsession')

or the even richer

La mer est ton miroir; tu contemples ton âme
  a m r   m r a r   ('L'Homme et la mer')

Ma jeunesse ne fut qu'un ténébreux orage,
  a ʒ   aʒ   ('L'Ennemi')

Notre âme est un trois-mâts cherchant son Icarie;
  tr ɑm   tr a mɑ   ('Le Voyage')

Examples of phonetic support for appositive metaphors (themselves fairly rare) are not particularly numerous, although the equivalences are rich and quite conspicuous:

Mon berceau s'adossait à la bibliothèque,
                  b bl ɛ

Babel sombre, où roman, science, fabliau,
b bɛl   b   ('La Voix')

Delacroix, lac de sang hanté des mauvais anges,
dəlak a   lakdə   ('Les Phares')

L'ennui, fruit de la morne incuriosité,
  ɥi   ɥi   ('Spleen')

De ses cheveux élastiques et lourds,
  s ʃ v

Vivant sachet, encensoir de l'alcôve,
v v s ʃ   ('Un fantôme')

It may be that the richness of the echoes in some way compensates for the absence of any direct grammatical indicator of comparison. The phonetic link is made even more conspicuous by the appositive closeness of the sound repetition in the first three examples immediately above; in the fourth it is further underlined by the parallel position in the verse-form.

It would not be wise to insist that Baudelaire was systematic in using the mechanism of phonetic logic (indeed if it were used so mechanically, the device would soon relate less to craft and more to technique), but it does seem that this feature of his imagery is important in several ways. Not only does this configuration of sound contribute to the rhythm of the verse in general and to the tightly-knit authority of the poet's lines, but it also appeals to the reader's ability to perceive imaginative analogies. This latter function has been recognized by such different commentators on poetry as William Empson, who says of a sound effect: 'I think myself its most important mode of action is to connect two words by similarity of sound so that you are made to think of their possible connections' (1961, 12) and the linguist Roman Jakobson, who states much the same idea: 'In poetry, any conspicuous similarity in sound is evaluated in respect to similarity and/or dissimilarity in meaning' (1960, 372). Baudelaire seems to have applied his own appreciation of this idea by successfully combining his feeling for phonetic association with his equally acute sense of analogy; in doing so, he has demonstrated a particularly rich exploitation of the properties of language.

The perspective so far has largely been that of the reader whom phonetic logic seeks to persuade. To adopt a different perspective for a moment (although I shall return to it in Chapter 4), it seems to me inevitable that Baudelaire's imagery, *in the act of composition*, must to some extent have been inspired by his keen ear for sound association. The poet himself in *Les Paradis artificiels* observes a result of drug-induced intoxication which has a curious relevance here: 'Des ressemblances et des rapprochements incongrus, impossibles à prévoir, des jeux de mots interminables ... jaillissent continuellement de votre cerveau' (I, 411). Although Baudelaire does not actually state that the 'rapprochements incongrus' are inspired by the 'jeux de mots', it appears very probable that the visual/conceptual and the auditory are interdependent and inspire each other. Absorbed in the more refined and willed intoxication of writing poetry, Baudelaire might well have followed an attenuated form of this process in which analogies can be called forth by auditory puns. In such a process the visual imagination is not necessarily primary but can be secondary to the promptings of sound association; thus, in a way similar to that in which the formalized demands of a rich rhyme may control the imagery, the constant appeal (however subconscious) of phonetic rhythm will certainly affect the poet's vision. I shall take as an illustration the amazing imagery from 'Le Beau Navire':

Ta gorge qui s'avance et qui pousse la moire,	17
Ta gorge triomphante est une belle armoire	18
Dont les panneaux bombés et clairs	19
Comme les boucliers accrochent des éclairs;	20

Boucliers provocants, armés de pointes roses!	21
Armoire à doux secrets, pleine de bonnes choses,	22
De vins, de parfums, de liqueurs	23
Qui feraient délirer les cerveaux et les cœurs!	24

These two stanzas, like the whole poem, are rich in imagery. The very first line evokes images of the woman as ship and the silken fabric pushed forward by her breasts as sails blown full by the wind. But the literal assertion of line 18 suggests an even more striking metamorphosis, that of the woman's bosom into an 'armoire'. The comparison may at first seem bizarre, but the 'gorge'/'armoire' metaphor has a respectable English equivalent in the dual meaning of the word 'chest'. Baudelaire wishes to suggest the *volume* of the woman's bosom. The second stage is the movement to simile, the comparison of 'panneaux' (now the tenor of the second image as well as vehicle of the first) with 'boucliers' (the second vehicle). At this point, the explicit reason for choosing 'boucliers' is that both shields and the curve of furniture panels catch the light (as does 'moire'). Hardly a convincing similarity, one might think. But its weakness is compensated for by the way in which the whole image of lines 19–20 is strengthened by the remarkable phonetic equivalences that link tenor and vehicle: 'les panneaux bombés et clairs'/'boucliers', [b-be e kl/b-kl-e]. The powerful rhythm overwhelms any over-prosaic reaction to the image. The structural justification for the 'panneaux'/'boucliers' simile is that it prepares the way for the direct, unmediated comparison of the woman's breasts with shields; her bosom is an 'armoire', parts of the 'armoire' resemble shields, the woman's breasts are shields (line 21). Apart from this structural reason for introducing the simile, I hazard the guess that it was suggested to Baudelaire by the close sound association of 'armoire' with *armoiries*, which are the designs on the *écu d'armes* (normally shield shaped). It is possible that the absent word, *armoiries*, helped the poet to visualize the panels as shields. The third stage is the full exploitation of the real potentialities of the 'bouclier' simile. The shields become the woman's breasts by metaphor (line 21) and indicate their aggressive and triumphant shape (whereas the 'armoire' metaphor stresses their intimate and generous volume). Finally the latent sound-association of 'armoire'/*armoiries* comes to the surface in the phonetic equivalence of 'armés' (line 21) and 'armoire' (line 22), which effects the transition back to the original metaphor (lines 22–4). This brilliantly interwoven imagery illustrates how phonetic patterns can strengthen the logic of a potentially weak comparison (lines 19–20), can possibly suggest an image by sound association ('armoire'/*armoiries*), and can bind together the dual movement of a complex metaphor ('armés'/ 'armoire').

Foregrounding

The second method by which phonetic patterns can affect an image is foregrounding. This section examines the way in which Baudelaire foregrounds his similes by giving them as a whole or in part a distinctive sound pattern which characterizes, and makes the reader aware of, the simile-unit. There is no longer any question of a strict phonetic parallel of the metaphorical process; the logic proposed in the previous section is not applicable to a line such as

> Ils me disent, tes yeux, clairs comme le cristal:
> kl r   kr l
> ('Sonnet d'automne')

What we have instead is a pattern which highlights the syntactical interdependence between the ground and vehicle, whether it be between adjective and noun, as in the example above, or verb and noun, as in

> Dont la moustache pend comme les vieux drapeaux.
> p   p
> ('Le Vin des chiffonniers')

The foregrounding of ground (adjective) and vehicle (noun) is fairly common in Baudelaire and can be compared to the foregrounding of adjective–noun couplings examined on pp. 46–7. Some examples amongst many would be: 'tendus comme une toile' ('Le Voyage'), 'singuliers comme les somnambules' ('Les Aveugles'), 'radieux comme des yeux' ('A une mendiante rousse'). Ground (verb) and vehicle (noun) are coupled phonetically in 'monte comme la mer' ('Causerie'), 'flam-boie . . . comme une forge' ('Madrigal triste'), 'marchant comme une chasseresse' ('A une dame créole'), 'tout en chancelant comme une enfant chétive' ('Confession'). The phonetic equivalence between ground and vehicle is a useful device which imposes a neat authority on the simile, making the vehicle seem inescapably linked to its ground so that it appears natural and indeed necessary that 'somnambules' should be 'singuliers', 'des yeux', 'radieux' etc.

Of all the ingredients of a simile, the most distinctive and important is obviously the vehicle, since it is the vehicle which reveals the poet's perception of analogy. The vehicle-containing phrase is essential to the image, but it is nearly always redundant syntactically. The fact that a sentence may very well stand without it tends to isolate the phrase, as in

> Toi qui, comme un coup de couteau,
> Dans mon cœur plaintif es entrée;   ('Le Vampire')

The isolation stresses the unity and importance of the phrase. Phonetic patterns, by foregrounding the vehicle, can achieve the same effect. Multiple examples are given in Chesters 1975, 80–2; a few must suffice here:

> Comme du chêne la chenille?
>   n   n   ('L'Irréparable')

> Comme au jeu le joueur têtu,
>   ʒø   ʒ   œ t t   ('Le Vampire')

> Comme des chariots ou des socs déchirants;
> kɔ   de ʃ rj   de ɔk de ʃ ir
>   ('Femmes damnées: Delphine et Hippolyte')

> Vers le ciel quelquefois, comme l'homme d'Ovide,
>   ɔm   ɔm   ('Le Cygne')

> Lesbos, où les baisers sont comme les cascades
>   k   k k   ('Lesbos')

> Et serrant sur leur flanc, ainsi que des reliques,
>   i k   ik
>   ('Les Petites Vieilles')

> Tes yeux, illuminés ainsi que des boutiques
>   i k   ik
>   ('Tu mettrais l'univers entier . . .')

> Pour partir; cœurs légers, semblables aux ballons,
>   blabl   bal   ('Le Voyage')

In all these examples, the phonetic pattern runs more or less parallel with the syntagm which contains the vehicle of the image.

There are some cases where all the components of an image (tenor, ground and vehicle) are involved in a single sound pattern:

Il est des parfums frais comme des chairs d'enfants,
    de   rf |frɛ| de   ɛr d f

                                           ('Correspondances')

      Sur ton beau corps poli comme le cuivre.

            kɔr | ɔli|kɔ   l k i r   ('Le Léthé')

These are comparatively rare instances in which the whole image is contained within a single line. Usually the tenor, ground and vehicle are more widely spaced, and, as a consequence, the patterns more involved. The following lines from 'Danse macabre' provide a good example:

      Dans un trou du plafond la trompette de l'Ange
      Sinistrement béante ainsi qu'un tromblon noir.

The tenor ('trompette') and the vehicle ('tromblon') display the richest equivalence [trɔ̃p/trɔ̃b], but in fact the whole simile is unified by a more intricate series of echoes based on the consonants [t, r, b, p] and the vowels [ɔ̃, ɑ̃]. The series can be represented thus:

Tenor	Ground	Vehicle
trompette de l'Ange	Sinistrement béante	tromblon noir
tr p t	tr b t	tr b r
ɔ̃ ɑ̃	ɑ̃ ɑ̃	ɔ̃ ɔ̃

The same kind of analysis could be used to examine the sonorous distinctiveness of

      Est fait pour inspirer au poète un amour
      Eternel et muet ainsi que la matière.   ('La Beauté')

or

      Dans une ténébreuse et profonde unité,
      Vaste comme la nuit et comme la clarté,

                                          ('Correspondances')

Whether it concerns the whole simile or only some of its constituents, foregrounding would seem to have two important related effects on the image. Firstly, by highlighting the syntactical relationship between words, it reinforces in the reader's mind the idea of unity; words are made to belong to the same syntagm not only by reason of their sense and grammatical function but also by reason of their sound. Phrases are isolated by their own phonetic rhythm, so that, rather than appear composed of random words, they take on an air of organized seemliness, a tidy poetic unit which has the ability to imprint itself in the receptive mind. What Mallarmé has to say of a line of poetry may well be seen to apply to the foregrounded similes of Baudelaire:

Le vers qui de plusieurs vocables refait un mot total, neuf, étranger à la langue et comme incantatoire, achève cet isolement de la parole: niant, d'un trait souverain, le hasard demeuré aux termes malgré l'artifice de leur retrempe alternée en le sens et la sonorité, et vous cause cette surprise de n'avoir ouï jamais tel fragment ordinaire d'élocution, en même temps que la réminiscence de l'objet nommé baigne dans une neuve atmosphère. (Mallarmé 1945, 368)

'Cet isolement de la parole' is precisely what Baudelaire achieves with his foregrounding; the fact that by this isolation it can, as Mallarmé says, awaken an imaginative response to the object named ('baigne dans une neuve atmosphère') leads us to the second effect. Foregrounding makes us aware of the form of words, and, more especially in the above examples, of the form of similes; and, in so doing, it leads us away from the normal referential function of language. Poets, more than anyone, are aware of the staleness which surrounds words in their everyday communicative role. They have the task of inducing the reader to look at words as words, to appreciate the medium of sound; they must nudge him out of his automatic concentration on the message so that he can not only savour the corporality and texture of words but also view things anew basking in their fascinating objectivity. Naturally, such a revolt against the normal prosaic mood can only enhance the power of imagery, which, likewise, is concerned with revealing not the commonplace vision but the hidden mystery of what Baudelaire called '*l'analogie universelle* ou ce qu'une religion mystique appelle *la correspondance*' (*Corres.*, I, 336).

The two effects of foregrounding imply a poet searching (partly by intuition, partly by acquired skill) for that coincidence of form and content, of sound-rhythm and grammar, which can help to give imagery its appeal and poetry its memorability.

4
SOUND PATTERNS AND THE SECRETS OF COMPOSITION

It is no doubt the Faustian dream of many critics to obtain access to the workings of the poet's mind, to enter into what Baudelaire calls 'le sanctuaire de l'art' (I, 185). Baudelaire's publisher certainly thought that the public would find useful an account of the poet's creative process, but in a projected reply designed to figure in a preface to *Les Fleurs du Mal*, Baudelaire rejects the request to 'expliquer pourquoi et comment j'ai fait ce livre, quels ont été mon but et mes moyens, mon dessein et ma méthode' (I, 185). This refusal to divulge the secrets of composition to the crowd (and even to the few 'esprits amoureux de la rhétorique profonde') has not prevented some penetration of the creative sanctuary. Variant readings permit a minimal glimpse of the process of choice; the poet may betray changes of mind in manuscripts, proofs or various published versions of the same poem. Analysis of variants, although never of course allowing one to approach in any measurable way the true complexity of creation (how many words never reach the page? how many rough copies are consigned to the waste-paper basket?), does at least provoke a more firmly-grounded sense of participation and set in some relief the distinctive features of the chosen version.[1]

A typology of variants

It is a relatively simple task to establish a typology of variants, 'une linguistique (et non une stylistique) des corrections' in Barthes's terms:

Les retouches que les écrivains apportent à leurs manuscrits se laissent aisément classer selon les deux axes du papier sur lequel ils écrivent; sur l'axe vertical sont portées les substitutions de mots (ce sont les 'ratures' ou 'hésitations'); sur l'axe horizontal, les suppressions ou ajouts de syntagmes (ce sont les 'refontes'). Or les axes du papier ne sont rien d'autre que les axes du langage. Les premières corrections sont substitutives, métaphoriques, elles visent à remplacer le signe initialement inscrit par un autre signe prélevé dans un paradigme d'éléments affinitaires et différents . . . Les secondes corrections (correspondant à l'ordre horizontal de la page) sont associatives, métonymiques; elles affectent la chaîne syntagmatique du message, en modifiant, par diminution ou par accroissement, son volume, conformément à deux modèles rhétoriques: l'ellipse et la catalyse.   (Barthes 1972, 138)

This linguistic model enables us, Barthes argues, to distinguish three main types of correction (he is talking only of prose):

(i) *substitutive*
The writer replaces one segment (a word or a phrase) with another, normally belonging to the same grammatical class (paradigm) and sharing the same syntactic function. For example, in 'A celle qui est trop gaie', Baudelaire replaced the adjective in the line 'Et, délicieuse douceur' with 'vertigineuse'. Less frequently, the replacement seems to have strayed from an alien syntactic group; this is the case in the Alexandrine from 'A une passante',

> Dont le regard m'a fait soudainement renaître

where the adverb ousted the infinitive and conjunction 'souvenir et'. In a comparison of the following two versions of the same stanza from 'L'Ame du vin':

> En toi je tomberai, végétale ambroisie,
> Comme le grain fécond tombe dans le sillon,
> Et de notre union naîtra la poésie,
> Qui montera vers Dieu comme un grand papillon
>
> (1851 version)

> En toi je tomberai, végétale ambroisie,
> Grain précieux jeté par l'éternel Semeur,
> Pour que de notre amour naisse la poésie
> Qui jaillira vers Dieu comme une rare fleur!   (1861 version)

one notices different types of substitution. There is a direct replacement of 'union' by 'amour', of 'montera' by 'jaillira', of 'un grand papillon' by 'une rare fleur' (presumably because 'grain' cannot produce butterflies); the syntactic correlation between both sets remains undisturbed. Even the change from coordinating conjunction ('Et') to subordinating conjunction ('Pour que'), despite the consequential switch from 'naîtra' to 'naisse', is relatively straightforward. But the second line is an example of complex substitution (appositive description replaces clause of comparison), possible here because simile and appositive phrases are nearly always grammatically redundant; they can slip into and out of texts without damaging the syntagmatic chain. In this odd sense they belong to the same functional

60

paradigm, that is, they can often present themselves as possible candidates in the same context.

(ii) *diminutive* and (iii) *augmentative*

The writer subtracts or adds to his material. I class these together since it is evidently in the nature of French verse that poet who subtracts words (and therefore syllables) from his line must reinstate an equal number of syllables. Thus when Baudelaire decides against the following couplet in an early version of 'Le Vin des chiffonniers':

> Et libre, sans souci des patrouilles funèbres,
> Seul épanche son âme au milieu des ténèbres

and chooses in its stead

> Et sans prendre souci des mouchards ténébreux,
> Epanchant tout son cœur dans l'air silencieux

he suppresses 'libre' (diminutive correction) but necessarily adds compensation elsewhere, expanding the next independent phrase by the insertion of 'prendre'; he likewise suppresses 'Seul' and makes good the syllabic loss by the emphatic 'tout' (a solution not possible if the feminine 'âme' had remained). Other alterations in the couplet – largely made necessary by a reshuffle in the surrounding rhyme-scheme, which now demands a masculine rhyme – are substitutive ('mouchards' for 'patrouilles' etc.). There are nevertheless (rare) instances when subtraction and addition can operate independently: complete metrical units (couplets or stanzas) can in certain circumstances be removed or inserted. Examples can be found in 'Le Vin des chiffonniers' (1861 text), 'L'Albatros' and 'La Rançon'.

To Barthes's three main categories, I would add a fourth:

(iv) *permutative*

The writer rearranges the order of the material, making no other changes. One can take as an example the modification from

> Est, comme son corps, mûr pour le savant amour

to

> Est mûr, comme son corps, pour le savant amour
>
> ('L'Amour du mensonge')

Of the four categories of variant, the most frequent in Baudelaire (and in most poets) is the substitutive. This predominance is hardly surprising given that formal impositions will hinder both diminutive and augmentative corrections. These same formal impositions will also of course generally determine the paradigm from which the substitution will be chosen; for the candidates in the paradigm must share not only semantic and syntactic properties but also syllabic features (and, if the rhyme is to be replaced, phonetic features too). The correction of a poetic text asserts the poet's freedom while reminding him of his restriction. Of all the principal characteristics of any word (syntactic, semantic, prosodic, phonetic), one can say that the prosodic claim is absolute; that the syntactic claim is powerful (although, as we have seen, 'soudainement' replaces 'souvenir et' in 'A une passante'); the semantic allows a fair measure of flexibility (the variant may be synonymous, antonymous or indeed related by nothing more striking than the fact that both it and the word it replaces make sense in the same context); only the phonetic texture of the word is denied any *a priori* claim on the poet's attention. But any reader of poetry knows (and the earlier chapters of this book have, I hope, confirmed this knowledge) that the phonetic properties of a word do assert themselves, even if the patterns they produce are modestly inessential to the act of composition (again with the exception of rhyme). What I wish to examine is the role played by sound patterns in the choice made between variant readings. There are dangers here: while there are strong arguments for supposing that when Baudelaire, writing of Cybèle in 'J'aime le souvenir . . .', prefers 'Abreuvait' to an earlier 'Suspendait' in

> Mais, louve au cœur gonflé de tendresses communes,
> Abreuvait l'univers à ses tétines brunes

he does so because of phonetic reasons (the [br] alliterates with the rhyme, the [vɛ] preludes that of 'univers'), one would not wish to deny the enhancement given to the meaning by the new verb ('Abreuvait' contains the idea of 'Suspendait' and adds the notion of fulfilment). The convergence of phonetic and semantic richness would appear to have dictated the change. This cautionary example makes it clear how rash it would be to profess that something as gratuitous as sound patterns *governs* the poetic choice; on the other hand, it also illustrates how such sound patterns can *influence* that choice.

Variants, sound and metre

Any analysis of sound repetition needs to be based on the way in which it interacts with other structuring features within the poem: metrical and syntactic. I have tried to show in earlier chapters the impressive level of coincidence between phonetic, metrical and syntactic patterns in Baudelaire's verse. An examination of variants will show how this coincidence is often skilfully contrived. Thus the framing effect of the internal rhyme [ɔr] in

> Au bord d'un lac de sang, sous un grand tas de morts
> ('La Cloche fêlée')

lends to the line a cohesive phonetic authority which it lacked in its earlier form:

> Auprès d'un lac de sang, sous un grand tas de morts.

And the word 'bord' is also visually more evocative. In the following lines from 'La Béatrice':

> J'aurais pu (mon orgueil aussi haut que les monts
> Domine la nuée et le cri des démons)
> Détourner simplement ma tête souveraine

the choice of 'simplement' rather than the replaced 'froidement' impresses partly because the initial alliteration in [s] between two syllabically equal words balancing each other on caesura and rhyme helps to stabilize a movement (already dislocated by parenthesis) in which the poet with arrogant confidence proposes a superior vision of himself (soon to be shattered). The opening of 'Spleen':

> Je suis comme le roi d'un pays pluvieux,
> Riche, mais impuissant, jeune et pourtant très vieux,
> Qui, de ses précepteurs méprisant les courbettes . . .

was alive with [p] alliteration, even before 'méprisant' replaced 'dédaignant', a close synonym; as well as adding to this larger configuration (echoing also in a near-rhyme 'impuissant' [pɥisɑ̃/p-izɑ̃]), the new word gives body to the centre of the line through its rich link with 'précepteurs' [presɛp-r/epr-z]. One particularly instructive alteration between proof and publication is found in 'Allégorie'; Baudelaire, listing the qualities of 'une femme belle et de riche encolure', first wrote:

> Elle rit à la mort et nargue la débauche,
> Ces monstres dont la main, qui toujours gratte et fauche,
> Dans ses cruels ébats a toujours respecté
> De ce corps ferme et droit la rude majesté.

Eliminating the inelegant and inexpressive repetition of 'toujours', yet preserving the paradoxical bite of 'cruels ébats', he recast the third line thus:

63

Dans ses jeux destructeurs a pourtant respecté

The 'pourtant', which stresses the unexpected preservation of the woman's physical beauty, forges a compound doublet in [p-t] with 'respecté'; the 'jeux destructeurs', promoting cruelty to the caesura, establishes a strong terminal echo with the rhyme [-str-kt-r/r-s-kt]. The final version also exhibits a four-fold repetition of [t], three of which fall in conspicuous pretonic positions [-tœr/-tã/-te]. It is surprising how poetically loaded a common adverb such as 'pourtant' can be. The remorse of omission in

> La servante au grand cœur dont vous étiez jalouse,
> Dort-elle son sommeil sous une humble pelouse?
> Nous aurions déjà dû lui porter quelques fleurs
>
>   ('La servante au grand cœur . . .')

gives way in a later version to the more positive promise of a neglected duty about to be fulfilled:

> La servante au grand cœur dont vous étiez jalouse,
> Et qui dort son sommeil sous une humble pelouse,
> Nous devrions pourtant lui porter quelques fleurs.

Here the 'pourtant', in a line now joined to the opening couplet by the loose, conversational syntax, contains a subtle hint of admonishment aimed at the 'vous' (the poet's mother): 'in spite of your jealousy and her humble grave, we still ought to take her some flowers'. From our point of view, the adverb is integrated beautifully into the context by the medially prominent cluster in [p-rt/p-rt].

The last five examples (to which could be added many more) all illustrate variants in which phonetic qualities have played their part; and in each case the resulting sound pattern has gained prominence through its partnership with the dynamics of the Alexandrine, producing either a defining cluster ('bord'/'morts'), terminal echoes ('simplement'/'souveraine', 'destructeurs'/'respecté'), medial clusters ('précepteurs méprisant', 'pourtant porter') or a terminal cluster ('pourtant respecté').

Variants, sound and syntax

Sound patterns, as we have seen, often run in parallel with syntactical units, so that the poet stresses the form not only of his verse but also of his syntagms. Baudelaire's verse is alive with this mechanism of foregrounding and many of his variants show a careful manipulation designed to achieve, amongst other things, a persuasive overlap between sound and syntax. When the 'réseau de cercles bleu' in 'La Pipe' gives way to 'réseau mobile et bleu', the poet creates a compound doublet in [b, l] which clasps together the two adjectives. Two nouns are similarly welded in

> Et charmer les loisirs d'un pontife ou d'un prince
>
> ('Le Masque')

where an earlier 'Mécène' abdicated in favour of 'pontife'; the always powerful *initial* alliteration held sway over the [s] doublet ('Mécène'/ 'prince') and the syntactically independent [me] pattern ('charmer'/ 'Mécène'). One of the poet's most characteristic uses of foregrounding is that involving noun and adjective. The first example comes from 'Remords posthume'. The line

> Et tes flancs qu'assouplit un vivant nonchaloir

lacks music compared with

> Et tes flancs qu'assouplit un charmant nonchaloir,

a version that ends with an enhanced phonetic spell [ʃar/ʃa-ar] to accompany the disturbing superimposition of a lover's compliment on a necrophilic description (already made ironic by the pun on 'nonchaloir', meaning 'nonchalance' but suggesting here 'lack of warmth'). Sometimes the foregrounding effect is arrived at after evident hesitation: the cohesive adjective–noun unit that concludes the first quatrain of 'Le Reniement de saint Pierre'

> Il s'endort au doux bruit de nos affreux blasphèmes
>
>   z af   as f

appeared only after 'sombres blasphèmes' and 'tristes blasphèmes' had been tried. Neither 'sombres' nor 'tristes' (although phonetically integrated) has the incisive paradoxical contrast with 'doux'; 'affreux' works perfectly on all levels. The syntactical bond between noun (whether subject or object) and verb is strengthened or preserved by judicious alterations in the following examples (the earlier version is bracketed underneath):

> De tout le feu qui pour nous flamboya.
>
>   f   f   ('Un fantôme')
>
> (De tout ce qui pour nous a flamboyé)
>
> A travers les lueurs que tourmente le vent
>
>   ã   ã
>
>   ('Le Crépuscule du soir')
>
> (A travers les lueurs que fatigue le vent)

Quand elle y veut baigner sa beauté nonchalante
         b   e   b   e   ('Le Vin du solitaire')

(Quand elle y veut tremper sa beauté nonchalante)

Dans le fiel; son regard aiguisait les frimas
             g   g   ('Les Sept Vieillards')

(Dans le fiel; son regard redoublait les frimas).

In the last example Baudelaire had tried and rejected 'augmentait', which, like 'aiguisait', gave the [g] doublet but lacked any power of evocation; the discovery of both metaphor and sound pattern brought by 'aiguisait' was a real *trouvaille*.

If one needed further evidence to maintain that Baudelaire often constructs his lines in what might be called phonetic cells, a variant from 'Les Aveugles' provides it. The second tercet began with the nicely euphonic

Cherchant la jouissance avec férocité
    ʃ   ʃ ã   ʒ   ã

which nevertheless needed alteration because of the unjustified repetition of 'chercher' in the final line of the sonnet. The replacement:

Eprise du plaisir jusqu'à l'atrocité
 epriz   p ɛzir

exhibits the same compactness of sound, but adds through the grimaced repetition of the taut [i], a hint of that underlying viciousness which explodes in 'jusqu'à l'atrocité'. The phonetic mechanism survives the variant, as it does when 'crispé' is substituted for 'tremblant' in

Moi, je buvais, crispé comme un extravagant
                     ('A une passante')

The link between ground and vehicle exists in both versions: 'tremblant'/'extravagant' [tr-ã/tr--ã]; 'crispé'/'extravagant' [kr-s/ks-r]. Similarly nothing is lost in the orchestration of the simile from 'Lesbos':

Comme une sentinelle à l'œil fidèle et sûr
             ɛl   ɛl

when 'perçant' takes the place of 'fidèle':

Comme une sentinelle à l'œil perçant et sûr
       sã   ɛ   ɛrsã   s r

In each instance the sacrifice of one sound pattern is redeemed by the substitution of another.

Variants and broader sound patterns

So far I have mainly restricted examples to those in which the sound patterns have kept within the limits of a single line. Yet in Baudelaire one often finds (as we have seen) a basic dominant sound or group of sounds around which the internal phonetic unity of a whole stanza is built. The chosen variant may enter the poem partly because of its contribution to the weave of a more expansive phonetic fabric. The greater suggestion of narrow city perspectives weighs in favour of 'entrevois' against the earlier 'aperçois' in

> Et lorsque j'entrevois un fantôme débile
> Traversant de Paris le fourmillant tableau,
> Il me semble toujours que cet être fragile
> S'en va tout doucement vers un nouveau berceau;
>
> ('Les Petites Vieilles')

yet it is also difficult to resist the conclusion that the poet's ear was influenced by the reverberations set up throughout the quatrain:

> entrevois / traversant / être fragile / S'en va tout
> ᾱ trəv a   trav rsᾱ   trə fra   s ᾱ va t

(And these are simply the main chords.) The ousted 'aperçois' could also have claimed echoes, but not such persistent ones. In 'Mœsta et errabunda', the establishing of a stanza-pattern is worked at in successive versions. In its first publication (June 1855), the penultimate verse read:

> Mais le vert paradis des amours enfantines,
> Les courses, les chansons, les baisers, les bouquets,
> Les violons mourans derrière les collines
> Avec les pots de vin, le soir, dans les bosquets,
> – Mais le vert paradis des amours enfantines.

In 1857, the 'pots de vin', which risked ambiguity (a 'pot-de-vin' is a bribe), give way to 'brocs de vin', which threads nicely with the initial alliterations of 'baisers', 'bouquets' and 'bosquets'; in 1861, the 'mourans' stepped aside for 'vibrant', plaintively onomatopœic, enhancing the [v], [i] and [b] patterns within and beyond the line. Both additions, it will be noticed, contain the consonantal cluster [br], all the more conspicuous because relatively uncommon.

The late alterations made to 'Le Vin des amants' at proof-stage before the 1857 edition shows the poet manœuvring his syllables to musical effect, tautening the resonances at the centre of his sonnet:

Proof   1857 publication

Comme deux anges que torture   Comme deux anges que torture
L'irrésistible calenture,   Une implacable calenture,
A travers l'azur du matin,   Dans le bleu cristal du matin
Suivons le mirage lointain!   Suivons le mirage lointain!

Nous laissant emporter sur l'aile   Mollement balancés sur l'aile
Du tourbillon intelligent,   Du tourbillon intelligent,
Dans un délire parallèle   Dans un délire parallèle

The internal rhyme of 'calenture'/'azur' has gone but is compensated by the subtler [blək/bløk] of 'implaca*ble c*alenture'/'*bleu c*ristal', the chiastic echo [lak/kal] in 'imp*lac*able *cal*enture' and the general proliferation of [l, a, k, t] patterns. The introduction of 'balancés' continues the [b-l] series (the three alterations between proof and publication all contain these phonemes) and shares the [alɑ̃] configuration with '*calen*ture'. There is support in this tercet for Henri Meschonnic's contention (Meschonnic 1973) that a visual pattern can operate independently of a phonetic pattern: the *b* and *l* in 'tourbillon' could be seen as yet another element in the 'implacable'/'bleu'/'balancés' series. And is it a coincidence that, after the insertion of 'Mollement', these three lines contain four occurrences of the double letter *ll*, the only double consonants in the whole poem apart from *mm* in 'Comme'? The other major alteration between proofs and publication was the removal of the word 'selle' from line 2 of the poem, so that the densely-packed

Sans éperons, mors, selle ou bride

became

Sans mors, sans éperons, sans bride.

And 'irrésistible' is replaced by 'implacable'. Thus two of the three remaining double consonants outside the first tercet disappear, leaving it to impose its conspicuous quasi-monopoly. The excision of 'laissant' also means that this monopoly is narrowed to just one set of double consonants, *ll*. Here surely is a rare case in which a dominant idea present in the text (that of parallelism; *cf.* 'délire parallèle' and 'côte à côte' in line 12 of the sonnet) is visually imitated by the graphic design of the letters. The importance of the letter *l* is signposted by its pronounced and actual presence in 'l'aile' [lɛl], not to mention the internal echo found in 'int*ell*igent'. The study of 'Le Vin des amants' reveals a Baudelaire quite ingeniously taking advantage of suggestive graphic effects years before Mallarmé – and curiously in a tercet with a distinctly Mallarmean tonality (suspended subject, cerebral adjective attached to physical noun, metaphoric use of 'aile', part of an octo-syllabic sonnet).

The modifications wrought on the stanzas from 'Les Petites Vieilles', 'Mœsta et errabunda' and 'Le Vin des amants' demonstrate the scope of phonetic influence in Baudelaire's poems, ranging beyond the line and even beyond the stanza.[2] And it is understandable how, in practice, variants can spring from a common phonetic source; a series such as that in 'Le Vin des amants' ('implacable', 'bleu cristal', 'balancés') has a unity possibly born of the fact that the revisions were made at the same time. Words are brought together in a relationship which the original process of composition may not necessarily have favoured. One specu-lative illustration of such a relationship is found in one of the seven versions of 'Les Sept Vieillards'. In the third manuscript of the poem,[3] Baudelaire writes as his second line:

> Les fantômes le jour raccrochent le passant

and then thinks again:

> Où le spectre en plein jour raccroche le passant!

– a change 'sans doute pour éviter la répétition de ce dernier mot [fantômes] qui figure déjà au titre [at that time 'Fantômes parisiens'], ce qui lui permet d'accéder à la formule finale, plus ample, plus générale, plus frappante' (Leakey and Pichois 1973, 274). Then in line 15, we find an alteration from 'habit' to 'aspect', in

> Et dont l'aspect aurait fait pleuvoir les aumônes.

Is it not possible that the emergence of these two variants at the same time owes something to the graphic similarity between 'spectre' and 'aspect'? (I am not suggesting that this similarity necessarily affects the reader, for whom the two words are distant, but rather that it influenced the writer, for whom, in a process of revision, the words were brought closer.)

Variants and expressiveness

The superiority of one variant over another may also depend on the greater expressiveness of its sound. Alison Fairlie (1981, 234) comments on the onomatopœic force given by the word 'cris' (replacing 'pleurs') to the line from 'Le Vin de l'assassin':

> Ses cris me déchiraient la fibre
>   kri   ir   i r

And what would Malherbe have thought of the daringly expressive, almost primitive beat of the first hemistich in

Entends-tu retentir les refrains des dimanches
ã t ã   t   r t ã t r   ('L'Ame du vin')

where the much safer 'résonner' has been displaced? The hissing of the snake, which is the sinister accompaniment to the opening lines of 'Les Métamorphoses du vampire', is rendered by the proliferation of sibilants:

La femme cependant, de sa bouche de fraise,
En se tordant ainsi qu'un serpent sur la braise,
Et pétrissant ses seins sur le fer de son busc

an effect by no means noticeable when line 3 read, less erotically:

Et faisant lutiner sa hanche avec son busc

The new participle 'pétrissant' adds another member to the already rich series:

cependant / se tordant / serpent / pétrissant
səp ã d ã   sə t rd ã   s rp ã   p tr s ã

One of the most remarkably subtle of Baudelaire's imitative effects was conceived when he revised 'Un voyage à Cythère' for publication in *Les Fleurs du Mal*. In the *Revue des Deux Mondes* (1 June 1855), the five lines containing the appositive description of Cythère ran thus:

Belle île aux myrtes verts, pleine de fleurs écloses,
Vénérée à jamais par toute nation,
Où tous les cœurs mortels en adoration
Font l'effet de l'encens sur un jardin de roses

Ou du roucoulement éternel d'un ramier!

The repetition of 'toute'/'tous', the poetic feebleness of 'mortels' and the long-winded method of indicating comparison ('Font l'effet de') all suggest a certain laxness in construction. Baudelaire reworks the lines superbly:

Belle île aux myrtes verts, pleine de fleurs écloses,
Vénérée à jamais par toute nation,
Où les soupirs des cœurs en adoration
Roulent comme l'encens sur un jardin de roses

Ou le roucoulement éternel d'un ramier!

The unashamed onomatopœia of 'roucoulement', already made doubly suggestive through simile (evoking the cooing of the bird *and* the sighs of the worshippers), finds itself heralded by a cluster of pre-echoes:

Où les / Roulent / Ou le / roucoulement
u l   r u lə   u lə ru u lə

none of which existed in the 1855 version. The support given to the meaning by the 'absent' words *houle* and *coule* (both present phonetically) has its effects here; the impression of waves of scent and sound is irresistible. The revisions achieve three objectives: (i) they establish a rich sound pattern the structure of which could, without reference to the character of the repeated phonemes, be said to be expressive of wave-like recurrence; (ii) they establish a sound pattern, [ul], the character of which expands the naturally expressive 'roucoulement'; and (iii) they establish a sound pattern which, through sound association, strongly suggests a swell-like movement.[4]

Variants and phonetic survivors

Another (rarer) form of substitutive variant is that in which the sound of the substitute word or phrase seems to be influenced not simply by the phonetic context into which it is inserted but also by the sound of the word or phrase replaced, some of whose phonetic characteristics survive. An example, by now familiar, will illustrate the point:

> Dont le regard m'a fait soudainement renaître
> (souvenir et)

The final choice of 'soudainement' in this line from 'A une passante' alters the syntax but retains several of the phonetic elements of the original [s, u, ə, n]. A second example from a line already quoted would be the replacement of 'pots' [po] by 'brocs' [bro] ('Mœsta et errabunda'). Doubts about the syllabic count of 'scorpions' in 'Au Lecteur' led Baudelaire to correct a private copy given to Bracquemond, changing the initial

> Les singes, les scorpions, les vautours, les serpents

to

> Les ours, les scorpions, les singes, les serpents

By permutating the list and by the amusing expedient of removing the 'vaut-' of 'vautours', the poet preserves the sound [ur], changes animals from vultures to bears and rectifies what he believes to be a fault in versification. (Second thoughts on the diæresis allowed the original to remain in the 1861 text.) The stressed vowels [ɔ̃, u] and the terminal echo in [r] of

> Au fond des carrefours, où pendent aux masures
> 5   u r   r

survive the revisions:

> Le long du vieux faubourg, où pendent aux masures
> 5   u r   r ('Le Soleil')

When correcting the proofs of 'Le Léthé' in *Les Epaves* (1866), Baudelaire changed what had already been published twice:

> Je veux dormir! dormir plutôt que vivre!
> Dans un sommeil douteux comme la mort,
> J'étalerai mes baisers sans remords
> Sur ton beau corps poli comme le cuivre

by taking out 'douteux comme la mort' and putting in an adjective very different semantically but oddly contained in '*dou*teux'. The revised second line then read:

> Dans un sommeil aussi doux que la mort

The new version avoids the repetition of the rhythm and structure of 'poli comme le cuivre' in the last line of the stanza. 'Le Vin des chiffonniers', a poem which went through several transformations, closed its 1854 text with the stanza:

> Pour apaiser le cœur et calmer la souffrance
> De tous les innocents qui meurent en silence,
> Dieu leur avait déjà donné le doux sommeil:
> Il ajouta le vin, fils sacré du soleil.

By the time of the corrected 1857 proofs of *Les Fleurs du Mal*, this had been changed to:

> Pour noyer la rancœur et bercer l'indolence
> De tous ces vieux maudits qui meurent en silence,
> Dieu, saisi de remords, avait fait le sommeil;
> L'Homme ajouta le Vin, fils sacré du Soleil!

Much could be said about this vital transformation, but what concerns us here is the ironic survival of the word 'cœur' in 'rancœur'.

Variants and rhyme

This last type of substitutive strategy brings us close to the one domain in which phonetic equivalence between variants is not arbitrary or voluntary but necessary: that of rhyme. The deciding factor in the

process of choice seems more often than not to be a matter of richness –
as in the following (the rejected alternative is bracketed):

Et des meubles volu*ptueux*,
... Qui traînent à plis som*ptueux*
        (paresseux)   ('Une martyre')

Et cependant, à voir la maigreur élé*gante*
... La hanche un peu pointue et la taille frin*gante*
        (pliante) ('Une martyre')

Ce n'était pas un temple aux ombres boc*agères*,
... Entrebâillant sa robe aux brises pass*agères*
        (à des brises légères) ('Un voyage à Cythère')

The prospect of enriching the rhyme is sometimes so alluring that the
poet reworks the whole line to accommodate the new word, as in

Les hiboux se tiennent *rangés*,
Ainsi que des dieux é*trangers*
(Comme des idoles de jais)   ('Les Hiboux')

La gerbe épan*ouie*
... Où Phœbé ré*jouie*
(Où la lune pâlie)   ('Le Jet d'eau')

Race d'Abel, chauffre ton ventre
A ton foyer patriar*cal*

Race de Caïn, dans ton antre
Grelotte comme un vieux cha*cal*
(Accomplis ton destin final)   ('Abel et Caïn')

These lines from 'Abel et Caïn' provide a fine example of how the
search for a rich rhyme acts as a stimulus to creative vision; the first
version is poetically impoverished with its air of tautology, whereas the
discovery of 'chacal' provokes a grimly physical image which confirms
the role of the 'race de Caïn' as earth-bound, beast-like victims of a
wrathful God. The consequent change from 'Accomplis' to 'Grelotte',
with its suggestions of cold, sharpens the contrast between Abel
('chauffe ton ventre') and the shivering Caïn. The vertical enrichment
of the rhyme in the third line of 'La Mort des amants' induces a
horizontal correction:

Nous aurons des lits pleins d'odeurs lé*gères*,
... Et d'étranges fleurs sur des é*tagères*
(Et de grandes fleurs dans des jardinières).

The 'étagères' not only rhymes richly but supplies a compound echo of the newly-inserted 'étranges', [etr-ʒ/et-ʒ-r]. The pressures from both horizontal and vertical axes have some control over the change from 'pesantes' to 'luisantes' in the opening rhyme of 'Bohémiens en voyage':

> Les hommes vont à pied sous leurs armes luisantes
> (pesantes)
> Le long des chariots où les leurs sont blottis,
> Promenant sur le ciel des yeux appesantis
> Par le morne regret des chimères absentes.

The 'pesantes' is scored out because, one presumes, it is too close to the rhyme in line 3, 'appesantis' (itself sharing several phonetic features with 'absentes' of line 4, [ap-zɑ̃/apsɑ̃t]). The new 'luisantes' provides a satisfactory rhyme and gains strength by being the third member of a hurrying triplet in [l-z], 'les hommes'/'leurs armes'/ 'luisantes'.

I may well have given the impression that Baudelaire invariably chooses the phonetically richer of two variants, as if the sound value were always the decisive factor. Such an overstatement is refuted by examples. The enticements of sound and sense cause the poet to waver over the rhyme in 'Les Métamorphoses du vampire':

> Je suis, mon cher savant, si docte aux voluptés,
> Lorsque j'étouffe un homme en mes bras redoutés.

The 'redoutés' is present in an 1852 manuscript and the first proofs of *Les Fleurs du Mal*; the second proofs replace the rhyme with 'veloutés', retained in the first edition, in the 1864 publication in *Le Parnasse satyrique du XIXe siècle* and in the proofs of *Les Epaves*, at which point Baudelaire reinstates 'redoutés'. Although the adjectives are close phonetically, sharing [-ute], 'veloutés' has the added advantage of bringing consonantal reinforcement to the rhyme with 'voluptés' [v-l-te/v-l-te]. But no doubt 'redoutés' stresses more unambiguously the sexual authority of the woman (*cf.* the earlier 'seins triomphants'). The abandoning of 'veloutés' is nevertheless to be regretted, for its sound value and also for its ironic suggestion of a texture at once soft and suffocating.

Le mot juste

The study of Baudelaire's variants, from the phonetic viewpoint, opens the door minimally on to the 'poulies' and 'chaînes' of the poet's art. The glimpse reveals a deliberate craftsman, finely working even the most arbitrary properties of his raw material. Indeed it is easy to imagine that the feeling of having conquered randomness is at its most intense when an inessential pattern dovetails sweetly with the demands of convention, when the sound, meaning and syllabic structure of a word are *just right*. The importance that Baudelaire attaches to the *mot juste* is evident from his first essay on Théophile Gautier, in which he argues that the right word evokes 'ce sentiment de l'ordre qui met chaque trait et chaque touche à sa place naturelle' (II, 117). The very corrections I have briefly studied show that Baudelaire himself did not possess the enchanting facility he attributes to Gautier. The scientist–poet believes in certainty and, unless he has Gautier's natural gift, will tirelessly seek out the *mot juste* as if it were a mathematical solution. The solution, although logical, will be none the less miraculous, giving the text a 'justesse qui ravit, qui étonne, et qui fait songer à ces miracles produits dans le jeu par une profonde science mathématique' (II, 118). I would argue that this 'justesse' is consistently (not invariably) found in Baudelaire, even if it is arrived at in a hesitating duel with words; and that the examination of variants thrills one with 'la sensation de la touche posée juste, du coup porté droit', producing, as Gautier's style did in Baudelaire, an admiration which 'engend[re] une sorte de convulsion nerveuse' (II, 118). The illicit glance behind the scenes enhances the *plaisir du texte*.

5

RHYMES

Background: theory, Sainte-Beuve, Banville

On the opening page of Cassagne's book on Baudelaire's versification (1906), we read:

> Il est impossible de ne pas commencer par des observations sur la rime cette étude sur la versification et la métrique de Baudelaire. L'époque où Baudelaire composait ses premières poésies et se constituait sa poétique particulière (1840–1850) était justement celle où s'établissait tyranniquement le dogme de la rime riche obligatoire, et surtout, ce qui est plus important encore, le dogme parent de la rime 'seul générateur du vers français'.   (Cassagne 1906, 1)[1]

Cassagne is no doubt right to draw attention to the conjunction of the poet's apprenticeship and the cult of rhyme; Baudelaire could not possibly have ignored the vigour and passion with which the theorists and practitioners of rhyme argued their case. Of the theorists, Wilhem Ténint published his *Prosodie de l'école moderne* in 1844 with a *lettre–introduction* by Victor Hugo and a preface by another poet, Emile Deschamps; of the practitioners, Sainte-Beuve had included the famous 'A la Rime' in his *Poésies de Joseph Delorme* (1829), Le Vavasseur, Baudelaire's acrobatic friend, wrote an *Epître* (1845) on rhyme, and Banville was busy practising in *Les Cariatides* (1842) and *Les Stalactites* (1846) what he was to preach in his *Petit Traité de poésie française* (1872). But we must beware of overestimating what might be meant by 'le dogme de la rime riche obligatoire' or of accepting in all its hyperbole an expression such as 'seul générateur du vers français' or Sainte-Beuve's 'Rime, l'unique harmonie/Du vers'. Rich rhyme, for instance, consists in Ténint's minimal definition of two phonemes one of which must be the consonant that launches the final syllable: 'profond'/'font', 'amie'/'endormie'. The *consonne d'appui* thus characterizes rich rhyme. On the other hand, for Landais and Barré in their *Dictionnaire des rimes françaises* (1853),[2] the *consonne d'appui* in a rhyme such as 'beauté'/'clarté' does no more than make the rhyme *suffisante*; in a definition such as this, richness depends on a further phoneme (as in 'éternité'/'nudité', for example). Banville goes even further in what one hopes is a moment of ironic excess:

Sans consonne d'appui, pas de Rime et par conséquent, pas de poésie; le poète consentirait plutôt à perdre en route un de ses bras ou une de ses jambes qu'à marcher sans la consonne d'appui. (Banville 1872, 57)

Since the minimal rhyme contains a *consonne d'appui*, Banville's rich rhyme must by implication always infiltrate further back into the line than the *consonne d'appui*; it follows that 'ténèbres'/'funèbres' would not strictly be any more than a minimal rhyme. I have cited only three theoretical texts, but they are sufficient to show that the definition of rich rhyme was by no means stable, even at a time when its use was supposedly tyrannical. There are two further points to be made about the tyranny of rich rhyme. Firstly, it was never obligatory in an absolute sense; Ténint states grudgingly, 'Rime riche pour tous les mots qui ont beaucoup de rimes ... Rime suffisante AU BESOIN pour les autres' (Ténint 1844, 98); Landais and Barré concede that 'la rime que l'on appelle *suffisante* n'est que tolérée, et cela par une invincible nécessité' (1853, xxii). Secondly, the dogma avoided the assertion that the richer the rhyme the better; indeed Ténint argues that 'il faut éviter les rimes trop riches, qui, au lieu de reproduire seulement la dernière syllabe ou les deux dernières du vers précédent, reproduisent trois ou quatre syllabes, et souvent tout un long mot' (1844, 98); Landais and Barré, likewise, are careful to warn that 'il faut prendre garde de tomber dans des exagérations contraires et de rimer à trois ou quatre syllabes' (1853, xxii). Aspiring poets were doubtless grateful for such concessions. Whatever the complexities of definition, there is no doubt concerning the awe in which rhyme was held. Nor can one mistake the highly prescriptive tone adopted in writings on it: 'rime suffisante AU BESOIN', 'il *faut* éviter', 'il *faut* prendre garde' (italics mine).

Although the minutiae of theory may of course have had little precise effect on Baudelaire, it is unlikely that he would have been able to escape the general favour which rhyme enjoyed. Indeed, Le Vavasseur in a poem addressed to Ernest Prarond, a mutual friend, recalls very specifically Baudelaire's attitude to rhyme in the 1840s:

Ce fut vers ce temps-là que, d'une amour fervente,
Nous aimâmes aussi la Muse et sa servante;
Nous nous mîmes à quatre à hanter la maison.
Vous et moi, mon ami, Baudelaire et Dozon,
Nous aimions follement la Rime; Baudelaire
Cherchait à l'étonner plus encor qu'à lui plaire.
Avait-il peur de voir, par un soin puéril,

L'originalité de sa Muse en péril,
Et son indépendance était-elle effrayée
De suivre en cette amour une route frayée?
– Peut-être, parmi ceux d'hier et d'aujourd'hui,
Nul ne fut moins banal ni moins naïf que lui. (Cited in I, 1232)

The tension implied in Le Vavasseur's view of his friend's attitude to rhyme would be typical of Baudelaire: on the one hand a passionate advocacy of rhyme, that most traditional of poetic devices, and on the other a fear of conformity and an acute awareness of the need to preserve his independence. The consequence of this tension was, according to Le Vavasseur, a search for *étonnement* in rhyme rather than a pleasing technical elegance ('Baudelaire/Cherchait à l'étonner plus encor qu'à lui plaire'); the effect would result from a highly conscious cultivation of 'l'originalité de sa Muse'. Whether Le Vavasseur was correct in his judgement we shall see when we look more closely at examples of Baudelaire's rhyming practice.

The general adulation of rhyme was partly inspired by the persuasive voice of the established Sainte-Beuve. The brilliant opening stanzas of 'A la Rime' would have been more seductively influential on a young poet than any theoretical announcement:

> Rime, qui donnes leurs sons
>   Aux chansons;
> Rime, l'unique harmonie
> Du vers, qui sans tes accents
>   Frémissants,
> Serait muet au génie;
>
> Rime, écho qui prends la voix
>   Du hautbois
> Ou l'éclat de la trompette;
> Dernier adieu d'un ami
>   Qu'à demi
> L'autre ami de loin répète;
>
> Rime, tranchant aviron;
>   Eperon
> Qui fend la vague écumante;
> Frein d'or, aiguillon d'acier
>   Du coursier
> A la crinière fumante:
>
> Agrafe, autour des seins nus
>   De Vénus
> Pressant l'écharpe divine,
> Ou serrant le baudrier

78

Du guerrier
Contre sa forte poitrine;

Col étroit, par où saillit
Et jaillit
La source au ciel élancée,
Qui, brisant l'éclat vermeil
Du soleil,
Tombe en gerbe nuancée:

Sainte-Beuve's apostrophes to rhyme ('Rime, l'unique harmonie/Du vers', 'Rime, écho qui prends la voix/Du hautbois/Ou l'éclat de la trompette', 'Rime, tranchant aviron', etc.) seek to define its essential qualities in a dazzling series of images. But the excitement of these images, as they multiply, should not disguise the careful nuances of the poet's view of rhyme. The tumbling metaphors may represent enthusiasm but they also point to a desire to discriminate between the multiple functions; they proceed from an awareness of an alternative or a need to adjust. Hence the repeated use of 'ou' in the attempts at definition. Rhyme may sound as soft as an oboe or have the blare of a trumpet; it may spur the poem onwards ('aiguillon d'acier') or draw it backwards ('frein d'or'); it may suggest constraint ('col étroit') while at the same time offering the springboard for lyricism ('par où saillit/Et jaillit/La source au ciel élancée'). The superiority of Sainte-Beuve's eulogy over prosodic debate lies partly in its insistence on the variability of rhyming effects; it acknowledges the importance of context whereas theory necessarily leans towards the abstract and universal.

Sainte-Beuve's influence on the young Baudelaire has long been recognized; indeed it was proclaimed by the poet himself in a poem sent to Sainte-Beuve in late 1844 or early 1845, 'Tous imberbes alors . . .' The poem contains explicit references to Baudelaire's absorption of the older poet's works:

– C'était dans ce vieux temps mémorable et marquant,
Où forcés d'élargir le classique carcan,
Les professeurs encor rebelles à vos rimes,
Succombaient sous l'effort de nos folles escrimes,

. . . Ce fut dans ce conflit de molles circonstances,
Mûri par vos sonnets, préparé par vos stances,
Qu'un soir, ayant flairé le livre et son esprit,
J'emportai sur mon cœur l'histoire d'Amaury.

But Baudelaire pays the poet of 'A la Rime' a subtler compliment by producing 39 couplets of which 28 are linked by rich rhyme (in Ténint's definition). It is another matter to argue that the poem is successful, even as an exercise in rhyming. There are signs, for example, that the rhymes have too much controlled the sense: the temptation of the rich 'marquant'/'carcan' leads to the tautology of 'vieux temps mémorable et marquant', and the relative rareness of rhymes in [fy] produces a lame *cheville* in

> – Livre voluptueux, si jamais il en fut.
> Et depuis, soit au fond d'un asile touffu

But, on the whole, the *pastiche d'éloge* makes its effect. The opening rhyme, [dəʃɛn], the richest of the poem, fanfares its presence:

> Tous imberbes alors, sur les vieux bancs de chêne,
> Plus polis et luisants que des anneaux de chaîne,

and, although it combines the syntactically similar (preposition plus noun), it does yoke together the normally different textures of wood and metal, here suggestively assimilated. And later in the poem, one might pick out the rare rhymes which highlight firstly the main character of Sainte-Beuve's *Volupté* ('esprit'/'Amaury') and secondly Chateaubriand's Romantic hero *par excellence* ('entraîné'/'René'). The evidence of 'Tous imberbes alors . . .' points to Baudelaire's awareness of the contemporary cult of rhyme; indeed one could almost say that the poem is a proclamation of that cult, partly in its overt praise of one of its founders and partly in its exemplary use of rich rhyme.

Sainte-Beuve, as the critic Brunetière remarked, was not himself exceptionally gifted with the 'imagination de la rime'.[3] Théodore de Banville, on the other hand, was a virtuoso of rhyme who rhymed so richly that one unfavourable critic, Abel Ducondut, numbered him amongst 'les Crésus de la rime' (1863, 102). Ultra-rich rhymes there certainly are in Banville's poetry, but the impression of virtuosity stems at least as much from three other features: firstly, the use of multiple rhymes (in virelais or ballades, for example); secondly, the use of short lines which at the same time bring rhyming partners closer together and allow them to occupy a proportionately greater space than, say, an Alexandrine would; and thirdly, the shock of unexpected rhyme-words. Baudelaire's admiration for Banville is eloquently expressed in his essay on him published in Eugène Crépet's *Anthologie des poètes français* (1862). Perhaps significantly, Baudelaire dwells less here on Banville's technical brilliance than on his lyrical power; he does however refer to the 'mille gymnastiques que les vrais amoureux de la Muse peuvent seuls apprécier à leur juste valeur' (II, 163). The verbal acrobatics are taken seriously. But as early as 1845 Baudelaire had written of his respect for his friend's precocious technical gifts in a sonnet, 'A Théodore de Banville'. The second quatrain reads:

> L'œil clair et plein du feu de la précocité,
> Vous avez prélassé votre orgueil d'architecte
> Dans des constructions dont l'audace correcte
> Fait voir quelle sera votre maturité.

Banville's poems offer Baudelaire a model of architectural ambition which combines boldness and correctness – expressions, if one wishes, of the radical and the conservative.

If Sainte-Beuve and Banville are cited, it is not because it is somehow necessary to find precise direct influences on Baudelaire during the 1840s; it is rather to illustrate the general tenor of the times with respect to poetic (and particularly rhyming) technique. It might be appropriate to conclude this short survey of prosodic debate by lingering over a text that brings together both Sainte-Beuve and Banville, 'Le Renard et les Raisins', a prose modernization by Banville of La Fontaine's fable published in *Dames et Demoiselles* (1886). It is the fictional story of two young poets, Denorus and Lafra, who supposedly published their first works in 1855. Denorus, envying Lafra's brilliant gift for rhyme, pours out his jealousy to the established critic, Secrétan, a thinly disguised Sainte-Beuve. His main complaint is that to rhyme richly is no more than a clever skill, akin to that of the 'jongleur impeccable' or the 'saltimbanque japonais'. The critic's reply is worth analysing at some length, since we may suppose that it points to the older Banville's view of the mature Sainte-Beuve's conclusions on rhyme:

> S'il ne s'agissait que de trouver et d'assembler des rimes riches, le jeu, en effet, serait sans doute assez facile! et encore, je n'en jurerais pas. Peut-être méprisez-vous trop les acrobates, et faire n'importe quoi avec une absolue perfection est toujours malaisé. (Banville, 1886, 300)

The 'mille gymnastiques', in Baudelaire's words, are not necessarily achieved with ease even by the accomplished acrobat; perfection implies a difficulty appreciated only by the 'vrais amoureux de la Muse' (II, 163).

> Mais là n'est pas la question, et la Rime de Lafra est bien autre chose que riche! Elle est variée, diverse, changeante comme un Protée femelle; elle sait prendre tous les tons, profondément française, parce qu'elle est toujours spirituelle; appropriée à l'effet qu'elle veut produire, riche s'il le faut, ténue et comme pauvre, si le cas l'exige . . . Vous vouliez bien me parler de mes propres œuvres poétiques. Eh bien! si j'ai voulu exprimer nuances de sentiment d'une ténuité excessive, j'ai donc bien rimé, dans le grand sens du mot, en faisant soupirer des rimes comme effacées et fuyantes. (Banville 1886, 300–1)

The critic's comments here seem to me more fundamental to an understanding of rhyme than any of the several theoretical treatises.

The argument develops that already implied in 'A la Rime': *context is all*.[4] The function of rhyme changes according to the effect required; in the right circumstances, an attentuated rhyme ('comme pauvre') can claim to be as effective as a rich rhyme. The timid, scarcely audible rhyme may be a perfect vehicle to convey the subtlety of a mood.

Vous vous imaginez, avec une naïve innocence, que l'art du rimeur consiste à trouver deux mots qui riment bien ensemble; mais alors, il se réduirait à rien, puisque ces deux mots vous sont offerts par tous les dictionnaires. Ce dont il s'agit, c'est de trouver entre eux un rapport *nouveau*, inattendu, étonnamment juste . . .   (Banville 1886, 301)

The secret of good rhyming also lies in the surprise of the semantic clash of two words brought together by some arbitrary phonetic resemblance. This surprise may be caused by the rareness of the rhyme, for example, the use of a proper name as in 'entraîné'/'René' or the appearance of an obscure word as in 'torture'/'calenture' (from Baudelaire's 'Le Vin des amants'); but it may also arise from an original harnessing of the most banal of partners. It is the 'rapport' that matters and that, of course, depends on context. To clinch his point, Secrétan quotes a stanza from Hugo:

> Cette trace qui nous enseigne,
> Ce pied blanc, ce pied fait de jour,
> Ce pied rose, hélas! car il saigne,
> Ce pied nu, c'est le tien, amour!

in which the 'jour'/'amour' cliché is given new life through the descriptive boldness of 'ce pied fait de jour'.

The importance of this whole passage is three-fold: it joins together in a single text Sainte-Beuve and Banville, two commonly acknowledged influences on French rhyme when Baudelaire was writing; by its measured, mature suggestiveness, it puts into their place the passionate but ultimately limited pronouncements of theorists such as Ténint, Landais and Barré, and Ducondut; and its stress on the creative variability of rhyme supplies a perspective in which to view aspects of Baudelaire's own rhyming practice. This we shall now do.

Practice

Rhyme as theme: 'Je te donne ces vers . . .'; 'A une Madone'

Somewhere between the territory of theory and that of practice, with a foot in each, stands a work such as Sainte-Beuve's 'A la Rime', a self-conscious and self-illustrating embodiment of theory within practice. No Baudelaire poem goes this far, but in two of the valedictory poems in which he bids farewell to the mistress who has inspired a particular cycle of poems, he reminds his dedicatees that their immortality is assured by the durability of poetic form. The sonnet that closes the so-called Jeanne Duval cycle, 'Je te donne ces vers . . .', claims that her memory will be linked to his verse, 'pendue à mes rimes hautaines'. In 'A une Madone', the poet wishes to construct for his mistress an imaginary, inner altar at which he can worship her as a sacred statue:

> Avec mes Vers polis, treillis d'un pur métal
> Savamment constellé de rimes de cristal,
> Je ferai pour ta tête une énorme Couronne;

The materials for this shrine are of course verbal. The image is powerfully suggestive: the lines of poetry against a white page are likened to the filigree intricacies on a royal crown, while the rhymes are at once like stars ('constellé') and like precious stones, set expertly in positions of sharp prominence to catch the light and the attention. Both poems pay homage to the mistresses but also to the power of rhyme, the first alluding to its sense of its own privilege, the second to its incisive, decorative richness. Unlike Sainte-Beuve, Baudelaire is not making a statement about rhyme in general but rather extolling the virtues of his own rhymes. If he chooses to boast of the quality of his rhymes in the poetry itself (even if one understands that he is seeking to impress the woman), it is worth asking to what extent his rhymes deserve such praise. One might wonder, for instance, why in the very sonnet in which he speaks of his 'rimes hautaines' he uses two sets of weak rhymes, 'nom'/'aquilon', 'profond'/'répond', aggravating the apparent *négligence* by the resort to the same nasal vowel in each case (indeed six out of the first ten lines end in [ɔ̃]). Let us look at the context:

> Je te donne ces vers afin que si mon nom
> Aborde heureusement aux époques lointaines,
> Et fait rêver un soir les cervelles humaines,
> Vaisseau favorisé par un grand aquilon,
>
> Ta mémoire, pareille aux fables incertaines,
> Fatigue le lecteur ainsi qu'un tympanon,
> Et par un fraternel et mystique chaînon
> Reste comme pendue à mes rimes hautaines;
>
> Etre maudit à qui, de l'abîme profond
> Jusqu'au plus haut du ciel, rien, hors moi, ne répond!
> — O toi qui, comme une ombre à la trace éphémère,

Foules d'un pied léger et d'un regard serein
Les stupides mortels qui t'ont jugée amère,
Statue aux yeux de jais, grand ange au front d'airain!

As well as the weakness of the rhymes in [5], there is even a hint that 'aquilon' suits the demands of rhyme better than the demands of sense; the favourable climate connoted by 'vaisseau favorisé' leads one to expect, as Pichois says, 'le zephyr et non l'aquilon, qui est un vent du nord, et violent' (I, 904). The contradiction between the assurance of the boastful versifier and the uncertainty of the weak rhymes teases the reader into a quest for explanation. One tempting suggestion would point to the clash within the text (at least in lines 1–11) between the relative confidence of the poet (his reputation reaches future generations, provokes their imagination and is generally 'favorisé') and the ambiguity of the woman's success (memory of her echoing as in some hazy legend will intone obsessively 'ainsi qu'un tympanon', irritating the reader). The contrast is enshrined in the A-rhymes of the second stanza, where 'incertaines' qualifies indirectly the woman's memory and 'hautaines' evokes the poet's belief in the efficacy of his verse. But the muffled and repeated beat of the rhymes in [5], including the weak ones, could well be seen as expressive of the uncertain yet persistent presence of her memory. Such a recuperation would cheer the heart of Banville's Secrétan, who might recognize an example of a rhyme which is 'ténue et comme pauvre, si le cas l'exige' (Banville 1886, 300). If one is suspicious of such expressiveness (and it is normally wise to be suspicious of expressiveness), then the least one could propose as explanation is that the oddness of the rhymes in such a self-reflexive poem adds piquancy to an altogether unusual sonnet. Unusual in that, while the quatrains offer a more or less traditional promise to the poet's mistress, the tercets veer away from this theme to stress her superior contempt of society's judgement. The switch of focus is so dramatic (much more pronounced than the conventional shift after line 8 of a sonnet) that Claude Pichois wonders whether the two halves were not composed as separate entities and then daringly brought together in order to extract 'de leur juxtaposition un effet particulièrement heureux qui résulte de la tension ainsi créée' (I, 904).[5]

The rhymes of 'A une Madone' do little to contradict the poet's description of them as 'rimes de cristal':

Je veux bâtir pour toi, Madone, ma maîtresse,
Un autel souterrain au fond de ma détresse,
Et creuser dans le coin le plus noir de mon cœur,
Loin du désir mondain et du regard moqueur,
Une niche, d'azur et d'or tout émaillée,   5

84

Où tu te dresseras, Statue émerveilléé.
Avec mes Vers polis, treillis d'un pur métal
Savamment constellé de rimes de cristal,
Je ferai pour ta tête une énorme Couronne;
Et dans ma Jalousie, ô mortelle Madone,   10
Je saurai te tailler un Manteau, de façon
Barbare, roide et lourd, et doublé de soupçon,
Qui, comme une guérite, enfermera tes charmes;
Non de Perles brodé, mais de toutes mes Larmes!
Ta Robe, ce sera mon Désir, frémissant,   15
Onduleux, mon Désir qui monte et qui descend,
Aux pointes se balance, aux vallons se repose,
Et revêt d'un baiser tout ton corps blanc et rose.
Je ferai de mon Respect de beaux Souliers
De satin, par tes pieds divins humiliés,   20
Qui, les emprisonnant dans une molle étreinte,
Comme un moule fidèle en garderont l'empreinte.
Si je ne puis, malgré tout mon art diligent,
Pour Marchepied tailler une Lune d'argent,
Je mettrai le Serpent qui me mord les entrailles   25
Sous tes talons, afin que tu foules et railles,
Reine victorieuse et féconde en rachats,
Ce monstre tout gonflé de haine et de crachats.
Tu verras mes Pensers, rangés comme les Cierges,
Devant l'autel fleuri de la Reine des Vierges,   30
Etoilant de reflets le plafond peint en bleu,
Te regarder toujours avec des yeux de feu;
Et comme tout en moi te chérit et t'admire,
Tout se fera Benjoin, Encens, Oliban, Myrrhe,
Et sans cesse vers toi, sommet blanc et neigeux,   35
En Vapeurs montera mon Esprit orageux.

Enfin, pour compléter ton rôle de Marie,
Et pour mêler l'amour avec la barbarie,
Volupté noire! des sept Péchés capitaux,
Bourreau plein de remords, je ferai sept Couteaux   40
Bien affilés, et, comme un jongleur insensible,
Prenant le plus profond de ton amour pour cible,
Je les planterai tous dans ton Cœur pantelant,
Dans ton Cœur sanglotant, dans ton Cœur ruisselant!

There is only one weak rhyme ('bleu'/'feu'), and only five lack the *consonne d'appui*; on the other hand, one finds rich rhymes throughout ('maîtresse'/'détresse', 'mon cœur'/'moqueur', 'rachats'/'crachats', 'admire'/'Myrrhe', for example). More impressive, however, than the overall richness of the rhymes is the sinister way in which they reinforce the inevitability of the dramatic conclusion. If, in lines 1–36, the rhymes are part of the materials with which the poet constructs the shrine for his beloved, in lines 37–44 they become just as surely the accomplices in her destruction. Here the poetics of closure play an important role: the gap before line 37, the sight of the last line define this 'paragraph' as *dénouement*. The emphatic 'Enfin, pour compléter ...' provokes and confirms expectations of closure. In such an atmosphere, the second rhyme of the couplet seems to carry an extra charge of inevitability, offering a hint of that completion the reader awaits. And Baudelaire takes beautiful advantage of it in order to stress with the slow relish of the sadist the process of his madonna's destruction. The response to the virginal 'Marie' is the violence of 'barbarie'; the second rhyme of 'capitaux'/'Couteaux' produces the instruments of her death; the 'cible' of line 42 offers the target of the poet's fury and 'ruisselant' the result. In the midst of this savagery, the poet describes himself as a 'jongleur insensible', using an image often applied to the expert rhymester. The woman is the victim of his rhymes, of a calculated, versified ritual murder. The glint of crystal rhymes has taken on the glint of blades.

Few of Baudelaire's poems invite reflection on their rhymes by explicit allusion to their presence as in 'Je te donne ces vers ...' or 'A une Madone'. But rhymes, by their very nature, can draw attention to themselves to varying degrees in any poem. The self-advertisement may depend most obviously on richness of rhyme, but this need not be so: rhymes may strike the reader through the rareness of the coupling or indeed through their brazen banality; the poverty of the rhymes (as in some lines of 'Je te donne ces vers ...') may impress more than their richness.

Rich and rare rhymes

For Banville, (ultra-)rich rhymes formed an essential ingredient of his wit; they were a part of his 'comique rimé', a device to 'faire vibrer la corde bouffonne'. Baudelaire was not temperamentally drawn to 'la corde bouffonne' and wit gives way to an irony that stems from a sense of the grotesque and the ridiculous. But late in his life, he did write three poems which were published in the collection *Les Epaves* (1866) under the title 'Bouffonneries'. The second poem, 'A propos d'un importun', is a witty anecdote which tells of a garrulous Belgian who plagues the poet with his incessant chatter:

Il me dit qu'il était très riche,
Mais qu'il craignait le choléra;
– Que de son or il était chiche,
Mais qu'il goûtait fort l'Opéra;   4

– Qu'il raffolait de la nature,
Ayant connu monsieur Corot;
– Qu'il n'avait pas encor voiture,
Mais que cela viendrait bientôt;   8

– Qu'il aimait le marbre et la brique,
Les bois noirs et les bois dorés;
– Qu'il possédait dans sa fabrique
Trois contremaîtres décorés;   12

– Qu'il avait, sans compter le reste,
Vingt mille actions sur le *Nord*;
– Qu'il avait trouvé, pour un zeste,
Des encadrements d'Oppenord;   16

– Qu'il donnerait (fût-ce à Luzarches!)
Dans le bric-à-brac jusqu'au cou,
Et qu'au Marché des Patriarches
Il avait fait plus d'un coup;   20

– Qu'il n'aimait pas beaucoup sa femme,
Ni sa mère; – mais qu'il croyait
A l'immortalité de l'âme,
Et qu'il avait lu Niboyet!   24

– Qu'il penchait pour l'amour physique,
Et qu'à Rome, séjour d'ennui,
Une femme, d'ailleurs phtisique,
Etait morte d'amour pour lui.   28

Pendant trois heures et demie,
Ce bavard, venue de Tournai,
M'a dégoisé toute sa vie;
J'en ai le cerveau consterné.   32

S'il fallait décrire ma peine,
Ce serait à n'en plus finir;
Je me disais, domptant ma haine:
"Au moins, si je pouvais dormir!"   36

Comme un qui n'est pas à son aise,
Et qui n'ose pas s'en aller,
Je frottais de mon cul ma chaise,
Rêvant de le faire empaler.   40

Ce monstre se nomme Bastogne;
Il fuyait devant le fléau.
Moi, je fuirai jusqu'en Gascogne,
Ou j'irai me jeter à l'eau,   44

Si dans ce Paris, qu'il redoute,
Quand chacun sera retourné,
Je trouve encore sur ma route
Ce fléau, natif de Tournai.   48

No-one would claim much poetic merit for this light-hearted piece. It is useful none the less to illustrate the contribution rhyme can make to comic effect: by the unlikely and rare conjoining of 'choléra'/'Opéra', by the playful richness of 'la brique'/'fabrique', 'physique'/'phtisique' (with the suggestion that the only difference between sexual activity and illness is the single letter 't'), by the improbable rhyming of proper names ('retourné'/'Tournai', 'le *Nord*'/'Oppenord', 'Luzarches'/ 'Patriarches', 'croyait'/'Niboyet', 'Bastogne'/'Gascogne'). The poem can be considered a Banvillesque extreme in Baudelaire's work. It is a space he scarcely visited (for which posterity can be grateful); but the virtuosity displayed does throw doubt on the view that he was simply incapable of such dexterity, lacking in 'invention verbale', suffering from 'une véritable indigence verbale' and inescapably 'pauvre en tournures' (all conclusions reached in the chapter on rhyme in Cassagne 1906, 23). The burlesque, caricatural potential of rich and rare rhyme, realized so blatantly in the above poem, can be put to subtler use.

Banville himself, in his 1857 preface to his *Odes funambulesques*, frames a critic's question: 'Est-ce pour peindre quelque chose, s'il vous plaît, que vous affectez ces mètres extravagants, ces césures effrontées, ces rimes d'une sauvagerie enfantine?' and answers with the one word, 'Paroxysme', borrowed from the celebrated journalist Nestor Roqueplan who had used it to define the spirit of the age. Formal extravagance matches and expresses the frantic intensity of mid-nineteenth-century Paris. If this is so, one might expect to find evidence for it in Baudelaire's 'Tableaux parisiens', the section of *Les Fleurs du Mal* that deals precisely with the magnified dynamics of the French capital. A prime example of a poem that combines 'paroxysme' and Parisian décor (the fashionable ball) is 'Danse macabre', in which the poet reflects on a statuette of a costumed skeleton sculpted by Ernest Christophe. To what extent does the form, particularly the rhymes, contribute to the allegorical caricature of Death?

88

Fière, autant qu'un vivant, de sa noble stature,
Avec son gros bouquet, son mouchoir et ses gants,
Elle a la nonchalance et la désinvolture
D'une coquette maigre aux airs extravagants.   4

Vit-on jamais au bal une taille plus mince?
Sa robe exagérée, en sa royale ampleur,
S'écroule abondamment sur un pied sec que pince
Un soulier pomponné, joli comme une fleur.   8

La ruche qui se joue au bord des clavicules,
Comme un ruisseau lascif qui se frotte au rocher,
Défend pudiquement des lazzi ridicules
Les funèbres appas qu'elle tient à cacher.   12

Ses yeux profonds sont faits de vide et de ténèbres,
Et son crâne, de fleurs artistement coiffé,
Oscille mollement sur ses frêles vertèbres.
O charme d'un néant follement attifé!   16

Aucuns t'appelleront une caricature,
Qui ne comprennent pas, amants ivres de chair,
L'élégance sans nom de l'humaine armature.
Tu réponds, grand squelette, à mon goût le plus cher!   20

Viens-tu troubler, avec ta puissante grimace,
La fête de la Vie? ou quelque vieux désir,
Eperonnant encor ta vivante carcasse,
Te pousse-t-il, crédule, au sabbat du Plaisir?   24

Au chant des violons, aux flammes des bougies,
Espères-tu chasser ton cauchemar moqueur,
Et viens-tu demander au torrent des orgies
De rafraîchir l'enfer allumé dans ton cœur?   28

Inépuisable puits de sottise et de fautes!
De l'antique douleur éternel alambic!
A travers le treillis recourbé de tes côtes
Je vois, errant encor, l'insatiable aspic.   32

Pour dire vrai, je crains que ta coquetterie
Ne trouve pas un prix digne de ses efforts;
Qui, de ces cœurs mortels, entend la raillerie?
Les charmes de l'horreur n'enivrent que les forts!   36

Le gouffre de tes yeux, plein d'horribles pensées,
Exhale le vertige, et les danseurs prudents
Ne contempleront pas sans d'amères nausées
Le sourire éternel de tes trente-deux dents.   40

Pourtant, qui n'a pas serré dans ses bras un squelette,
Et qui ne s'est nourri des choses du tombeau?
Qu'importe le parfum, l'habit ou la toilette?
Qui fait le dégoûté montre qu'il se croit beau.   44

Bayadère sans nez, irrésistible gouge,
Dis donc à ces danseurs qui font les offusqués:
"Fiers mignons, malgré l'art des poudres et du rouge
Vous sentez tous la mort! O squelettes musqués,   48

"Antinoüs flétris, dandys à face glabre,
Cadavres vernissés, lovelaces chenus,
Le branle universel de la danse macabre
Vous entraîne en des lieux qui ne sont pas connus!   52

"Des quais froids de la Seine aux bords brûlants du Gange,
Le troupeau mortel saute et se pâme, sans voir
Dans un trou du plafond la trompette de l'Ange
Sinistrement béante ainsi qu'un tromblon noir.   56

"En tout climat, sous tout soleil, la Mort t'admire
En tes contorsions, risible Humanité,
Et souvent, comme toi, se parfumant de myrrhe,
Mêle son ironie à ton insanité!"   60

The theme of extravagance and exaggeration is established from the beginning ('aux airs extravagants', 'sa robe exagérée', etc.) and is soon realized structurally in the phonetic web of the poem: the hyperbolic rhyming of 'caricature'/'armature' (ll. 17–19), echoing the not-too-distant 'stature'/'désinvolture' of the first stanza; the self-illustrative, mocking excess of 'clavicules'/'ridicules' (ll. 9–11); the brazen over-exposure of the rhyming adverbs, 'abondamment' (l. 7), 'pudiquement' (l. 11), 'artistement' (l. 14), culminating in the exorbitant 'mollement'/ 'follement' (ll. 15–16);[6] the superfluity of 'funèbres' (l. 12) heralding its almost inseparable partner 'ténèbres', here yoked to 'vertèbres' as its end-rhyme. (Given the virtuosity of this display, it is perhaps not surprising that Banville, in a newspaper article, chose to quote lines 9–16 to illustrate Baudelaire's descriptive prowess.)[7] The rare, impudent rhyming of 'alambic'/'aspic' (ll. 30–2) preludes a stanza (ll. 33–6) which can be interpreted as an oblique reflection on the poet's own activity. The poet's own creation has advertised itself coquettishly in its phonetic display; the poetic 'coquetterie', like that of the skeleton, is the result of careful effort, and yet the irony of the verbal artifice may, again like that of the skeleton, go unnoticed by those readers/dancers insensitive to 'les charmes de l'horreur'. To support this reading one could turn to Baudelaire himself, who, describing Leconte de Lisle's rhymes, calls them 'exactes sans trop de coquetterie' (II, 179), evoking the image of rhyme as the flirtatious woman seeking to catch the eye. What is remarkable in 'Danse macabre' is the sustained appeal of the rhyming. The linkage of 'offusqués'/'musqués' is not only very rich (four elements in common) but has the virtue of repeating the unusual 'squ' orthography found in the key-word, 'squelettes'. The search for the phonetically and orthographically bizarre is evident in lines 49–52, where we find 'Antinoüs', 'dandys' and 'lovelaces' as well as the rare '-avres' ending (only two other French words have this ending); and the rhyme 'glabre'/'macabre' is one of a very restricted number possible. Together with the near anagram of 'vernissés' and 'universel', these features of the *signifiant* all contribute to a sense of *outrance*, a linguistic disorientation which takes the reader 'en des lieux qui ne sont pas connus'. Baudelaire reserves his richest (but not his most surprising) rhyme, 'Humanité'/'insanité', for his concluding stanza, in which Death powerfully passes judgement on the ridiculousness of Mankind and voices explicitly the theme of irony which has been present throughout. The ironic coquettishness of the skeleton, like the stylized rituals and fashion of the dancers at a Parisian ball – indeed like the varnished artifice of the poem itself – is no more than a masquerade which does nothing to hide the inevitable reality of Death.

'Danse macabre' is a hyperbolic *tour de force*, illustrating a masterly adaptation of form and content and a particular ability to functionalize the use of rich and rare rhyme. I move now to an example which will confirm this ability, the sonnet 'Sed non satiata':

> Bizarre déité, brune comme les nuits,
> Au parfum mélangé de musc et de havane,
> Œuvre de quelque obi, le Faust de la savane,
> Sorcière au flanc d'ébène, enfant des noirs minuits,   4
>
> Je préfère au constance, à l'opium, au nuits,
> L'élixir de ta bouche où l'amour se pavane;
> Quand vers toi mes désirs partent en caravane,
> Tes yeux sont la citerne où boivent mes ennuis.   8
>
> Par ces deux grands yeux noirs, soupiraux de ton âme,
> O démon sans pitié! verse-moi moins de flamme;
> Je ne suis pas le Styx pour t'embrasser neuf fois,   11
>
> Hélas! et je ne puis, Mégère libertine,
> Pour briser ton courage et te mettre aux abois,
> Dans l'enfer de ton lit devenir Proserpine!   14

The title, taken from Juvenal and alluding to the insatiable sexual appetite of Messalina, preludes two themes of the poem: firstly that of sensual extravagance (the woman's lust for the plural implied in line 11, her desire for a female lover implied in line 14) and secondly that of foreignness, evoked by the use of Latin. The first line immediately confirms this hint of the unusual, not only by the actual word 'Bizarre' or the choice of the rare 'déité' rather than *déesse*, but also by the oddness of comparing singular with plural (when 'brune comme la nuit' would equally have suited the metre); and, even though French has *sur la brune* for 'at dusk', the use of the 'les nuits' as a vehicle to epitomize the colour suggested by 'brune' is again disconcerting. The rhymes play an important role in producing and supporting this sense of the rare and the bizarre. Long ago, Cassagne (1906, 13–14) consulted his Landais and Barré rhyming dictionary and revealed the interesting fact that, if Baudelaire had chosen to rhyme in '-ane', he would have had over 160 words at his disposal, if he had chosen to rhyme in '-vane' he would have had only seven, and finally, by choosing the very rich '-avane', he limited himself to the the only four words available: 'havane', 'savane', 'pavane' and 'caravane'. The feminine rhymes of the quatrains are therefore not only sumptuously rich but also extremely rare; and the connotations of all these rhyme words tint the poem with a touch of exoticism. It is not too difficult to imagine how the lure of the rich rhyme must have provoked a fascinating compositional battle in which form and content struggled not so much against each other as with each other in order to find a perfect fit.[8] Baudelaire talks of 'rimes puissamment colorées, ces lanternes qui éclairent la route de l'idée' (II, 11). These rhymes in '-avane' radiate their power so conspicuously that the thematic journey of the reader through the quatrains seems guided by their inevitability (as the poet's journey was in the act of composition, no doubt). The first rhyme ('havane') connotes foreignness and masculinity and forges what Claude Pichois, in his excellent notes on the sonnet, calls a 'curieuse alliance d'un parfum d'origine animale avec le tabac des dandys' (I, 884). The second rhyme ('savane') maintains the *dépaysement*, and echoes the primitive associations of the rare word 'obi', a kind of witch-doctor/magician. The third rhyme ('pavane') flaunts its richness in a phonetic display worthy of the peacock from which the word derives ('se paonner'=to strut like a peacock) to express the aggressive sensuality of the woman. The fourth rhyme ('caravane') is likewise metaphorically creative, transforming the desires of the European love-poet into exotic travellers. Although commentators have largely been drawn to the poetic fertility of the feminine rhymes, the masculine rhymes deserve almost equal attention. Vocalically the semi-vowel plus the tight, closed [i] form a distinctive contrast with the full, open vowels of [-avan], a contrast that reinforces structurally a thematic opposition between the sunlit tropical associations of the feminine rhymes and the dark suggestions of 'nuits'/'minuits'/'ennuis'. It is as if the masculine rhymes pull into focus the sombre danger of the mysterious, dark-skinned mistress. These rhymes are not so rich phonetically as their neighbours, but visually 'nuits'/'minuits' share as many common elements as '-avane'. I have already commented upon the oddness of the plural 'nuits' in the opening line; the plural 'minuits' is equally unusual, conjuring here visions of a repeated magic ritual. But possibly more disorientating than either is the appearance of 'au nuits' in line 5. We may know that 'le nuits' is a wine from Nuits-Saint-Georges (just as 'le constance' is also a wine, this time from South Africa), but this knowledge does little to absorb the double linguistic shock of seeing a masculine, singular form ('au') before what looks like a feminine, plural noun ('nuits'). A similar comment could be made about 'au constance', where, as well as the direct gender clash with *la constance*, there is a semantic clash full of irony, setting together the high moral quality of steadfast, faithful perseverance and the intoxicating wine which, in this context, might suggest totally opposite qualities. The ambiguity of the genders can be taken as a forerunner of the more or less explicit reference to the ambiguous sexuality of the mistress in the second tercet: both 'nuits' and 'constance' are, as it were, bisexual. What is more, the play of singular and plural forms in 'au nuits' is a subtle foregrounding of the dilemma of a lover who cannot meet the plural demands of the woman; the 'failed' plural of 'au nuits' preludes the poet's failure. The fourth masculine rhyme of the quatrains closes the pattern with the plural of the key-word 'ennui'. Paradoxically, the plural risks weakening the force of the singular, with pathological tedium giving way to much more mundane troubles. But Baudelaire uses the plural frequently in his poetry and sometimes to express repeated bouts of severe boredom, *e.g.* in 'Sur l'esprit gémissant en proie aux longs ennuis' ('Spleen'). This stronger meaning prevails here.

The rhyming in the tercets is noticeably less *recherché*. Indeed the pairing of 'âme'/'flamme' is positively banal. In this context, however, it is rescued by the audacity of Baudelaire's mixed metaphor: the air-vents or skylights of the soul, which outrageously describe the woman's eyes, cannot (prosaically) pour flame. Only the most literal-minded reader would object to such *inconséquence*. Its surrealism adds rather to the hyperbolic strangeness of the poem, as well as demonstrating how to rejuvenate old rhymes. The reinforced rhyme 'libertine'/'Proserpine' ([ɛr-in]) ends the sonnet with a sonorous exclamation, the last syllable of which ('-pine') has been seen by Pichois to smuggle into the poem a common obscenity ('la pine'/'penis'). If this reading is accepted, then the inclusion of the phallus in the female name and the feminine rhyme emphasizes the theme of bisexuality in a totally unexpected way.

In the concentrated space of the sonnet, rhymes can carry a high poetic charge, particularly when the quatrains employ only two rhymes. In 'Sed non satiata', Baudelaire extracts every advantage from these privileged phonemes, making them work above all to produce some of his most memorable images: 'ces images, au lieu de se suivre par ressemblance, comme dans nos rêveries paresseuses, ont l'air de venir, grâce à la rime, des coins les plus éloignés de la fantaisie' (Prévost 1953, 324). There could be no better example of the creative power of rhyme. Within the poem, they function excellently and suggestively as generators of theme through their excess, bizarreness and ambiguity.

Weak rhymes

So far, the discussion has tended to centre on Baudelaire's richer rhymes. But effects can be drawn from juxtaposing the rich and the not-so-rich, and even the poorest of rhymes can steal attention. Baudelaire's longest poem, 'Le Voyage', written in 1859, a wonderfully creative year for the poet, provides a wealth of material for the study of rhyme. There is space here for only three examples. The first is the opening quatrain of section IV in which the travellers reply to the eager question of the stay-at-homes, 'Dites, qu'avez-vous vu?':

> Nous avons vu des astres
> Et des flots; nous avons vu des sables aussi;
> Et, malgré bien des chocs et d'imprévus désastres
> Nous nous sommes souvent ennuyés, comme ici.

The reply is deliberately bathetic; the growing anticipation of the 'nobles histoires' to be told by the travellers meets with the dispiriting news that travel cannot shake loose 'ennui'. The sights seen consist, in the first two lines, of no more than the highly predictable stars, waves and sand; and even the unpredictable (the 'chocs' and 'imprévus désastres') cannot stave off the return of boredom. Bathos is built into the structure of the rhymes: the feminine rhymes are amongst the richest in Baudelaire, *'vu des astres'/'d'imprévus désastres'* giving nine elements in common ([vydezastr]), whereas the masculine rhymes have a minimal two shared elements ([si]). The numerical contrast matches the thematic contrast between the poetic and cosmic aura of 'des astres' and the high drama of 'imprévus désastres' on the one hand, and the banality of 'aussi' and 'ici' on the other. The mock-heroic star-gazing is pulled inexorably back to the tedium of reality. In this quatrain the clash of the very rich and the barely sufficient rhymes mimics the theme.

In the next example from section II of 'Le Voyage', the weak rhyme 'où'/'fou' functions expressively as a part of a quite extraordinary phonetic madness based on the sound [u]:

> Nous imitons, horreur! la toupie et la boule
> Dans leur valse et leurs bonds; même dans nos sommeils
> La Curiosité nous tourmente et nous roule,
> Comme un Ange cruel qui fouette des soleils.
>
> Singulière fortune où le but se déplace,
> Et, n'étant nulle part, peut être n'importe où!
> Où l'Homme, dont jamais l'espérance n'est lasse,
> Pour trouver le repos court toujours comme un fou!

The poet–moralist despairs of Man's frenzied and tortured search for a spiritual haven, and the lines which express this despair, rather than displaying a euphonic harmony, are characterized instead by an obsessive, unsettling repetition of the [u], reaching a crescendo in the last line, where it occurs no less than six times. The weak rhyme is only weak in theory; in context, it allows the dominant [u] to occupy alone the privileged rhyme-space. Three stanzas deeper into the poem, the same vowel conspires in another weak rhyme:

> Tel le vieux vagabond, piétinant dans la boue,
> Rêve, le nez en l'air, de brillants paradis;
> Son œil ensorcelé découvre une Capoue
> Partout où la chandelle illumine un taudis.

Here the weak rhyme (reinforced by the penultimate vowel 'la b*oue*'/ '*Capoue*') is recuperated by its thematic function which serves to highlight the contrast between reality ('la boue') and imagination (the legendary wealth of 'Capoue'). This exquisitely structured quatrain plays an ABBA thematic pattern (mud/paradise/wealth/hovel) against an ABAB rhyme-scheme, with the result that each pair of rhymes carries the contrastive charge (not only 'la boue'/'Capoue' but also 'paradis'/'taudis'). Such examples are typical of the complex ambition that Baudelaire shows in the rhymes of 'Le Voyage'.

The suggestion arising out of this brief study of examples of weak rhymes is that Baudelaire compensates for their phonetic frailty by endowing them with a thematic function, whether this be achieved through expressiveness or through structural contrast. If one thinks of weak rhymes as being phonetically frail, what is one to make of the so-called *rimes normandes?* These rhymes can scarcely be said to be rhymes at all: examples would be 'aimer'/'la mer' and 'hiver'/'s'élever' in the following quatrains.

> Rubens, fleuve d'oubli, jardin de la paresse,
> Oreiller de chair fraîche où l'on ne peut aimer,
> Mais où la vie afflue et s'agite sans cesse,
> Comme l'air dans le ciel et la mer dans la mer. ('Les Phares')

> Il est amer et doux, pendant les nuits d'hiver,
> D'écouter, près du feu qui palpite et qui fume,
> Les souvenirs lointains lentement s'élever
> Au bruit des carillons qui chantent dans la brume. ('La Cloche fêlée')

> Elle était donc couchée et se laissait aimer,
> Et du haut du divan elle souriait d'aise
> A mon amour profond et doux comme la mer,
> Qui vers elle montait comme vers sa falaise. ('Les Bijoux')

In each of these stanzas, we find what were by Baudelaire's time (and indeed much earlier) incorrect rhymes,[9] tolerated by the verse canon for historical reasons (there was a time when, in Normandy, the -er infinitive was pronounced [ɛr]). Baudelaire's love of *étrangeté* might well have been sufficient reason for him to have used such rhymes, which exude a sense of the archaic and whose phonetic mismatch contradicts their visual correctness. It is worth noting that in 'Les Phares' and 'La Cloche fêlée' they occur in the opening stanza, that is before the rhyme-scheme has become established; their reluctance to rhyme defers the fulfilment of the reader's expectations. In all three examples, the orchestration of sound patterns *within* the lines provides compensatory internal rhymes: 'chair', 'air' and an internal 'mer' in 'Les Phares', 'amer' in 'La Cloche fêlée' and 'vers' (twice) in 'Les Bijoux'. Yves Bonnefoy, the poet and critic, argues in a complex and demanding analysis of the stanza from 'Les Phares' that the lines express the ultimate futility of artistic creation: 'Cet espace où la vie afflue, mais s'agite en vain, car son rivage lui manque, c'est la création artistique. Prémonition de la vanité de l'effort: "aimer", qui est le fait de la rive, ne rime pas avec "mer"' (Bonnefoy 1969, 104). Although the *rime normande* in 'Les Bijoux' is not recuperable through this kind of (always risky) mimetic interpretation, such an interpretation works persuasively with the quatrain from 'La Cloche fêlée', where the inadequate rhyme signals the theme of disharmony and poetic flaw that dominates the title and the poem.

Concluding remarks

Rhyme foregrounds its own activity in other ways than those exemplified above. We have already seen Baudelaire's use of reinforced, similar and internal rhymes in Chapter 2. Three further aspects that have almost escaped mention relate to the gender of rhymes, the disposition of rhymes and the grammar of rhymes. A book devoted solely to Baudelaire's rhyming practice would examine these at some length; I intend simply to point the reader in their direction.

Rhymes are either masculine or feminine (masculine describes a rhyme that does not end in a mute e, feminine a rhyme that does). Roy Lewis (1982, 140) and Clive Scott (1980, 108–13) both write interestingly on this distinction, a critical one in strict prosody because of the requirement that masculine and feminine rhymes alternate. The principle of alternation, based as it is on historical reasons, is a fact of versification which yields very little interpretative fruit. Scott argues that

the potential expressive or tonal distinction between masculinity and femininity is lost when alternation is a mechanical process, when the placing of masculine and feminine rhymes is not a strategic act.   (Scott 1980, 109)

When can such placing become a strategic act? It might be, to offer one possibility, that in 'La Chevelure' Baudelaire exploits the rhyme-scheme of the quintil, ABAAB, to allow the feminine rhymes to dominate. By making the first line of the poem end in a feminine rhyme, the poet ensures that three out of every five rhymes throughout the poem will be feminine. Feminine rhymes, because of the characteristic mute e, have a greater capacity for prolongation (Scott talks of 'vibrancy': 1980, 110). In a stanza such as the following, from 'La Chevelure':

> Je plongerai ma tête amoureuse d'ivresse
> Dans ce noir océan où l'autre est enfermé;
> Et mon esprit subtil que le roulis caresse
> Saura vous retrouver, ô féconde paresse,
> Infinis bercements du loisir embaumé!

the dominant feminine rhyme resonates perfectly to enhance the mood of blissful indolence.

A clearer example of a strategic decision would be when the poet refuses to conform to the principle of alternation. Baudelaire is guilty of this insubordination in two poems, 'Ciel brouillé' and 'A une mendiante rousse'. In both cases, he uses masculine rhymes throughout. In the first, Scott implies that the decision to use solely masculine rhymes reflects an interest in 'isolating moods and exploring their extensions into obsession and neurosis' (1980, 110). This may be so, although one has to say that there are many more poems which explore obsession and neurosis while obeying the principle of alternation. 'Ciel brouillé' should be seen therefore as experimentation, an attempt perhaps to eradicate the sense of distinction implied by alternation and thereby evoke the undifferentiated impression of a 'ciel brouillé'. (This reading receives some support from the ambiguity of the stanza form – quatrains with a rhyme-scheme of AABB, CCDD, etc; since couplets, of themselves, cannot define stanzas, the visual gap is the only indicator of stanzaic form. The usual auditory differentiation supplied by the inward pattern of a rhyme scheme is absent.) In 'A une mendiante rousse', the decision to use masculine rhymes exclusively relates the general archaism of the poem, alluding to an earlier period of French verse when the principle of alternation had not taken firm root. Curiously, the poem mentions Ronsard, one of the major proponents of alternation in the Pléiade school of Renaissance poets; and it owes a good deal to his example in other ways (Pichois argues that the rhythm is inspired by two Ronsardian odes: I, 999). Is the refusal of alternation an assertion of Baudelairean independence, a deliberate stepping away from the dominant model?

The disposition of rhymes into *rimes croisées*, *rimes embrassées* and *rimes plates* need not detain us long. Clive Scott (1980, 128–36) strives hard to suggest that a rhyme-scheme has an 'ability to mean', whilst making the very necessary caveat that the abstract meaning that one might attach to a scheme has no universal applicability. In an ABBA scheme, for example, the B-couplet might seem parenthetic with the second A-line superseding the observation and revelling in its own finality. There are a few instances in Baudelaire where the B-couplet is genuinely parenthetical but it is much more common to find a sense of finality attached to the second A-line. This is hardly surprising since it not only closes the rhyme-scheme but also the stanza; and, in the great majority of cases, it will also effect syntactic closure, given the overwhelming tendency in French verse to match syntactical and metrical units (be they hemistichs, lines or stanzas). Roy Lewis (1982, 112) insists that an ABBA scheme 'gives each stanza its self-contained mental rhythm', whereas an ABAB scheme produces a stanza which is less self-contained, very suitable 'when the poet wishes to establish a high degree of continuity in his poem while exploiting the advantages of stanza-division'. Scott likewise sees the ABAB scheme as less mono-lithic: it is more a question of the eye 'coming and going', a 'progression with hesitation, with room for circumstance and qualification'; the scheme is a 'scheme of losing *and* remembering, of changing in order to recur'. This particular scheme is that most commonly found in Baudelaire and it is perhaps inevitable that one should discover some excellent illustrations of Scott's point. The quatrains of 'Le Chat' seem designed to act as models:

> Viens, mon beau chat, sur mon cœur amoureux;
>> Retiens les griffes de ta patte,
> Et laisse-moi plonger dans tes beaux yeux,
>> Mêlés de métal et d'agate.
>
> Lorsque mes doigts caressent à loisir
>> Ta tête et ton dos élastique,
> Et que ma main s'enivre du plaisir
>> De palper ton corps électrique

In the first stanza, the A-lines suggest approach and intimacy whilst the B-lines suggest possible threat and impenetrability; in the second stanza, the A-lines contain the instruments of the poet's caress, the B-lines its object. In both cases, the alternation is of course reinforced by the oscillation between decasyllables and octosyllables. In the second quatrain the progression within alternation is stressed by a parallelism which implies an increasing excitement in its move from fingers to hand, from head and back to the whole body, from surface caress to a deeper fondling and from leisurely enjoyment to a more intoxicating, sexual pleasure.

The disposition of rhymes is inevitably bound up with the definition of stanza form; the completion of a rhyme-scheme signals the probability that the stanza has run its course. The denial of this probability in some of Baudelaire's five-line stanzas (quintils) is worth examining. In 'Le Poison', for example, the ABBAA scheme could be seen as a quatrain in *rimes embrassées* to which has been added an extra A-line; there is a strong sense of excess, created by the subverting of the closural expectations aroused by the dominant ABBA quatrain model. It would be difficult not to accept some clear expressive link between the structural extension of the rhyme-scheme and the theme of spiritual and sensual expansion in

> L'opium agrandit ce qui n'a pas de bornes,
>> Allonge l'illimité,
> Approfondit le temps, creuse la volupté,
>> Et de plaisirs noirs et mornes
> Remplit l'âme au-delà de sa capacité.

The conspicuous run-on of the syntax between the fourth and fifth line enhances the refusal to close the ABBA scheme and increases the impression of going beyond the limits. 'Le Poison' (poem 49 in *Les Fleurs du Mal*) should be compared with its close neighbour 'Réversibilité' (poem 44); this ostensibly has the same rhyme-scheme, but as the first stanza will illustrate there is an important difference:

> Ange plein de gaieté, connaissez-vous l'angoisse,
> La honte, les remords, les sanglots, les ennuis,
> Et les vagues terreurs de ces affreuses nuits
> Qui compriment le cœur comme un papier qu'on froisse?
> Ange plein de gaieté, connaissez-vous l'angoisse?

Roy Lewis, discussing the repetition of the first line as the fifth line of a quintil, says that in such cases 'the normal representation of the rime-scheme by letters proves inadequate' (1982, 116), since a word cannot rhyme with itself. Whereas in 'Le Poison' there is a genuine supplementation of the rhyme-scheme which militates against the closural assumptions of *rimes embrassées*, in 'Réversibilité' the fifth line, through its circular return to the substance and rhyme-word of the first line, actually strengthens the sense of closure already evoked by the *rimes embrassées*. This argument could be made for each of the poem's five stanzas. The unvarying refrains suggest an increasing desperation, offering an inescapable sameness rather than the possibility of exciting and expansive difference. There is no sense of exaltation but rather one of the poet's imprisonment in depressing solitude, rendered the more cruel by the presence of the 'Ange plein de bonheur, de joie et de lumières' from whom he implores first understanding and then prayers.

The quintil with refrains is a form that is more characteristic of Baudelaire than of any other French poet; as well as in 'Réversibilité', he uses it in 'Le Balcon', 'L'Irréparable', 'Mœsta et errabunda', 'Lesbos' and 'Le Monstre ou le paranymphe d'une nymphe macabre'. With the exception of 'Réversibilité', all these poems are written in an ABABA rhyme scheme. The difference is important and sheds light on what was said above about the relative self-containedness of ABBA and ABAB stanzas. As examples of ABABA quintils, I shall quote stanzas three and four from 'L'Irréparable':

> Dis-le, belle sorcière, oh! dis, si tu le sais,
>   A cet esprit comblé d'angoisse
> Et pareil au mourant qu'écrasent les blessés,
>   Que le sabot du cheval froisse,
> Dis-le, belle sorcière, oh! dis, si tu le sais,
>
> A cet agonisant que le loup déjà flaire
>   Et que surveille le corbeau,
> A ce soldat brisé! s'il faut qu'il désespère

D'avoir sa croix et son tombeau;
Ce pauvre agonisant que déjà le loup flaire!

The weaker impression of closure inherent in the alternating rhyme-scheme is decisively confirmed here: 'froisse' is followed by the open-spiritedness of a comma, the repeated first line does not merely look backwards in a movement of introversion but presses forward to the next stanza, establishing that 'high degree of continuity' identified by Roy Lewis as characteristic of poems with alternating rhyme-schemes; and the refrain of the second stanza quoted is subtly varied through the inversion of 'le loup' and 'déjà'. This variation signals progression and intensification (and it is a tactic adopted elsewhere in this poem as well as in the other ABABA quintils). The unconventionality of the quintil pulls into focus the question of rhyme-schemes and stanza forms and their possible functioning; the quintil defines a fair measure of its effect against the assumed dominance of the quatrain and, as such, forces the reader to look more closely at the pre-eminent features of the normal four-line stanza. In these paragraphs on the disposition of rhymes, it has again proved more interesting to examine the unusual rather than the usual, the rare quintil rather than the omnipresent quatrain. The exception provokes the reader into a search for reasons, whereas the norm might hide its potential functionality under its very need to repeat itself. As Roy Lewis warns in his discussion on the differences between quatrains in *rimes embrassées* and *rimes croisées*:

While the theoretical distinction between these two types of quatrain may be perfectly clear, its practical effect is less so, and the student called on to assess the significance of one rime-scheme rather than another in a particular poem will be compelled to use his own judgement to decide whether the poet has made any real use of their potential.   (1982, 113)[10]

Such a gap between theoretical tenet and practical effect is illustrated again when one considers the grammar of rhymes. Theory holds that rhyme should yoke different parts of speech. One of the main reasons for Cassagne's conclusion that Baudelaire is only a mediocre rhymer is that there is a high frequency of rhymes using the same part of speech. He presents as evidence the irrefutable fact that, for example, 90 per cent of the rhymes of 'Hymne' (from *Les Epaves*) link words of the same grammatical function. But one wonders if Cassagne really believes in the theoretical position, when, having detected so-called rhyming weaknesses in 'Bohémiens en voyage', he admits with disarming common sense:

On remarquera que cette défectuosité ne l'empêche d'ailleurs pas d'être un morceau superbe, et on aura par là, soit dit en passant, la mesure de l'importance toute relative de ces observations.   (Cassagne 1906, 22–3)

The same attitude could be taken to almost all prescriptive comments on rhyme. What matters is the practical realization of potential within a context. But the stricter rules of rhyme cannot be lightly ignored; they help to provide a system of regularity and propriety which can be exploited as system or as the area of transgression. They are designed to elevate the principle of pattern to the dominant principle of French verse. The question of how Baudelaire views and applies such a prosodic model will be examined in my next chapter.

6

PATTERN, EXPECTATION, SURPRISE

Theory

In Baudelaire's *Salon de 1859*, an essay in art criticism based on the Louvre exhibition of that year, the poet suddenly digresses from his main line of argument (concerning an artist's method of composing his painting) to comment provocatively on the role of rhetoric and versification:

> Car il est évident que les rhétoriques et les prosodies ne sont pas des tyrannies inventées arbitrairement, mais une collection de règles réclamées par l'organisation même de l'être spirituel.   (II, 626–7)

Versification ('prosodies') is not an arbitrary invention designed simply to make the poet's life more difficult or, after successful completion, to persuade an audience of his skill. According to Baudelaire it *satisfies a need* which has deep roots in the human psyche: the rules correspond to the complex web of our inner being. The patterning of language answers at one level to the desire for order, a desire to stabilize the self. Elsewhere, Baudelaire claims that it is possible to 'considérer toute infraction ... au beau moral comme une espèce de faute contre le rythme et la prosodie universels' (II, 113). The 'beau moral' alludes to the existence of a spiritual state whose moral perfection is at the same time an aesthetic perfection; a flaw in this moral ideal would be like a gross error of versification. These two quotations both suggest that versification is a great deal more than a frivolous language-game. As well as responding to man's psychical needs (and physiological needs too, perhaps), prosody acts as a model for – or is modelled on – states of aesthetic or spiritual grace. The phrase 'rythme universel' occurs again in Baudelaire's writings, this time in an essay on hashish, at a point where the drug-taker ('le rêveur') has reached a state of euphoria:

> L'harmonie, le balancement des lignes, l'eurythmie dans les mouvements, apparaissent au rêveur comme des nécessités, comme des *devoirs*, non seulement pour tous les êtres de la création, mais pour lui-même, le rêveur, qui

103

se trouve, à cette période de la crise, doué d'une merveilleuse aptitude pour comprendre le rythme immortel et universel. (I, 432)

The outside world seems governed by a metrical perfection, and everything, including 'le rêveur', has a duty to accept the dictates of this overwhelming musical harmony; in this ecstatic vision, the subject (the 'rêveur') and the object ('tous les êtres de la création') are united in a single rhythm. Baudelaire goes on to say that one should not believe for a moment that, even if the 'rêveur' himself is less than perfect, he will see himself as 'une note discordante dans le monde d'harmonie'. The drug persuades him otherwise: 'les sophismes du hachisch sont nombreux et admirables'. But the very clear suggestion is that the 'rêveur' is being deluded and that in reality he is indeed 'une note discordante', just as Baudelaire proclaims himself to be 'un faux accord dans la divine symphonie' in 'L'Héautontimorouménos'. The picture of a universal euphonic pattern is darkening: the implication that the 'rêveur' is deluded about himself suggests that the flaw in the system is Man. What now happens to the prosody metaphor? Will a prosody which, in the quotations above, is synonymous with harmony still be workable in an imperfect creation? Can the poet continue to claim that his poetic harmonies are models for – or modelled on – some universal harmonies, when at the centre of his perception his own self is like a 'cloche fêlée'? It is arguable of course that poetic harmony can be a reminder of some 'paradis perdu', an earlier age when the heart of Man and the Universe beat at the same rhythm; or that it projects a future ideal. But Baudelairean lucidity does not permit the poet to accept harmony as the sole form of poetic expression: nostalgia and idealism do not allow sufficiently for Baudelairean irony, a willed dissonance and exploitation of flaw. In his *Journaux intimes*, Baudelaire launches into a brief exploration of Beauty:

Ce qui n'est pas légèrement difforme a l'air insensible; – d'où il suit que l'irrégularité, c'est-à-dire l'inattendu, la surprise, l'étonnement sont une partie essentielle et la caractéristique de la beauté. (I, 656)

Beauty, Baudelaire's 'unique reine', includes – in this definition at least – deformity, however slight, within its essence. The perfect harmony of the regular seems 'insensible' and not easily assimilated to the human condition. Baudelaire has transposed this mistrust of the perfect into narrative form in a prose-poem, 'Portraits de maîtresses', in which one of the story-tellers recounts how he murdered his mistress because she was perfection itself, offering herself as a devastating and intolerable model. She provoked in him the desire to scream, as he strangled her: 'Sois donc imparfaite, misérable!' Perfection intimidates. The ideal, a

useful goal perhaps, would not guarantee happiness once found – quite
the contrary according to Baudelaire:

Les poètes, les artistes et toute la race humaine seraient bien malheureux, si
l'idéal, cette absurdité, cette impossibilité, était trouvé. Qu'est-ce que chacun
ferait désormais de son pauvre *moi* – de sa ligne brisée?   (II, 455)

Reverting to the prosodic analogies which began this chapter, one must
then ask how the idea of flaw (the 'note discordante', the 'faux accord',
the 'cloche fêlée', the 'légèrement difforme', the 'ligne brisée') can
translate into versification. For one must infer from Baudelaire's
analogy between prosody and being that he will at times wish his form to
mime the human condition, and at other times he will wish it to
transcend it. A partial response would be that prosody must not simply
generate pattern, expectation that the pattern will continue, and then
satisfaction of that expectation, but must also use that expectation to
create the conditions for surprise, irregularity and frustration of
pattern. Versification must allow for the disturbance of its own drive
towards order. In so doing, it recognizes the innate tensions of the
human psyche: 'le rythme et la rime répondent dans l'homme aux
immortels besoins de monotonie, de symétrie et de surprise' (I, 182). In
its exaggerated form, the argument would run as follows: just as Man
would be wretchedly unhappy in an ideal world in which all tension, all
dialectic would disappear, so the reader would be left unfulfilled by a
poem which offered simply 'monotonie' and 'symétrie'. The irregular,
the surprising and the unexpected – which can only exist in the
company of 'monotonie' and 'symétrie' – provide a prosodic reminder
of Man's 'ligne brisée'.

Practice

A verse text

I should like to illustrate the dynamics of pattern, expectation and
surprise in Baudelaire's verse by looking specifically at one text, 'Les
Petites Vieilles', a late poem (1859) which shows Baudelaire in the
full maturity of his craft. As an urban poem from 'Tableaux parisiens', it will act as an introduction to the more developed discussion of urban poetics to be found in Chapters 8 and 9. What follows
is intended to be not an *explication de texte* but rather an attempt to
elucidate some of the forces at work in the reading of a single
poem.

105

LES PETITES VIEILLES
A Victor Hugo

I

Dans les plis sinueux des vieilles capitales,
Où tout, même l'horreur, tourne aux enchantements,
Je guette, obéissant à mes humeurs fatales,
Des êtres singuliers, décrépits et charmants.   4

Ces monstres disloqués furent jadis des femmes,
Eponine ou Laïs! Monstres brisés, bossus
Ou tordus, aimons-les! ce sont encor des âmes.
Sous des jupons troués et sous de froids tissus   8

Ils rampent, flagellés par les bises iniques,
Frémissant au fracas roulant des omnibus,
Et serrant sur leur flanc, ainsi que des reliques,
Un petit sac brodé de fleurs ou de rébus;   12

Ils trottent, tout pareils à des marionnettes;
Se traînent, comme font les animaux blessés,
Ou dansent, sans vouloir danser, pauvres sonnettes
Où se pend un Démon sans pitié! Tout cassés   16

Qu'ils sont, ils ont des yeux perçants comme une vrille,
Luisants comme ces trous où l'eau dort dans la nuit;
Ils ont les yeux divins de la petite fille
Qui s'étonne et qui rit à tout ce qui reluit.   20

– Avez-vous observé que maints cercueils de vieilles
Sont presque aussi petits que celui d'un enfant?
La Mort savante met dans ces bières pareilles
Un symbole d'un goût bizarre et captivant,   24

Et lorsque j'entrevois un fantôme débile
Traversant de Paris le fourmillant tableau,
Il me semble toujours que cet être fragile
S'en va tout doucement vers un nouveau berceau;   28

A moins que, méditant sur la géométrie,
Je ne cherche, à l'aspect de ces membres discords,
Combien de fois il faut que l'ouvrier varie
La forme de la boîte où l'on met tous ces corps.   32

– Ces yeux sont des puits faits d'un million de larmes,
Des creusets qu'un métal refroidi pailleta . . .
Ces yeux mystérieux ont d'invincibles charmes
Pour celui que l'austère Infortune allaita!   36

II

De Frascati défunt Vestale enamourée;
Prêtresse de Thalie, hélas! dont le souffleur

Enterré sait le nom; célèbre évaporée
Que Tivoli jadis ombragea dans sa fleur,   40

Toutes m'enivrent; mais parmi ces êtres frêles
Il en est qui, faisant de la douleur un miel,
Ont dit au Dévouement qui leur prêtait ses ailes:
Hippogriffe puissant, mène-moi jusqu'au ciel!   44

L'une, par sa patrie au malheur exercée,
L'autre, que son époux surchargea de douleurs,
L'autre, par son enfant Madone transpercée,
Toutes auraient pu faire un fleuve avec leurs pleurs!   48

III

Ah! que j'en ai suivi de ces petites vieilles!
Une, entre autres, à l'heure où le soleil tombant
Ensanglante le ciel de blessures vermeilles,
Pensive, s'asseyait à l'écart sur un banc,   52

Pour entendre un de ces concerts, riches de cuivre,
Dont les soldats parfois inondent nos jardins,
Et qui, dans ces soirs d'or où l'on se sent revivre,
Versent quelque héroïsme au cœur des citadins.   56

Celle-là, droite encor, fière et sentant la règle,
Humait avidement ce chant vif et guerrier;
Son œil parfois s'ouvrait comme l'œil d'un vieil aigle;
Son front de marbre avait l'air fait pour le laurier!   60

IV

Telles vous cheminez, stoïques et sans plaintes,
A travers le chaos des vivantes cités,
Mères au cœur saignant, courtisanes ou saintes,
Dont autrefois les noms par tous étaient cités.   64

Vous qui fûtes la grâce ou qui fûtes la gloire,
Nul ne vous reconnaît! un ivrogne incivil
Vous insulte en passant d'un amour dérisoire;
Sur vos talons gambade un enfant lâche et vil.   68

Honteuses d'exister, ombres ratatinées,
Peureuses, le dos bas, vous côtoyez les murs;
Et nul ne vous salue, étranges destinées!
Débris d'humanité pour l'éternité mûrs!   72

Mais moi, moi qui de loin tendrement vous surveille,
L'œil inquiet, fixé sur vos pas incertains,
Tout comme si j'étais votre père, ô merveille!
Je goûte à votre insu des plaisirs clandestins: 76

Je vois s'épanouir vos passions novices;
Sombre ou lumineux, je vis vos jours perdus;

107

Mon cœur multiplié jouit de tous vos vices!
Mon âme resplendit de toutes vos vertus!   80
Ruines! ma famille! ô cerveaux congénères!
Je vous fais chaque soir un solennel adieu!
Où serez-vous demain, Eves octogénaires,
Sur qui pèse la griffe effroyable de Dieu?   84

Versification and transgression

Even before we read this poem, we are prepared for pattern: our
previous knowledge of French verse has taught us the apparently
unremarkable facts that if the first line has twelve syllables there is a
strong possibility that all the rest will have twelve syllables; that quatrain
will follow quatrain; and that the rhyme-scheme will remain inviolable.
Even the reader's visual apprehension of the page confirms these
presuppositions: the blocks of verse *look* regular. It is as if we are
entering a world governed by some authoritarian verbal regime: ideal
circumstances for a poet who wishes to subvert the predictable.

The truth that rhyme creates pattern and expectation of pattern risks
making it seem a rather dull creature – whereas, paradoxically, most
good rhymes are a mixture of surprise and predictability. Baudelàire,
talking of Leconte de Lisle's rhymes, says that they 'répondent
régulièrement à cet amour contradictoire et mystérieux de l'esprit
humain pour la surprise et la symétrie' (II, 179). The symmetry of
rhyme is self-evident: it allows a fairly simple process of anticipation
and satisfaction, both as the rhyming partner echoes its herald and as
the rhyme-scheme repeats itself from stanza to stanza. The richer the
rhyme, the more enhanced the sense of symmetry. The game of
call-and-echo is played beautifully by Baudelaire in 'Les Petites
Vieilles'. Two particular features can be singled out. Firstly, there is his
use of the homophones: 'cités' (cities)/'cités' (cited) (lines 62/64) and
'murs' (walls)/'mûrs' (ripe) (lines 70/72). Rhyme theory in Baudelaire's
time promoted the excellence of such rhymes since they combined total
phonetic identity between words with semantic difference. Secondly,
and more strikingly, there is Baudelaire's cultivation throughout the
poem of rhymes of the type 'novices'/'vices' (lines 77/79), where one
element is a complete word chiming with the last syllable of its rhyming
partner. The other instances are: 'discords'/'corps' (lines 30/32),
'souffleur'/'fleur' (lines 38/40), 'frêles'/'ailes' (lines 41/43), 'tombant'/
'banc' (lines 50/52), 'règle'/'aigle' (lines 57/59), 'incivil'/'vil' (lines
66/68) and 'adieu'/'Dieu' (lines 82/84). I doubt if any other poem by
Baudelaire achieves a similar concentration of such rhymes, in which,

one might note, the shorter word always comes second, acting like a truncated echo. These rhymes enhance symmetry through their rich neatness, but they also point to the surprise of rhyme. This can lie in the coming together of words and their concepts which share – quite by chance in most cases – common phonemes or syllables. The poet's ingenuity provokes a momentary thrill and quiver, as two words are plucked out of the vocabulary to be press-ganged into the prosodic system. The truncated echoes above multiply the effect because the phonetic identity engages a whole word, like a pun which relies on the fragmentation of the first rhyme-word. The listening mind is encouraged to apprehend the concept of the flower hidden clandestinely and surrealistically in the word for a theatrical prompter ('souffleur') or vice lurking perversely in the innocence of 'novices'. These rhymes thus engage meaning in a more obvious way than most rhymes, although the semantics of all rhyme-words can play a part in the surprise of rhyme. The rare rhyme 'omnibus'/'rébus' (lines 10/12) welds together in the unreality of poetic language two very mundane details more likely to be found in a Realist novel; the yoking of 'larmes'/'charmes' (lines 33/35) expresses succinctly the paradox of discovering enchantment in the despair of the old women, these 'êtres singuliers, décrépits et charmants'. Nineteenth-century rhyme-theory maintained also that rhymes gained in colour and surprise if the words were of different grammatical function: thus, 'iniques' (line 9), an adjective, rhymes more surprisingly with 'reliques' (line 11) the noun, than 'blessés' (line 14) does with 'cassés' (line 16).[1]

But these types of surprise are not essentially disruptive. Baudelaire himself, in his description of Leconte de Lisle's rhymes, uses the word 'régulièrement' to qualify their occurrence. In Baudelaire, rhyme can disrupt its own system in other ways. We have already examined the insubordinate activity of internal rhymes: in 'Les Petites Vieilles', lines 69–72 provide excellent examples ('Honteuses'/'Peureuses', 'humanité'/'éternité'). And there is a conspicuous refusal to produce a harmonic differentiation between A- and B-rhymes in lines 17–20, where, in a stanza shrill with [i] sounds, the juxtaposition of 'vrille'/'nuit'/'fille'/'reluit' on the rhymes is insistently cacophonous. Of equal interest, however, is the architecture of the rhymes in section II of the poem. The A- and B-rhymes of the first of these three stanzas recur – against all theoretical precepts – in the third: 'enamourée'/'évaporée' is echoed in the assonance of 'exercée'/'transpercée', and 'souffleur'/'fleur' is taken up by 'douleurs'/'pleurs'. The second stanza, parenthesized almost, proclaims its own difference through the similar rhymes 'frêles'/'miel'/'ailes'/'ciel'. These three stanzas, isolated typographically by Baudelaire, advertise their independence through the taut, inward-turning structure of the rhymes (I shall look at their syntax later). The degree of disruption, whatever the method (internal rhyme, similar rhymes, a structural challenge to the dominant rhyme-scheme), is undeniably limited in these examples. Baudelaire never went so far as to alter a rhyme-scheme fundamentally in mid-course (as Verlaine was to do) or miss out a rhyme altogether (as Valéry was to do);[2] what he was seeking was the 'légèrement difforme'. The three stanzas in section II, for example, do not display total prosodic dislocation; it is simply that, by breaking the normally expected pattern and by using the rhyme-scheme to foreground their isolation, they take on a certain idiosyncratic bizarreness. Within a relatively long poem such as 'Les Petites Vieilles', Baudelaire's passion for the short, tautly woven unit (so evident in his preference for the sonnet) is preserved through the use of subdivisions in general and the stressed isolation of section II in particular. Through such arrangements, the poet accommodates his mistrust of the long poem, a phrase which he considered, as Poe did, a contradiction in terms.

The other great creator of prosodic pattern is of course metre (or, in Baudelaire's words and inaccurately, 'le rythme'), here in 'Les Petites Vieilles' the Alexandrine with its characteristic integrity as a thought-containing unit. It is expected of the poet that he will be able to trim his syntax and thought within its boundaries; and he will count his syllables carefully to make sure that the sixth will coincide with some natural break in the chain of language. This Classical notion of the Alexandrine dominates numerically the work of every French poet who has used the line, no matter how revolutionary the poetry may be in other ways. The very predictability of the major characteristics (the syntax/metre parallel, the central caesura) provides a perfect climate for surprise, an ambushing of expectations. The key device is enjambement, which works its disruptive effect at three different boundaries: that between line and line, that between stanza and stanza and that between first and second hemistich.

As an example of transgression of the first boundary we can take lines 38–40:

> Prêtresse de Thalie, hélas! dont le souffleur
> Enterré sait le nom; célèbre évaporée
> Que Tivoli jadis ombragea dans sa fleur,

Claude Pichois comments that the *rejet* (the isolated word or words which are thrown over to the next line, here 'Enterré') stresses a deliberate ambiguity: 'enterré le souffleur, parce qu'il est au-dessous de la scène et, depuis lors, sous la terre' (I, 1020). A supplementary point might call upon the expressiveness of spacing in verse: as the eye dips to the next line it enacts the movement down from stage to the prompter's booth below. The cumulative artifice (the rhyme, the space to its right, the capitalized new line, but especially the unnatural separation of noun and adjective) encourages the study of lines such as these and is likely to generate the kind of interpretative strategies adopted in this paragraph. One is tempted to find reasons for having one's expectations thwarted.

As an example of transgression of the boundary between stanzas it is impossible not to cite again lines 15–18:

> Ou dansent, sans vouloir danser, pauvres sonnettes
> Où se pend un Démon sans pitié! Tout cassés
>
> Qu'ils sont, ils ont des yeux perçants comme une vrille,
> Luisants comme ces trous où l'eau dort dans la nuit:

The audacity of this stanzaic enjambement drew such unflattering comment from one Belgian critic of the time that the young Verlaine felt obliged to come to the defence of the greatly admired Baudelaire:

> Et à ce propos, je me souviens d'avoir lu – en Belgique, il est vrai ('Pauvre Belgique!' décidément), – un article de revue où l'on raillait, avec une grâce et superficialité parfaites, justement ce rejet d'une strophe à l'autre:
>
> .... Tout cassés
>
> Qu'ils sont ....
> Vraisemblablement, le critique belge ignore ce que c'est qu'une onomatopée, 'grand mot qu'il prend pour terme de chimie'.   (Verlaine 1972, 610–11)

I doubt if many nowadays would use onomatopœia to describe the effect (the irony misfires), but it is not difficult to see the basis of Verlaine's defence: the dislocation of the verse-form is expressive of, enacts, the awkward, even grotesque, movements of the old women. The expectation is that the B-rhyme, 'cassés', should click shut the ABAB scheme of the quatrain; instead, it propels the reader forward in an unbalancing lurch towards the phrase that will fulfil the demands of syntax. Stanzaic enjambement will always display tension between a sense of closure (suggested by the completion of rhyme, the visual terminus and the precedent of syntax/metre parallels) and a need to pursue meaning beyond the formal boundary.

Transgression of the medial break within an Alexandrine is a much more subdued affair; there is no visual boundary to leap and no rhyme to mark the limits. The convention of the 6+6 division inscribes itself on the reader's expectations through the repetition of its beat, a metronomic invariable (or almost) that ticks beneath the changing syntax and theme. The subtle variations wrought by the shifting secondary stresses of each hemistich do little to disturb the dominance of the central *coupe*, but occasionally (one should say rarely), the sixth syllable abandons its claims, creating a momentary prolapse of the line, as in line 53:

> Pour entendre un de ces concerts, riches de cuivre,

which is followed by three stabilizing 6+6 Alexandrines:

> Dont les soldats parfois inondent nos jardins,
> Et qui, dans ces soirs d'or où l'on se sent revivre,
> Versent quelque héroïsme au cœur des citadins.

The usurpation of the sixth syllable by the banal demonstrative 'ces' destroys the balance of the line; the impulse towards sense requires the mind to push beyond the central point to find what the demonstrative qualifies. The effect is interesting. For its first eight syllables, the line reads like prose, a slice of language destined not to find itself in an Alexandrine because of its prosodic shape; the prosaic quality is matched by the use of 'un de ces . . .', a phrase that invariably introduces the commonplace. Although the last four syllables, and the rest of the stanza, seek to restore a certain martial solemnity and *gloire* to the scene, the banality of the introduction casts a mocking irony over the description and encourages the cynical view of state-supplied heroism present in the last line.

The transgressions exemplified above all invite interpretation. They halt careful readers in their study of the poem and challenge their absorption of the regular.

Syntax and structure

Pattern and expectation of form do not just operate at the level of prosody. Two very powerful forces at work on the reader are those controlled by syntax and by a sense of a poem's overall structure. Just as we know that a sentence or part of a sentence will take shape according to the rules of syntax, so we sense that a poem will take shape and conclude according to some kind of structural syntax. The 'rules' governing the shape of a poem are, of course, much looser and more difficult to define; but, at the simplest level, most readers will have expectations, nurtured through experience, of beginnings, middles and ends.[3] They might see the plot of a poem as a smooth parabola, taking off from the void and returning to the void of the white space of the page. Such a model, partly because it is so rudimentary, is useful if it allows measurement of coincidence and digression.

Syntax in poetry has always been required to show its elasticity, its preparedness to make allowances for the demands of versification. The classic result is *inversion*, a violence done to the normal word-order of a sentence. The artifice foregrounds the syntax and affects the unproblematic reception of the message by the reader. Such momentary disorientation is recognized as a virtue by Louis Aragon in a vigorous (and self-illustrating) defence of inversion:

Où la syntaxe est violée, où le mot déçoit le mouvement lyrique, où la phrase de travers se construit, là combien de fois le lecteur frémit.   (Aragon, 1975, 9)

Aragon's sentence presupposes the principles that lie behind the discussion in this chapter: transgression, disappointment (of expectation), irregularity and reader-response. One would not have to look hard in 'Les Petites Vieilles' to find examples of inversion. We can return to the three stanzas of section II (lines 37–48) to see how inversion contributes to the syntactical patterning. There are at least three instances:

De Frascati défunt Vestale enamourée; (line 37)

L'une, par sa patrie au malheur exercée, (line 45)

L'autre, par son enfant Madone transpercée, (line 47)

In each of these lines, phrases remain in a state of critical abeyance until they are offered a syntactic chain which rescues them from non-sense. A section which launches itself with 'De Frascati défunt' presents the reader with a block of language demanding structural support from the following syntax; 'Vestale enamourée' resolves the suspense and explains retrospectively the function of the initial 'De'. The past participles which conclude the other examples fulfil the same function, giving the lines and their syntax some equilibrium. The aesthetics of inversion repay thought in that the dynamics of its curve from surprise (for example, the premature and unattached surge of the prepositions 'par' and 'au' in line 45) to expectation (how will sense be rescued?) to fulfilment can serve as a neat model for other, larger patterns of reader-response. Here, for instance, the 'Vestale enamourée' supplies only a provisional equilibrium, completing the particular segment of meaning contained within that line; it completes neither sentence nor clause and the semi-colon apparently blocks access to any obvious process of syntactical closure. Meaning is suspended until the mind recognizes the device of ternary enumeration, culminating in the summarizing '*Toutes* m'enivrent'. The search for sense finds its quarry thrown into the next stanza, where the simple juxtaposition of subject and finite verb clarifies the list in dramatic fashion. Baudelaire refuses, however, the stability that such a resolution might bring by declining (in this version at least) to capitalize 'mais', treating the exclamation mark as a minor stop to the flow of words. The poet wishes to subdivide the objects of his study, the 'petites vieilles', in order to concentrate on those whose pain has been spiritually productive. Exemplars of such suffering are listed in yet another ternary movement: 'L'une . . . L'autre . . . L'autre', leading to the climactic '*Toutes* auraient pu . . .'. The pattern of delay, summarized subject and finite verb repeats the broad tensions of lines 37–41, but with the difference (highlighted by the parallelism of structure) that the second list is unambiguously enumerative: visual appearance, thematic preparation ('Il en est qui . . .') and rhetorical preparation (lines 37–41 provide a model with which to 'rhyme') are all persuasive. Whereas the first list moves fitfully (disorientating bizarreness in its sudden beginning, odd segmentation by semi-colons, interpolated exclamation, enjambement, running beyond the stanza-unit), supporting a partly ironic view of these former actresses and their notorious frivolity, the second list unfolds in a more dignified rhythm (symmetry of initial stresses, use of the Alexandrine as a thought-containing unit, parallelism), reinforcing Baudelaire's view of the nobility of pain.

In the preceding analysis, I have concentrated on inversion and enumeration because the tensions underlying such figures feed off the reader's desire for completion: he expects the syntax to pattern itself into sense. Other, no less interesting, tensions underlie other rhetorical patterns (parallelism, chiasmus, apostrophe, apposition, for example) but inversion and enumeration sharpen best an awareness of the reader's expectation of syntactical wholeness.

I suggested earlier that this expectation of wholeness can be transferred to the level of the poem's structure. A poem can fall into many compositional patterns (although probably not as many as one might think), and, while it is not possible to predict the structure (except perhaps in fixed-form poems such as the sonnet or ballad, where the theme is often closely moulded in its development by the characteristics of the form), one does expect a pattern to emerge. It is certain, for example, that the reader of a poem will no sooner be launched into the text than he will be expecting it to conclude. How will the poem reach its end? How will the reader be taken there? How will he know that the poem is ending? Such questions remain unspoken, but they are useful starting-points for a brief consideration of a poem's overall structure.

Pattern, expectation, surprise

Before looking at the ending of 'Les Petites Vieilles', I want to consider the smoothness, or lack of it, of its narrative/descriptive parabola with reference to its first section. The opening stanza is economic exposition: location (line 1), the promise of a theme (line 2), the observer (line 3) and the observed (line 4). Lines 5–20, whilst defeminizing and dehumanizing the old women, end with the discovery of the brilliance and liveliness of their eyes. In an attempt to capture the paradox of the eyes, Baudelaire compares them to 'les yeux divins de la petite fille/Qui s'étonne et qui rit à tout ce qui reluit'. After images of 'monstres', puppets, wounded animals and bell-clappers, the affinity between the eyes of old women and those of little girls risks appearing as a rather sentimental counterweight – momentarily. In the parenthetical lines 21–32, any hint of sentimentality is eradicated. The old woman/child comparison is transferred by means of the word *petit* to an observation on the size of coffins; the brilliance of the eyes is extinguished by the images of death. Even within this parenthesis, however, the tone wavers. The picture of the old woman as a fragile being who 'S'en va tout doucement vers un nouveau berceau' implies yet again a rather sentimental observer, reflecting on the cyclical nature of life and the possibility of a new beginning. Such relative optimism is quickly shattered by the alternative stance:

> A moins que, méditant sur la géométrie,
> Je ne cherche, à l'aspect de ces membres discords,
> Combien de fois il faut que l'ouvrier varie
> La forme de la boîte où l'on met tous ces corps.

The women's bodies represent no more than a puzzle, a geometric problem for the undertaker. The *tiret* at the beginning of line 33 and the demonstrative 'Ces' (pointing backwards and over the obstacle of the digression) mark the end of the parenthesis and the re-joining of the interrupted description of the eyes. The eyes no longer evoke the child's gleam but are seen rather as the place of suffering, as the place of affinity with the poet, 'celui que l'austère Infortune allaita'. This first section is fascinating from the structural point of view, at once satisfying the descriptive expectations aroused by the title and yet subverting the expected linearity of description. The three parenthetical stanzas, with their own internal oscillation, are indisputably digressive, a tangent to the main parabola and a challenge to the simple progression of description. Their dislocation can be seen as a structural equivalent to the 'pas incertains' (line 74) of the old women, and, as such, a device which could be compared to the stanzaic enjambement of lines 16–17. Both unsettle the reader's path through the poem.

115

That path will inevitably suggest its own end. One of the commonest and oldest devices to signal closure is to repeat the introduction by way of conclusion. Conveniently, Baudelaire has given this principle a memorable, if fairly banal, formulation: 'Conclure, c'est fermer un cercle.' This return to the beginning can be *verbatim* or near *verbatim* repetition (as in many of Verlaine's or Valéry's poems) or can be a subtler echo, as in 'Les Petites Vieilles'. How do we know – apart from visually (and this obvious fact should never be underestimated) – that we are approaching the end of 'Les Petites Vieilles'? The 'Telles' (line 61) which opens section IV is a good summarizing word, signposting a satisfaction that some development has come or is coming to an end. As well as this initial indication, there are distant echoes of the opening section which enter the text, awakening the sense of a circle being closed. The locational line

> A travers le chaos des vivantes cités,

responds to the expository first line of the poem

> Dans les plis sinueux des vieilles capitales.

The earlier plea to love the old women, '*aimons*-les' (line 7), is recalled in a cruel antithesis by the 'ivrogne incivil' who insults the women 'd'un *amour* dérisoire' (line 67). And perhaps the most significant echo is found in the energetic re-emergence of the narrating 'moi'. The poet's voice has been implicit throughout (inevitably) and has occasionally asserted itself more openly ('Ah! que j'en ai suivi de ces petites vieilles!', line 49); but in this final section it is insistently present, switching the focus of the whole poem from the observed to the observer. The switch is emphatically introduced:

> Mais moi, moi qui de loin tendrement vous surveille,
> . . . Je goûte à votre insu des plaisirs clandestins.

This last line recalls through the opening syntax and the similarity of sound the third line of the poem:

> Je guette, obéissant à mes humeurs fatales.

In a poem where the 'je' form has been so rare, such a parallel is noticeable even at a distance. It not only helps to close the circle but also suggests the change wrought by the itinerary through the poem: the poet, no longer lying in wait, is now actively tasting the pleasures of his voyeuristic compassion. He has waited for his 'petites vieilles', has seen them, described them, been inspired by a feeling of empathy, and now says his good-bye:

116

Je vous fais chaque soir un solennel adieu!

There is a sense that the story, the day and the poem have run their course. But the last two lines reject the traditional equation of evening and closure and endow the poem with an unexpected open-endedness. The anticipation of a summarizing conclusion is frustrated and is replaced by the feeling of thematic irresolution which unanswered questions are likely to generate. The old women's tomorrow is the imaginative space which the reader is invited to ponder. This form of *l'inattendu*, the inconclusive conclusion, is one of Baudelaire's most important contributions to modern poetics. 'Le Balcon', 'Ciel brouillé', 'Mœsta et errabunda', 'Les Aveugles', 'La servante au grand cœur . . .' and 'Les Deux Bonnes Sœurs' all leave the reader pondering on questions that set the mind leaping beyond the poem:

Ces serments, ces parfums, ces baisers infinis,
Renaîtront-ils d'un gouffre interdit à nos sondes,
Comme montent au ciel les soleils rajeunis
Après s'être lavés au fond des mers profondes?
– O serments! ô parfums! ô baisers infinis!　　('Le Balcon')

O femme dangereuse, ô séduisants climats!
Adorerai-je aussi ta neige et vos frimas,
Et saurai-je tirer de l'implacable hiver
Des plaisirs plus aigus que la glace et le fer?　　('Ciel brouillé')

L'innocent paradis, plein de plaisirs furtifs,
Est-il déjà plus loin que l'Inde et la Chine?
Peut-on le rappeler avec des cris plaintifs,
Et l'animer encor d'une voix argentine,
L'innocent paradis plein de plaisirs furtifs?
　　　　　　　　　　　　　　　　('Mœsta et errabunda')

　　　　　　　　mais, plus qu'eux hébété,
Je dis: Que cherchent-ils au Ciel, tous ces aveugles?
　　　　　　　　　　　　　　　　　　('Les Aveugles')

Que pourrais-je répondre à cette âme pieuse,
Voyant tomber des pleurs de sa paupière creuse?
　　　　　　　　　　　　　　('La servante au grand cœur . . .')

And one should mention here that most famous example of open-endedness, the last line of 'Le Cygne':

Aux captifs, aux vaincus! . . . à bien d'autres encor!

Such refusals to click the poem shut are a form of thematic enjambement, transgressing the notion of organic unity.

117

Structuring the unpredictable: Baudelaire's prose-poems

By touching on rhyme, metre, syntax and overall structure, I have in this chapter tried to show some of the multiple patterns and expectations that underlie a single poem in all its parts. The discussion presupposes an attentive reader on the look-out not only for the pattern (the 'monotonie' and 'symétrie') but also for its collapse ('la surprise'). But how can this dialectical process work in Baudelaire's prose-poems – in a poetry which eschews metre and rhyme, the great structural foundations on which verse-patterns are built?

As a simplified introduction to the problem (and it is a problem: no one has yet succeeded in formulating a poetics of the prose-poem), one could say that, whereas in the predictable form of verse Baudelaire injects the unpredictable, in prose, where he is faced with a pervasive unpredictability, he tries to inject the predictable – to a certain extent. Unable to do so on the level of metre and rhyme, he concentrates particularly on patterns of *syntax and structure*. These are the weapons he uses to safeguard himself against the vertigo of structurelessness, a threat of which he was well aware:

... la fantaisie est d'autant plus dangereuse qu'elle est plus facile et plus ouverte; dangereuse comme la poésie en prose ... comme toute liberté absolue. (II, 644)

In the next page, I shall suggest briefly some simple patterning strategies adopted by Baudelaire to avert the dangers inherent in the absolute liberty of unstructured prose, before looking at the more complex poetics of a single poem, 'Un cheval de race'.

Some patterning strategies

Sometimes, the device Baudelaire uses to create expectation and satisfaction in the reader is relatively elementary. For example, in the long piece, 'Les Vocations', the poem opens with a scene in a twilit garden where 'quatre beaux enfants, quatre garçons, las de jouer sans doute, causaient entre eux'. The scheme that generates the pattern for the poem's development is primarily numerical: 'L'un disait . . .'; 'L'un des quatre enfants . . . dit tout à coup'; 'dit alors le troisième'; and the highly predictable 'Enfin le quatrième dit'. Added to this system of signals is a chronological subsystem, located at the beginning and end of the poem: the 'soleil automnal', which was reluctant to set, has disappeared by the closing paragraph, to be replaced by 'la nuit solennelle'. A not dissimilar enumerative system governs 'Les Tentations ou Eros, Plutus et la Gloire' and 'Portraits de maîtresses'.

The reverberations that are set up by the title of a poem are used to suggest form in several pieces. There is what seems a natural assumption that the body of a poem will, in time, justify its title. Baudelaire plays on this expectation by suspending the appearance of the title-word in the text itself and not revealing its exact relevance until the final or – more often – the penultimate paragraph. This exploitation of a pattern of suspense and fulfilment is found in 'L'Etranger', 'Un plaisant', 'Le Joujou du pauvre', 'Les Yeux des pauvres', 'Déjà' and 'Un cheval de race' (an example I shall examine in detail below). As a closural device, the return to the title can be compared to the conclusion that echoes the introduction, an arrangement seen above in 'Les Petites Vieilles'. It too is found in the prose-poems. In 'L'Etranger', for instance, the initial question, 'Qui aimes-tu le mieux, homme énigmatique, dis?' is rephrased with even greater insistence at the end: 'Qu'aimes-tu donc, extraordinaire étranger?' In 'Le Désir de peindre', the opening 'heureux l'artiste que le désir déchire!' is echoed in the final comment on the woman: 'celle-ci donne le désir de mourir lentement sous son regard'.

A prose text

But although the identification of such patterning strategies goes some way to appreciating the formal tension that can exist in the prose-poem, it does little justice to the specific complexities of a single poem. I choose as my example 'Un cheval de race', simply to illustrate the possibilities of pattern and expectation in this curious genre.

Un cheval de race

Elle est bien laide. Elle est délicieuse pourtant!

Le Temps et l'Amour l'ont marquée de leurs griffes et lui ont cruellement enseigné ce que chaque minute et chaque baiser emportent de jeunesse et de fraîcheur.

Elle est vraiment laide; elle est fourmi, araignée, si vous voulez, squelette même; mais aussi elle est breuvage, magistère, sorcellerie! en somme, elle est exquise.

Le Temps n'a pu rompre l'harmonie pétillante de sa démarche ni l'élégance indestructible de son armature. L'Amour n'a pas altéré la suavité de son haleine d'enfant; et le Temps n'a rien arraché de son abondante crinière d'où s'exhale en fauves parfums toute la vitalité endiablée du Midi français: Nîmes, Aix, Arles, Avignon, Narbonne, Toulouse, villes bénies du soleil, amoureuses et charmantes!

Le Temps et L'Amour l'ont vainement mordue à belles dents; il n'ont rien diminué du charme vague, mais éternel, de sa poitrine garçonnière.

Usée peut-être, mais non fatiguée, et toujours héroïque, elle fait penser à ces

chevaux de grande race que l'œil du véritable amateur reconnaît, même attelés
à un carrosse de louage ou à un lourd chariot.
  Et puis elle est si douce et si fervente! Elle aime comme on aime en automne;
on dirait que les approches de l'hiver allument dans son cœur un feu nouveau,
et la servilité de sa tendresse n'a jamais rien de fatigant.

Baudelaire immediately uses the reader's expectations that the title will
relate to what follows in order to create surprise. The thoroughbred and
the female pronoun 'Elle' clash. In poetry, an 'Elle' without a referent
traditionally alludes to a woman, normally the poet's beloved. The
conventions of female portraits are activated and the reader has to
attempt an adjustment of these conventions to the fact of the title. The
possibility of a woman/thoroughbred metaphor promises a resolution
(and indeed this supposition is validated in the penultimate paragraph –
but only then). The clash between the title and the curt opening
sentence is increased by the way in which the stress on ugliness
contradicts the ideas of grace contained in 'de race'; and the stress on
ugliness also contradicts the conventions of a female portrayal which
traditionally hymns the woman's beauty (here Baudelaire joins the
parodic tradition of *poésie satyrique*). Already the poem is vibrant with
tension. The second sentence revels in contradicting the first, showing
Baudelaire's delight in surprise and provocation. Yet paradox is itself a
pattern, and it soon becomes apparent that 'Un cheval de race' is
organized around its contradictory force-fields. The opening paragraph
thus offers the rhetorical figure which dominates the poem.

  In prose, the paragraph can fulfil similar functions to those of the
stanza in verse. The typography (final line falling short of the right-
hand margin, the indentation) emphasizes the integrity of the paragraph
as a unit of argument (in the widest sense), and, as with any foregrounded unit, prompts questions on the justification of its independence.
Baudelaire's first paragraph raises this issue in an acute form because of
its brevity: how can a development take place in such a minimal space?
But the explosiveness of the paradox is enhanced precisely because,
despite the brevity, it is given the status of a unit of argument.
Paragraphing insists not simply on the *integrity* of the unit but also on
the *difference* and *similarity* between units. What justifies the new
beginning? What is the relationship between the new unit and previous
ones? The reader is encouraged to look at the structuring process both
within and beyond paragraphs.

  The second paragraph identifies the agents which have caused the
ugliness, 'le Temps et l'Amour', destructive beasts of prey operating at
'chaque minute' (Time) and with 'chaque baiser' (Love), taking away
'jeunesse' (Time) and 'fraîcheur' (Love). The meticulous binarism of

the sentence (two main subjects, two main verbs, two subordinate subjects governing two direct objects) lends a verse-like polish to the paragraph and seals its independence.

The third paragraph clearly relates to the first: it begins in the same way and it uses the same grammatical simplicity in an attempt to define with a minimum of elaboration the qualities of the 'Elle'. And, in the same fashion, the grammatical simplicity contains the huge complexity of paradox, also enshrined in a transparently perfect form. The paragraph pivots around the crucial 'mais': on either side, in strict symmetry, one finds 'laide' balanced by 'exquise', and the triple 'fourmi, araignée . . . squelette' by 'breuvage, magistère, sorcellerie'. Even without the paradox, the minimal innocence of a formula such as 'elle est'+noun is violated by the choice of 'fourmi' and 'araignée', deliberately shocking in their stretching of the limits of metaphor. But the casual 'si vous voulez, squelette même' admits that the language-use is above all an exercise of the poetic will, producing instant metamorphoses. The rhetorical neatness certainly leaves the reader in no doubt that he is becoming intricated in a verbal system which is being generated before his eyes.

Just as paragraph 3 relates to paragraph 1, so paragraph 4 relates to paragraph 2. The ABAB pattern asserts itself with the authority of a rhyme-scheme. But whereas paragraph 3 repeated and developed on paragraph 1, paragraph 4 contradicts paragraph 2. The stress is now on the ineffectiveness of the ravages wrought by Time and Love, on the positive 'délicieuse' and 'exquise' rather than the 'bien laide'. The rhetoric of this paragraph beautifully enacts the content. The measured form, so characteristic of the poem so far, gradually breaks down under the pressure of the poet's enthusiasm and the woman's vitality. No hint of this breakdown is contained in the careful equilibrium of the first sentence; nor in the move from 'Temps' to 'Amour' which follows the order of paragraph 2; nor in the parallelism between these declarations of the woman's resistant charms. But the return to the failure of Time ('et le Temps n'a rien arraché . . .') invades a sentence which one feels should have been apportioned to Love alone. And the phrase 'son abondante crinière d'où s'exhale . . .' refuses to follow the clear pattern established within this paragraph of abstract noun+'de'+physical quality: 'l'harmonie pétillante de sa démarche . . . l'élégance indestructible de son armature . . . la suavité de son haleine d'enfant'. The deviation signals a shift into a less analytical mode. As in the verse-poem 'La Chevelure', the woman's hair acts as a powerful stimulus to the imagination, arousing an excitement that fits uneasily into the geometrically balanced prose of the first ten lines. The vitality finds its

121

formal outlet in the enumerated names of southern French towns, cited like the ingredients of a magic spell. Unlike the structures of binarism, parallelism, symmetry, paradox and repetition that have gone before, such a listing does not contain within itself a suggestion of how it might end; theoretically, it could go on for pages. The threat of the limitless lasts only a moment before the reader is reassured by the summarizing closure 'villes bénies du soleil, amoureuses et charmantes!' But the list succeeds in evoking the infinity of imaginative travel associated by Baudelaire with the scent of a woman's hair. Rhetorically, it eases the poem away from the dominance of the self-enclosed patterns.

Paragraph 5 disappoints any expectation of a continuing pattern of alternation (ABAB . . . A); instead it looks backwards to paragraph 2 in its exact repetition of 'Le Temps et l'Amour l'ont' and in its image of the beast of prey ('mordue à belles dents'), and also to paragraph 4 in its restatement of the woman's permanent and unaffected attraction, to the point of resurrecting the syntactical formula (set out above) in 'charme vague, mais éternel' (abstract noun) + 'de' + 'sa poitrine garçonnière' (physical attribute). It is as if Baudelaire is seeking to restore the earlier tone of analysis after the outburst of excitement; but there is an air of excess and displacement about this paragraph (which could easily have been inserted after, say, 'haleine d'enfant'). The rhetorical pattern is pushed too far and the effectiveness of its persuasion is tainted not by some dislocating intrusion but by its own persistence and *démesure*. This is not a criticism of Baudelaire – excess and exaggeration are part of the poem's theme.

Paragraph 6 abandons the opening strategies of the preceding paragraphs and proceeds to assert its difference. It breaks away from the alternative models offered in order to relate very specifically to the title: 'elle fait penser à ces chevaux de grande race . . .' An important expectation is satisfied, and in a manner which might have been predicted as early as line 1, although the extension of the metaphor goes beyond what one could have foreseen. The paragraph at once fulfils expectation and offers novelty in the detail of the fulfilment. The woman's innate grace survives the surface ravages of Time and Love: harmony, elegance, suaveness, vitality, charm remain intact and are instantly recognizable to the 'œil du véritable amateur' – just as the qualities of a thoroughbred could not be mistaken even if it were harnessed to a carriage or cart, or, one might say, just as the poetic can maintain itself within the confines of prose.

The echo of the title could be taken as the signal for closure. But the further paragraph deliberately postpones the conclusion through its enthusiastic 'Et puis . . .', its sudden return to the 'elle est' construction and the exclamation mark of the first sentence. The poet wants to say more, such is his fascination. This final paragraph attempts synthesis: it promotes 'Elle' as subject, echoing paragraphs 1 and 3, and it recalls and conjoins 'Le Temps' (in the seasonal imagery) and 'L'Amour' (in the repetition of 'aime' and the stress on renewed emotional ardour). Another closural point is reached with the suspension (by inversion) of 'feu nouveau'. After all, Baudelaire ends the final line of the final poem in *Les Fleurs du Mal* with 'pour trouver du *nouveau*!' The poem would have finished with a triumphant metaphor, proclaiming victory over Time, but instead Baudelaire adds an extraordinarily disconcèrting sentence: 'et la servilité de sa tendresse n'a jamais rien de fatigant'. On the level of syntax, there is a powerful reminder of the earlier pattern of paragraphs 4 and 5, but the parallel serves to highlight difference and deviation. Whereas in the earlier formulae the abstract noun embodies an essentially positive quality ('harmonie', 'élégance', 'suavité', 'charme'), now the quality is the condescending 'servilité'. There is a shift too from the physicality of 'démarche', 'armature', 'haleine' and 'poitrine' to the inner attitude of 'tendresse'. Gone too are the adjectival elaborations ('pétillante', 'indestructible', 'd'enfant', 'vague', 'éternel', 'garçonnière'), leaving the nouns to bare their difference. The double negation ('n'a jamais rien'), looking back again on the earlier model, is of course emphatic in mitigating the effects of 'servilité', but it cannot cancel out its existence. This concluding sentence, although fitting syntactically into an existing pattern, can hardly be expected. The pattern, one thought, had run its course and even exceeded its capacity to persuade. The last line with its comma and 'et' has an air of being tacked on, like a piece of debris from an earlier system.

The need to use such words as 'system', 'pattern', 'parallels' on the one hand, and 'difference', 'deviation', 'shift' on the other, indicates that in a prose-poem such as 'Un cheval de race' the aesthetics of regularity and irregularity, expectation and surprise can operate. Prose, within the characteristically short space of the prose-poem, can create its own predictability and its own dislocations. Although 'Un cheval de race' cannot be said to be a typical prose-poem in all respects (a typical prose-poem probably does not exist), the way in which it exploits both the reader's desire for order and the pleasure to be gained from disorientation can, I would argue, act as an index of the genre's potential for provoking formal tensions not totally dissimilar to those of verse.

The ambitious reader

To talk of pattern, expectation and surprise in poetry is to presume that the highest value of a poem lies in the nature of the reader's response. This may seem obvious. But there is a danger that criticism of a certain kind risks locating a poem's worth purely within the boundaries of the poem itself, as if the outside world, other literary texts, reading conventions did not exist. Yet effects – monotony, surprise, suspense, tension – are not self-defining features of a text but are the offspring of the reader's confrontation with the text. It is in the act of reading (beginning at the beginning, enjoying the drama of the poem, ending at the end) and re-reading (perhaps studying fragments before reconstituting the poem) that one should locate the true dynamics of a poem. Thus, for instance, the correct question for the critically aware reader to ask at any given point in a poem is not (say) 'What does the poet intend?', but rather 'What do I expect? Am I given what I expected?' There are dangers, of course, to such an approach. A reader's expectations will vary enormously, depending on linguistic and literary experience. To totally inexperienced readers, it is possible that all texts might appear chaotic; if that is so, there can be no expectations , no surprise and no tensions. It is true that they should be able to appreciate an intrinsic pattern (*e.g.* an unbroken series of rhyming couplets) and establish a set of expectations from the text itself (as we did in 'Un cheval de race' to some degree); but they may be completely unaware of extrinsic convention (*e.g.* that which requires a *ballade* to finish with an *envoi*). In this example, the *envoi* would come as a surprise, a break in a very clear pattern, yet to the knowledgeable reader, familiar with *ballades*, it would be a surprise if the *envoi* were absent. As students of poetry, we ought to be continually trying to move from the position of inexperience to one of knowledge, to perceive and assimilate the patterns and conventions of what we read, keeping them in a personal storehouse of expectations with which we can approach the next text. That is not to say, however, that we will approach that text with the hope that those expectations will be entirely satisfied; that would be to welcome cliché and to banish tension. Barbara Smith provides my conclusion for me in her outstanding book, *Poetic Closure*:

As we read a poem we are continually subjected to small surprises and disappointments as the developing lines evade or contradict our expectations. But far from annoying us, this toying with and teasing of our expectations is a major source of our 'excitement' – that is, our pleasure – in literature. If the surprises and disappointments are not finally justified, so to speak, by the total design, then to that extent the poem is a poor one. If, on the other hand, there have been no surprises or disappointments, if all our expectations have been gratified, the poem has been as predictable – and as interesting – as someone's reciting the alphabet. Art inhabits the country between chaos and cliché.

(Smith 1968, 14)

Baudelaire thrived in such territory.

7

'LAPSE' AND RECUPERATION

Whereas the admirer of Baudelaire perceives irregularities or the 'légèrement difforme' as devices designed to enhance the pleasure of a poem, his critic might well prefer to say simply that Baudelaire has produced a flawed poem and has done no more than to show himself to be a less than competent craftsman. This argument has to be taken seriously, if only because it has been advanced by such eminent literary critics of the past as Emile Faguet and Ferdinand Brunetière.

Lapses belong to two main categories. Firstly, there are those evident lapses when a poet fails to adhere to a prescribed canon (prosodic, grammatical). Secondly, there are lapses that offend a much vaguer set of principles: good taste, logical development, clarity, wholeness. Between these two categories there is a blurred area inhabited by undesirables such as weak rhymes and cacophony, technical blemishes that mar the tasteful harmony of 'good' verse. The fact that the principles governing the second category are vaguer than the rules of prosody or grammar does not mean that they have been held with less conviction. For a Faguet or a Brunetière, an obscurity in expression or argument was as much a fault as a technical error; both come very close to being moral lapses. Faguet and Brunetière turned their fire on Baudelaire in defence, one suspects, of some moral tradition, but this moral disapproval was soon deflected towards the poet's craftsmanship. The accusation levelled against Baudelaire as craftsman had not been uncommon in the last quarter of the nineteenth century, so Faguet (1910) was not saying anything very original when he observed of Baudelaire's verse: 'Ses vers sont souvent bourrés de chevilles et de propos insignifiants.' Charles Maurras calls the poet (more ambiguously) 'un effronté chevilleur' (cited in Carter, 1963, 171); the suggestion of shamelessness in 'effronté' will be touched on later. Louis Desprez, in his book L'Evolution naturaliste (1884), depicts the poet as a slave to prosody: 'Comme ce despotique est amené par la rime! . . . il cheville continuellement.' And one did not have to be a more or less hostile critic to question the competence of Baudelaire's verse. His

126

correspondence records the exchange between the poet and the editor of the *Revue contemporaine* who thought to 'correct' Baudelaire's lines saying that they had contained 'telles chevilles que vous auriez à coup sûr désavouées' (Pichois 1973, 70; Baudelaire refused to change anything). A related criticism was that, since Baudelaire was apparently embarrassed by the demands of versification, he lacked the easy gift of a true poet who could match form and idea with a graciousness that concealed art and (especially) artifice. Brunetière bemoaned Baudelaire's all too evident creative difficulty: 'Au moins, s'il était maître dans l'emploi de ses procédés! . . . Mais les vers de Baudelaire suent l'effort' (Brunetière 1887). In the 1890s it became commonplace to explain such inadequacy by supposing that Baudelaire, unlike true poets, thought in prose. Leconte de Lisle repaid Baudelaire's favourable article on him by a blunt assertion that 'Baudelaire n'est pas poète. Pour être poète, il faut sentir, il faut penser en vers. Lui commençait par traduire sa pensée en prose. C'était son procédé de travail' (cited by Brûlat, 1892). Brunetière again is highly critical: 'C'était un poète, auquel d'ailleurs il a manqué plus d'une partie de son art, et notamment . . . le don de penser directement en vers' (Brunetière 1894). And the poet Heredia is one of several who have looked upon Baudelaire's prose-poems as failed verse-poems: 'Baudelaire, qui faisait très difficultueusement les vers, laissa en prose . . . des poèmes auxquels il n'était pas arrivé à donner la forme poétique' (cited by Huret, 1891). Some of these criticisms (not all) ring with such a tone of vindictiveness that one has to understand the circumstances in which they were made, often in reaction to the idolatry accorded to Baudelaire by his Symbolist followers. But they are all the more interesting because, at their centre, there may lie a truth. It is a truth which, viewed from different premises, may provoke a different response. There is certainly evidence that Baudelaire found difficulty in writing.[1] His poetry *is* uneven. Anthology pieces such as 'L'Invitation au voyage', 'La Chevelure', 'Le Balcon' present a picture of a seductively harmonic Baudelaire, the Baudelaire cherished by Valéry; but there is another Baudelaire, the poet of 'Sisina' or 'Le Soleil' or 'Brumes et pluies', less impressive poems that reach no anthology that I know of and have stolen less critical attention. The unevenness does pose a problem and the 'lapses' do set a critical challenge.

The very notion of the lapse does presuppose some perfect prelapsarian poetic standard. The basic criteria that can be inferred from the criticisms of Baudelaire that I have just quoted are relatively straightforward: the poetic line must give the impression of 'naturalness', it must conceal creative effort (indeed it ought to convey the sense that inspiration has made effort unnecessary), technical exigencies must be obeyed with a skill that smoothes over their artificiality and the whole poem must persuade the reader that no word, phrase or line is in any way redundant. Poetry of this type – combined of course with a worthy theme – most easily convinces us of its divine source and promotes through its very form its own unique mode of idealism.

Baudelaire was familiar with this view of the poet and his creation; indeed, in many ways he accepted it and was envious of those poets who satisfied its criteria. How extraordinary it must be to be a poet who can create effortlessly and 'naturally'! How inconceivable it was for Baudelaire that an artist could be consistently and prolifically brilliant: listen to him on the English caricaturist, George Cruikshank, a formidably energetic creator: 'Cette verve est inconcevable . . . le grotesque coule incessamment et inévitablement de la pointe de Cruikshank, *comme les rimes riches de la plume des poètes naturels*' (II, 566; the italics are mine). As so often in Baudelaire's art criticism, the aside, the supplementary example, offers teasing revelations of his attitudes towards his own art. These 'poètes naturels' would include Gautier and Banville. Gautier, the 'magicien ès lettres françaises' (I, 3) to whom *Les Fleurs du Mal* is dedicated, possesses enviable qualities, 'des facultés innées': a knowledge of language 'qui n'est jamais en défaut', a mind which is like a 'magnifique dictionnaire', a sense of order and form, and a capacity which enables him 'sans cesse, sans fatigue comme sans faute, définir l'attitude mystérieuse que les objets de la création tiennent devant le regard de l'homme' (this and the preceding quotations: II, 117). In a word, Gautier the writer has the gift of facility. Baudelaire tells with admiration how Gautier could sit down at a table in a busy newspaper office and write at astonishing speed an immaculate critical article or even a chapter for a novel. Banville likewise had this creative gift. According to Baudelaire, Banville, on his first publication, 'apparaissait comme un de ces esprits marqués, pour qui la poésie est la langue la plus facile à parler, et dont la pensée se coule d'elle-même dans un rythme' (II, 162). In Brunetière's words one might say that he had 'le don de penser directement en vers'. For such natural talents, the complexities of the most recalcitrant verse-form hold no fear; in fact, the poet revels in them. Gautier and Banville are the natural craftsmen whose lines glide brilliantly over hindrances of form, sense and syntax, inspired not by some 'fine frenzy' but rather by a combination of supreme skill and lyrical disposition. And the created object – the poem – mirrors the ease and rhythm of its own creation. Gautier's poetry 'à la fois majestueuse et précieuse, marche magnifiquement, comme les personnes de cour en grande toilette' (II, 126); and in a following remark, Baudelaire goes on to locate the essential genius of all lyric poetry:

C'est, du reste, le caractère de la vraie poésie d'avoir le flot régulier, comme les grands fleuves qui s'approchent de la mer, leur mort et leur infini, et d'éviter la précipitation et la saccade. La poésie lyrique s'élance, mais toujours d'un mouvement élastique et ondulé. Tout ce qui est brusque et cassé lui déplaît . . .

(II, 126)

This link between the process of creation (seen as an effortless, natural force at work) and the characteristics of that which is created (an easy and elegant undulation in the rhythmical development) is one to which I shall return.

Gautier and Banville, as I have suggested, are correct poets. They have to be. A fault, a *cheville*, would dislocate the harmony and the *élan* of the verse, any awkwardness would cast doubt over the suppleness of the poets' Muse, whereas correctness guarantees an untrammelled passage to the receptive spirit of the reader. Formal correctness is often vaunted by Baudelaire. He attacks the notion that technically accomplished verse automatically lacks feeling (II, 150); and he describes as very odd (II, 175) the opinion that perfection prevents readers from having confidence in the poet's sincerity. But the fact that 'la critique vulgaire' is suspicious of an aristocratic correctness should cause no surprise, because in France unpopularity accompanies 'tout ce qui tend vers n'importe quel genre de perfection' (II, 177). The defence of correctness goes hand in hand with an impatience towards poets who are lax in the composition of their verse. Of Auguste Barbier he says:

C'est une chose douloureuse de voir un poète aussi bien doué supprimer les articles et les adjectifs possessifs, quand ces monosyllabes ou ces dissyllabes le gênent, et employer un mot dans un sens contraire à l'usage parce que ce mot a le nombre de syllabes qui lui convient. (II, 144)

This laxness, Baudelaire asserts, is common in poets obsessed with usefulness and moralizing – they allow the idea to dominate and think they can neglect the form. For Baudelaire such a bias would mean the end of poetry. Elsewhere he confesses to having been 'impatienté et désolé' by Marceline Desbordes-Valmore's verse because of 'la négligence, le cahot, le trouble' (II, 146). And he finds in Pierre Dupont's poetry, 'de nombreuses négligences de langage et un *lâché* dans la forme vraiment inconcevables' (II, 175). All these criticisms are not so far removed from those levelled at Baudelaire himself by Brunetière and Faguet. The conservative criteria with respect to form, the notion of the 'poète naturel', for example, bring victim and executioners into an ironical alliance. Baudelaire the victim of Brunetière and Faguet is also the executioner of Barbier, Desbordes-Valmore and Dupont.

However, as we know from 'L'Héautontimorouménos' ('Je suis la plaie et le couteau . . . Et la victime et le bourreau'), Baudelaire the victim is also Baudelaire the self-executioner. And one has to suppose that the poet, aware of the natural talents of Gautier and Banville, was by no means blind to his own failings, to his own lack of facility. At the very moment he is preparing the final manuscripts for Poulet-Malassis, the publisher of *Les Fleurs du Mal*, he is still seeking the solution to problems of expression: 'Je m'escrime contre une trentaine de vers insuffisants, désagréables, mal faits, mal rimants.' Significantly he contrasts himself to one of the 'poètes naturels': 'Croyez-vous donc que j'aie la souplesse de Banville?' (*Corres.*, I, 399). Three years later, preparing pieces for the second edition, he writes to Poulet-Malassis with a similar dissatisfaction: 'Je viens de relire ces vingt-cinq morceaux; je ne suis pas tout à fait content; il y a toujours des lourdeurs et des violences de style' (*Corres.*, II, 9). If Baudelaire achieves perfection, it seems as if it will be through a process of elimination, a scoring-out of imperfections, a struggle with the intractable. In a deflected self-portrait, he depicts just such a poet 'penché sur une table, barbouillant une page blanche d'horribles petits signes noirs, se battant contre la phrase rebelle' (II, 166). To illustrate how different Baudelaire's method of composition appears to be from that of the natural poets, we can look at 'Bribes', fragments of verse carefully copied out by the poet, a stockpile of available lines. Here one group of rhyming couplets begins:

> Ta jeunesse sera plus féconde en orages
> Que cette canicule aux yeux pleins de lueurs
> Qui sur nos fronts pâlis tord ses bras en sueurs,
> Et soufflant dans la nuit ses haleines fièvreuses,
> Rend de leurs frêles corps les filles amoureuses,

The absence of a rhyme for 'orages' suggests that the poet would need to work *backwards* in an 'unnatural' fashion. There is another point to be made about these lines. Line 1 is reminiscent of the opening of 'L'Ennemi' ('Ma jeunesse ne fut qu'un ténébreux orage'); the rest echoes closely two passages, one from an early poem dedicated to Sainte-Beuve ('Tous imberbes alors . . .'), the other from 'Lesbos'. The permutation and renovation of material already used are further evidence of the patient jigsaw approach to creation, of a poet piecing together units rather than sweeping along on a lyrical tide. The disordered snippets of lines which were to complete an Epilogue to the 1861 *Fleurs du Mal* are even more revealing. Stretching his 'goût passionné de l'obstacle' (I, 181) to the limits, Baudelaire attempts a *terza rima*. He managed to finish five stanzas but left material for a poem three times that length.

Amongst the debris, one finds:

> Tranquille comme un sage et doux comme un maudit,
>   J'ai dit:
> Je t'aime, ô ma très belle, ô ma charmante . . .
> Que de fois . . .

Here there is a rhyme which lacks the rest of its line ('J'ai dit'); and, given the *terza rima* scheme (ABA BCB CDC etc.), a whole line is missing between the rhymes, 'maudit'/'dit'. The third line above reverses the problem of the second line in that here the line lacks its rhyme. Elsewhere, there are lines boasting rhymes but in dispositions inconsistent with the *terza rima*:

> Et tes feux d'artifice, éruptions de joie,
> Qui font rire le Ciel, muet et ténébreux.
>
> Ton vice vénérable étalé dans la soie,
> Et ta vertu risible, au regard malheureux,
> Douce, s'extasiant au luxe qu'il déploie.

These examples are sufficient to give a glimpse of a creative process in which the idea and the form do not develop simultaneously. Unresolved technical problems are left to one side and their solution, if achieved, will inevitably bend the original idea. The suppleness of a Banville or the effortless accuracy of a Gautier would not have produced the stuttering fragments of this draft.

Faced with the constant threat of creative impotence, Baudelaire takes a dramatic and honest decision: he weaves the theme of such impotence into the structure of his collection. Poems early on in *Les Fleurs du Mal* bemoan the inadequacy of his Muse: 'La Muse malade', 'La Muse vénale', 'Le Mauvais Moine', 'L'Ennemi' all express a specifically artistic spleen, preparing the reader for a poetry which he will now know has been hard-won. And there are later reminders of this inadequacy: 'La Cloche fêlée', for example, with its 'voix affaiblie' and 'râle épais'; 'Paysage' with its stress on 'volonté' in poetic creation; 'Le Soleil' with its satirical picture of the poet as a victim of linguistic accident; and particularly 'La Mort des artistes', where the 'subtils complots' of poetic composition contribute to the gradual wearing away of the soul.

These 'confessions' of difficulty are confirmed time and time again in his correspondence and *Journaux intimes*. Claude Pichois has noted how he uses images of painful childbearing to refer to his writings: for example, he writes that his polemic against Belgium, *Pauvre Belgique!*, 'me coûte des douleurs d'enfantement égales à celles que j'ai toujours subies' (*Corres.*, II, 418). Waiting for inspiration was useless. The only solution was to be found in Work and the Will – not that Baudelaire was a compulsive worker (quite the opposite) or possessed an iron will (again quite the opposite). But at least he was capable of work and he did have sufficient will. And his critical writings show him to be sympathetic to other artists who suffered from similar creative difficulty – Pétrus Borel, for instance, who would spend hours perfecting an invitation or a trivial letter, agonizing over the least word (II, 154); or the painter Ingres, whose pictures, so patiently and laboriously constructed, are 'filles de la douleur [qui] engendrent la douleur' (II, 460; notice again the link between the processes of creation and reception); or Poe, whose poetry, 'condensée et laborieuse, lui coûtait sans doute beaucoup de peine' (II, 275). These are the artists who lack the natural gifts which make creation painless. But the pain of creation, as with all other pain in Baudelaire, contains its own redemption and its own enjoyment. Just as there are those in 'Le Cygne' who draw sustenance from pain ('ceux qui s'abreuvent de pleurs/Et tètent la Douleur comme une bonne louve'), or some 'Petites Vieilles' who 'font de la douleur un miel', just as the poet in 'Le Rêve d'un curieux' asks 'Connais-tu, comme moi, la douleur savoureuse' or declares in 'Bénédiction' 'Je sais que la douleur est la noblesse unique', so we find in Baudelaire's critical writings a refusal to accept pain as simply destructive. In an essay on Poe, for example, he talks of poetic composition as 'cette voluptueuse . . . douleur' (II, 275). The poet can gain satisfaction from the tormented battles with his material – and, what is more, the reader, sensing these battles, can likewise savour the creative struggle. The following is a key passage which it is worth quoting in full, since it gives superb expression to the crucial link between creation and reception. It opens a short *notice* on the actor Philibert Rouvière, and its very incongruity as an introduction to the essay betrays the importance of the theme and the compulsiveness with which it surfaces:

Voilà une vie agitée et tordue, comme ces arbres – le grenadier, par exemple – noueux, perplexes dans leur croissance, qui donnent des fruits compliqués et savoureux, et dont les orgueilleuses et rouges floraisons ont l'air de raconter l'histoire d'une sève longtemps comprimée. Il y a des gens par milliers qui, en littérature, adorent le style *coulant*, l'art qui s'épanche à l'abandon, presque à l'étourdie, sans méthode, mais sans fureurs et sans cascades. D'autres, – et généralement ce sont des littérateurs, – ne lisent avec plaisir que ce qui demande à être relu. Ils jouissent presque des douleurs de l'auteur. Car ces ouvrages médités, laborieux, tourmentés, contiennent la saveur toujours vive de la volonté qui les enfanta. (II, 60)

This model of literary production and reception needs to be contrasted with the image of the river. The river/lyric poem, having left its source, flows smoothly and of its own momentum towards the sea, its infinite destination. In that model (related to Gautier's poetry) the reader is so carried along by the elasticity of the verse that the source is forgotten. In the tree model, the produce, whether the 'fruits compliqués et savoureux' or the 'rouges et orgueilleuses floraisons', occupies the same field of vision as its source, – the tree is not hidden or forgotten, but is real evidence, in its contorsions, of the intricate process of creation. The redness of the flowers seems to fanfare their pride in difficulties overcome and even tell the story of their own genesis. The complex inner architecture of the pomegranate, for instance, presents itself as a system which can be savoured as a system, laboriously achieved. Far from admiring the art that conceals art, the reader of this literature admires the suggestion of artistic effort, the 'histoire d'une sève longtemps comprimée'; he acknowledges the author's struggles and responds to the exercise of the Will. This passage may be seen as a rationalization of a defeat, an attempt by the poet to turn creative difficulty into a virtue; even if it is accepted as such, the arguments advanced by Baudelaire constitute an interesting new aesthetics, a set of premisses the existence of which Brunetière and Faguet scarcely recognize. I want to argue that it is possible to enjoy the evident artifice of Baudelaire's verse as a signal of the creative battle, to consent to the so-called weaknesses of the verse as expressive tokens of defeat, bearing their own message beyond the simple semantics of the words.

I shall begin this process of recuperation by looking at 'Hymne à la Beauté', a poem written in 1859, a year which saw the writing of 'Le Cygne', 'Le Voyage', 'Les Sept Vieillards' and 'Les Petites Vieilles', all superb, mature poems.

Hymne à la Beauté

Viens-tu du ciel profond ou sors-tu de l'abîme,
O Beauté! ton regard, infernal et divin,
Verse confusément le bienfait et le crime,
Et l'on peut pour cela te comparer au vin.   4

Tu contiens dans ton œil le couchant et l'aurore;
Tu répands des parfums comme un soir orageux;
Tes baisers sont un philtre et ta bouche une amphore
Qui font le héros lâche et l'enfant courageux.   8

Sors-tu du gouffre noir ou descends-tu des astres?
Le Destin charmé suit tes jupons comme un chien;
Tu sèmes au hasard la joie et les désastres,
Et tu gouvernes tout et ne réponds de rien.   12

Tu marches sur des morts, Beauté, dont tu te moques;
De tes bijoux l'Horreur n'est pas le moins charmant,
Et le Meurtre, parmi tes plus chères breloques,
Sur ton ventre orgueilleux danse amoureusement.   16

L'éphémère ébloui vole vers toi, chandelle,
Crépite, flambe et dit: Bénissons ce flambeau!
L'amoureux pantelant incliné sur sa belle
A l'air d'un moribond caressant son tombeau.   20

Que tu viennes du ciel ou de l'enfer, qu'importe,
O Beauté! monstre énorme, effrayant, ingénu!
Si ton œil, ton souris, ton pied, m'ouvrent la porte
D'un Infini que j'aime et n'ai jamais connu?   24

De Satan ou de Dieu, qu'importe? Ange ou Sirène,
Qu'importe, si tu rends – fée aux yeux de velours,
Rythme, parfum, lueur, ô mon unique reine! –
L'univers moins hideux et les instants moins lourds? 28

The opening stanza begins with a Romantic commonplace, the morally ambiguous nature of Beauty, here shaped as alternative questions provoked by the apparent coexistence ('infernal *et* divin') of God and Satan in the same power. And it ends with a line which squanders its syllables on a comparison explicitly introduced and lacking any imaginative sparkle. The analogy between Beauty and wine is acknowledged as feasible ('l'on peut') and reasonable ('pour cela') but it is quickly dropped from the poem which presses on instead with the personification of Beauty as a woman whose very being seems composed of metaphors (lines 5–8).

The obviousness with which the wine comparison parades its own redundancy, an afterthought that breaks the *élan* of the description, forces one to admit that the critic who called Baudelaire 'un effronté chevilleur' was perhaps right. The need to rhyme is faced out brazenly. And what is the effect of this *cheville*? For the first three lines, the reader finds himself asked to overhear a hymn-like address, half-question, half-exclamation, by the poet to Beauty; a system of binary characteristics is speedily established, promising him a recognizable oratorical development. And then the rhetoric is deflated: the system snaps; the forward surge is checked by the 'pour cela' which invites the reader to look backwards to verify the grounds of the comparison; the devotional poet is displaced by an emotionless, analytic and generalized 'on'; and a clumsy comparison steals the climax of the stanza. The *cheville* reminds us of the poet as fabricator just when we were prepared to accept the illusion of poet as celebrant. The effect is likely to be one of frustration, disappointment and bewilderment. But paradoxically, the emptiness of the line is rich in suggestion: it casts a tinge of self-irony on the rhetorical ease of the opening movement, it mocks the poet's own dramatic pose and betrays the fragility of his 'inspiration' at the very moment he is invoking his muse. This interpretation of the line is not difficult to integrate into the interpretation of the whole poem. Its disruptive power helps to explain the later dislocation of the rhetorical flow by the insertion of a stanza (lines 17–20) which explores the major theme through a lateral shift. The images of the may-fly and the lover are displayed as supplementary demonstrations of a theme. By introducing another (and strange) 'toi'-figure (the candle), by implicating the reader as *voyeur*, they deflect the onward impetus of the hymn to Beauty. I am not suggesting of course that this stanza is as empty as line 4, but it again shows Baudelaire's bridling of rhetorical development and desire to try something more complex. The conclusion (lines 21–8) loosens the reins once more: even here the apostrophes, enumerations, parallelisms, rich rhymes, the suspensions of a climax, lead us not to a glorious final line but to one whose classical balance throws into expressive relief the most unclassical flaw of hiatus ('moins hideux') and stabilizes the poem on a note of mitigated spleen. The example of 'Hymne à la Beauté' illustrates how it is possible to recuperate the apparent lapse by accepting the irony of a *cheville* which the poet uses to puncture his own rhetoric. I shall return to this kind of perverse irony directed towards the self.

But I should now like to move to another example, 'Recueillement'.

Recueillement

Sois sage, ô ma Douleur, et tiens-toi plus tranquille.
Tu réclamais le Soir; il descend; le voici:
Une atmosphère obscure enveloppe la ville,
Aux uns portant la paix, aux autres le souci.   4

Pendant que des mortels la multitude vile,
Sous le fouet du Plaisir, ce bourreau sans merci,
Va cueillir des remords dans la fête servile,
Ma Douleur, donne-moi la main; viens par ici,   8

Loin d'eux. Vois se pencher les défuntes Années,
Sur les balcons du ciel, en robes surannées;
Surgir du fond des eaux le Regret souriant;   11

Le Soleil moribond s'endormir sous une arche,
Et, comme un long linceul traînant à l'Orient,
Entends, ma chère, entends la douce Nuit qui marche.   14

This is perhaps the most famous of all Baudelaire's sonnets; it has undeniable appeal and power of evocation. Yet, in a celebrated study, Valéry went so far as to call some lines inept:

Sur les quatorze vers du sonnet *Recueillement*, qui est une des plus charmantes pièces de l'ouvrage, je m'étonnerai toujours d'en compter cinq ou six qui sont d'une incontestable faiblesse. Mais les premiers et les derniers vers de cette poésie sont d'une telle magie que le milieu ne fait pas sentir son ineptie et se tient pour nul et inexistant. Il faut un grand poète pour ce genre de miracles.

(Valéry 1957, I, 610)

One must not be too harsh on Valéry. He does insist that 'Recueillement' is 'une des plus charmantes pièces de l'ouvrage', that the bad lines do not ruin the poem but rather miraculously leave its magic unaffected; only a great poet could achieve such an effect. Which, first of all, are the bad lines? These are normally taken to be lines 3/4–7/8 ('cinq ou six'). And what is wrong with them? Line 4 is facile, an easily manufactured balance and antithesis; line 5 has a rhyme-induced inversion, a cliché in the adjectival substantive 'mortels'; line 6 has another touch of banality, 'sous le fouet du Plaisir', made worse by the uninformative 'bourreau sans merci' (someone with a whip is likely to be a 'bourreau' and a 'bourreau' is likely to be 'sans merci'); line 8 lacks a firm central caesura and is prosaic. Even if we were to agree with Valéry that these lines were 'd'une incontestable faiblesse', we might still be justifiably astonished that he has missed the point of Baudelaire's poetics, the point being that Baudelaire deliberately wrote weak lines with the express purpose of throwing into relief moments of high poetic charge. These lines, far from being inept, reveal an audacious new method of composition. There is an anecdote told by Baudelaire's friend, Asselineau:

J'ai entendu, dans un bureau d'imprimerie, le dialogue suivant entre le directeur d'un recueil des plus accrédités, comme on dit, et un poète célèbre: 'Ne trouvez-vous pas, monsieur, que ce vers est un peu faible? – Oui, monsieur, répondit le poète en se mordant la lèvre, et le vers suivant aussi est faible, mais ils sont là pour amener celui d'après, qui n'est pas faible du tout. – Je ne dis pas non, monsieur; mais il vaudrait bien mieux qu'ils fussent tous les trois d'égale force. Non, monsieur, répondit le poète, en colère cette fois; car alors où serait la gradation? C'est un art, monsieur, un art que j'ai mis vingt ans à apprendre et' – il n'osa pas ajouter: dont vous ne savez pas le premier mot.

(Cited in Fongaro 1973, 176)

It is not possible to say, of course, that the poem referred to in this conversation is 'Recueillement'; that is not really the point. But it is important to notice that this idea of *gradation* is something that it has taken Baudelaire twenty years to master. We know that he started writing poetry seriously around 1840–1; in other words we can situate the anecdote around 1859–60/1, close in any case to the date of composition of 'Recueillement'. It is thus quite possible to see in the sonnet a prime example of this perfected aesthetic of gradation. This aesthetic implies that the critic should judge a line or a verse in the context of the whole poem, *not* in isolation; judged in this light, the bad lines of 'Recueillement' become acceptable: even Valéry admits that in the context of the whole poem, 'le milieu ne fait pas sentir son ineptie et se tient pour nul et inexistant' and that this fact is a miracle. Sceptics might argue that Baudelaire was defending himself against criticism in the Asselineau anecdote by inventing a new aesthetic on the spot; that the art of gradation is no more than a rationalization of uneven inspiration. But the idea that a work of art should be judged as a whole occurs in Baudelaire's critical work and at a very early date. In the 1846 Salon, in his praise for Delacroix, he deliberately ignores the weaknesses of Delacroix's paintings:

à quoi bon relever des fautes de détail et des taches microscopiques? L'ensemble est si beau, que je n'en ai pas le courage.   (II, 441)

and again

une faute occasionnelle de dessin est quelquefois nécessaire pour ne pas sacrifier quelque chose de plus important.   (II, 432)

And at a much later date (1857), in a discussion of the merits of the short story (as perfected by Poe), he underlines the great advantage of 'l'unité d'impression, la *totalité* d'effet' (II, 329) which can be gained from a short story, even though prose may accommodate variety of tones, even dissonance of tones. The '*totalité* d'effet' is what saves 'Recueillement'.

Let us now leave the theory and return to the practice. In what way do the bad lines justify themselves? It will be noticed immediately that these lines coincide with the description of the outer world – and not only the description but with the moralizing form that the description takes. Lines 5–7 are an angry, brutal outcry against the pleasure-driven masses of the city, and as such they offer a dramatic contrast to the gentle admonitions of the opening line and the imaginative meditations of the tercets. These lines present a picture of dissipation, 'vaporisation'; and in Baudelaire's conceptual universe this negative idea is a necessary, antithetical partner to 'concentration', 'centralisation', 'recueillement'. Antithesis is one of the great driving forces behind Baudelairean creativeness, and here the antithesis operates on the level of content *and* on the level of poetic success: the picture of dissipation is drawn in clichés, the picture of 'recueillement' is drawn in deeply resonant images. The clichés are forgotten as soon as *our* imagination obeys the imperative 'viens par ici,/Loin d'eux', after which we enter an entirely different world. But the juxtaposition of bad and good lines, of the moralist and the meditator, works brilliantly, in that it *gradates* – very boldly – the movement into fruitful reflectiveness, the 'concentration productive' which Baudelaire saw as characteristic of the mature man; the impression of stepping into a deeper vein of poetry is inescapable.

Nevertheless, one might also ask, how bad are these lines? 'Mortels' in line 4 may be a threadbare alternative to people, but here the notion of death is truly relevant (see 'défuntes Années', 'Soleil moribond' and 'long linceul'). 'La multitude vile' may be thought tautologous, since 'multitude' already has such strong pejorative connotations that 'vile' appears to add little and to be there just for the rhyme; but 'multitude vile' had a particular resonance in the France of 1861. Nine years earlier, Thiers in a parliamentary speech decried 'la multitude, la vile multitude qui a perdu toutes les républiques', and the phrase became notorious. Baudelaire's use of it (inverted in obedience to the rhyme) would have evoked the political, moralizing wrath of the orator, and at the same time have confirmed these lines as cliché. The 'cueillir' of line 7 is not without merit; it echoes the title and throws the two activities (pleasure and contemplation) into ironic opposition. The second stanza is not bad, but one has to admit that it has nothing that can compare with the richness of the tercets.

The recuperation of 'Recueillement' relies largely on the mimesis of the lines: the bad lines mime the distaste the poet feels towards a group of people who deserve clichés.[2]

The 'lapse' in 'Recueillement' is perhaps all the more conspicuous because the poem is a sonnet; and sonnets, with all their formal rigour, should in theory admit no slackness in construction. As my third example I shall take another sonnet which has received adverse criticism and is dismally entitled 'Brumes et pluies':

Brumes et pluies

O fins d'automne, hivers, printemps trempés de boue
Endormeuses saisons! je vous aime et vous loue
D'envelopper ainsi mon cœur et mon cerveau
D'un linceul vaporeux et d'un vague tombeau.   4

'Lapse' and recuperation

Dans cette grande plaine où l'autan froid se joue,
Où par les longues nuits la girouette s'enroue,
Mon âme mieux qu'au temps du tiède renouveau
Ouvrira largement ses ailes de corbeau.   8

Rien n'est plus doux au cœur plein de choses funèbres,
Et sur qui dès longtemps descendent les frimas,
O blafardes saisons, reines de nos climats,   11

Que l'aspect permanent de vos pâles ténèbres,
– Si ce n'est, par un soir sans lune, deux à deux,
D'endormir la douleur sur un lit hasardeux.   14

Rachel Killick (1980, 34) comments on the final couplet, often the place of climax and poetic resonance:

The sonnet concludes with a somewhat intrusive comparison, which introduces another possible alternative for the obliteration of suffering. The chance sexual encounter may perform the same function as the absorption into the unchanging gloom of winter. An entirely new element is thus brought to the reader's attention with a detrimental effect on the atmosphere of unexpectant monotony the poet has been at pains to create. Moreover the lines are very ordinary and offer little in compensation. The 'soir sans lune' is a cliché and the construction 'si ce n'est' introduces a note of prosaic logic into the poem.

As a description, these comments would be generally acceptable, but there is more than a hint that, to the critic's ear, the poem has not succeeded. It is possible, however, to look upon the bathetic ordinariness of the couplet with more indulgence. The bathos is hardly accidental. The deliberateness of the dash that precedes the final couplet confirms its status as an afterthought that trivializes all that has gone before. These last two lines exude an air of cultivated perverseness that suggests the workings of Baudelairean irony, an irony that refuses the harmony of the unified sonnet, preferring instead to intrude destructively on what the poet has indeed been at pains to create. The relationship between the body and conclusion of the poem could be compared to that found in 'A une Madone' where the final lines obliterate thematically the idolized portrait of the woman which dominates the rest of the poem (or, to put it differently, the portrait has been drawn *in order* to be obliterated). In the conclusion of 'Brumes et pluies', Baudelaire risks his poem for the sake of irony; or, alternatively, one could say that the elaborate antiphrasis of lines 1–12 (a curiously over-emphatic eulogy of the weather of 'ennui') has been constructed *in order* to be trivialized. Whichever way one looks at it, the structure is genuinely audacious. But just as sexual risk (the 'lit hasardeux') palliates

139

pain, so poetic risk stimulates the imagination. It questions the easy unity of a poem and problematizes interpretation. One interpretation would be that the very ordinariness of the final couplet evokes the prosaic world of the Parisian prostitute (an evocation that justifies the inclusion of the poem in the 'Tableaux parisiens' section of *Les Fleurs du Mal*); and that, as in 'Recueillement', cliché is used to describe the banal.

For my fourth example, I turn to 'La Muse malade', one of that set of poems I mentioned earlier in which Baudelaire confesses his creative weakness. Here above all one might expect mimetic banality. After all, there is something suspect about a robust poem about not being able to write robust poems.

La Muse malade

Ma pauvre muse, hélas! qu'as-tu donc ce matin?
Tes yeux creux sont peuplés de visions nocturnes,
Et je vois tour à tour réfléchis sur ton teint
La folie et l'horreur, froides et taciturnes.   4

Le succube verdâtre et le rose lutin
T'ont-ils versé la peur et l'amour de leurs urnes?
Le cauchemar, d'un poing despotique et mutin,
T'a-t-il noyée au fond d'un fabuleux Minturnes?   8

Je voudrais qu'exhalant l'odeur de la santé
Ton sein de pensers forts fût toujours fréquenté,
Et que ton sang chrétien coulât à flots rythmiques,   11

Comme les sons nombreux des syllabes antiques,
Où règnent tour à tour le père des chansons,
Phœbus, et le grand Pan, le seigneur des moissons.   14

There are, I would argue, at least four features of the poem that display mimesis in the way in which I am using the word. Firstly, the repetition of what is already repetitive, the 'tour à tour' of lines 3 and 13. Secondly, the inability to produce the usual mixed rhyme-scheme in the tercets; the flatness of the couplets when one expects complication is disappointing. Thirdly, the monotony of the final rhyme which draws together exactly parallel syntactic structures, whereas nineteenth-century rhyme-theory demands syntactical variety of the rhymes. Fourthly, the fact that 'La Muse malade' contains the only grammatical mistake in *Les Fleurs du Mal* – in line 3, where 'réfléchis' should of course agree with 'la folie' and 'l'horreur', as 'froides' does. The technical problem is that the combination of vowel+mute e+written consonant is simply not allowed by the rules of versification then in force – so that 'réfléchies' in the feminine plural would not be admissible in French verse (unless it was at the rhyme).[3] So what Baudelaire has done is to observe the prosodic rule and sacrifice the grammar – and this mistake could easily have been avoided, as it was in the third edition of *Les Fleurs du Mal* (1868) where the line read

> Et je vois tour à tour s'étaler sur ton teint

But the third edition was seen through its publication by Asselineau and Banville, and Pichois hints that Banville made the correction, not Baudelaire (I, 855). The solution is easy – so why had Baudelaire let it through the proofs and final printing of the first and second editions? This is indeed odd, especially when one considers how meticulous the poet was in his proof-reading. I prefer to accept the mistake as an expressive confirmation of how enfeebled Baudelaire's Muse supposedly was – incapable of marrying prosody and grammar. Whatever the explanation, the mistake could not have happened in a more appropriate poem.

My final example is 'Le Soleil', a poem truly bizarre in its banality and in its structure.

Le Soleil

Le long du vieux faubourg, où pendent aux masures
Les persiennes, abri des secrètes luxures,
Quand le soleil cruel frappe à traits redoublés
Sur la ville et les champs, sur les toits et les blés,
Je vais m'exercer seul à ma fantasque escrime,   5
Flairant dans tous les coins les hasards de la rime,
Trébuchant sur les mots comme sur les pavés,
Heurtant parfois des vers depuis longtemps rêvés.

Ce père nourricier, ennemi des chloroses,
Eveille dans les champs les vers comme les roses;   10
Il fait s'évaporer les soucis vers le ciel,
Et remplit les cerveaux et les ruches de miel.
C'est lui qui rajeunit les porteurs de béquilles
Et les rend gais et doux comme des jeunes filles,
Et commande aux moissons de croître et de mûrir   15
Dans le cœur immortel qui toujours veut fleurir!

Quand, ainsi qu'un poète, il descend dans les villes,
Il ennoblit le sort des choses les plus viles,
Et s'introduit en roi, sans bruit et sans valets,
Dans tous les hôpitaux et dans tous les palais.   20

Felix Leakey argues that the two parts (lines 1–8 and 9–20) are so contradictory that they were written at different stages in Baudelaire's career and that the fragments have been badly welded together (Leakey 1969, 106–8). One can see what he means.

The sun of the title plays a very subordinate role in lines 1–8, and yet springs to the fore with no warning in line 9, with the casual demonstrative '*Ce* père nourricier' hardly justified. And what is more, the 'soleil cruel [qui] frappe à traits redoublés' suddenly becomes extraordinarily beneficent: knocking up sleepy earthworms, filling brains with honey, making lame old men as sprightly as young girls and generally being a splendid presence. All this is very odd – as perhaps one might expect if Baudelaire had simply juxtaposed fragments, with the occasional limp attempt at forging coherence (for example, the 'ainsi qu'un poète' of line 17 which brings together poet and sun, the main protagonists of sections 1 and 2 respectively). One might be happy to leave this as a 'failed' poem, were it not for the insistence on the *process of composition* to be found in the poem itself. Such self-reflexive observations as are to be found in lines 5–8 argue for a lucid artist who knows what he is doing and who is honest enough to confess the accidental nature of his 'inspiration'. Is it not odd – almost inconceivable – that Baudelaire should draw attention to the act of composition in a poem that so patently lacks coherence, unless the incoherence is part of the poem's meaning? The picture the poet paints of himself does not immediately promise coherence; the stress is on the arbitrary ('les hasards de la rime'), the accidental ('Trébuchant sur les mots') and the chance revelation ('Heurtant parfois des vers . . .'). The poet–swordsman sets out confidently, even if he admits that his exercise has something of the bizarre and capricious in it; but very soon he becomes the poet–buffoon. So it could be argued that the poem is self-illustrating – the incoherence being a part of the general satire directed at the poet's own creative self. Certainly at a local level, self-illustration is present: in lines 5–6, for example, when 'les hasards de la rime' bring together 'escrime' and 'rime'. Elsewhere the atmosphere of 'bouffonnerie' is maintained by the linguistic accident which brings together three times in four lines the word 'vers' with a different sense each time; or by the pun on 'soucis' meaning cares and marigolds. It would be wrong, in my view, to take this poem too seriously as an attempt at a conventionally logical piece of verse. The trope that might be used to summarize its structure is that of zeugma[4] – which is present in line 12 ('Et remplit les cerveaux et les ruches de miel'). The yoking of the appropriate (filling hives with honey) and the inappropriate (filling brains with honey) in a single structure (the sentence) is emblematic of what happens in the whole poem. Lines 9–20 are appropriate to a poem with the title 'Le Soleil', but they are yoked to lines 1–8, which are inappropriate. On both levels – that of the line (line 12) and that of the poem – there is a capricious clash, a willingness to risk the discordant.

These examples will have to suffice. I have chosen to look at them and to defend them because, in my view, there is still an exaggerated tendency to look upon Baudelaire as someone who sought without exception to write a poetry that would fulfil his own definition, 'le principe de la poésie est, strictement et simplement, l'aspiration humaine vers une beauté supérieure' (II, 334), a poetry akin to the harmonious swell of true lyric poetry as defined in his essay on Gautier, a poetry which was to win the admiration of Valéry, a poetry close to *la poésie pure*. Faguet and Brunetière did Baudelaire a service by pointing to the vastness of his failure if indeed the production of that type of poetry was his only aim. But it makes much more sense to accept the impurities of Baudelaire's poetry as a crucial ingredient, an ingredient which helps to give the whole of *Les Fleurs du Mal* a certain strangeness. We ought not to forget that in his *Journaux intimes* (I, 658) Baudelaire identified two fundamental literary qualities: 'surnaturalisme' and 'ironie'. By 'surnaturalisme', he means the poetic ability to experience moments of grace and plenitude when the senses penetrate the universal pattern; by 'ironie' he refers to the sequel to such epiphany, 'puis tournure d'esprit satanique'. The bitterness of satanic exile is at its most intense following moments of revelation; then the self is unable to suppress the sense of its own imperfection. The prospect of a beautiful garden in sunlight – a place which promises *le surnaturel* – is enough to goad the poet into satanic revenge: he destroys a flower; this incident forms part of 'A celle qui est trop gaie' which concludes with the imagined violation of the woman whose beauty and happiness provoke the same retaliation as the flower. And in 'L'Héautontimorouménos' the beauty of the woman incites the poet's sadism, which leads to a moment of self-awareness:

> Ne suis-je pas un faux accord
> Dans la divine symphonie,
> Grâce à la vorace Ironie
> Qui me secoue et qui me mord?

In these last two examples, the poet wields a vicious irony which refuses and degrades the perfection of the ideal, spurred on by the lucid vision he has of his own imperfection (the 'faux accord'). As 'L'Héautontimorouménos' makes clear, the irony is self-destructive too. One last example of the rape of perfection occurs obliquely but very suggestively in the essay on Banville. As he nears his conclusion, Baudelaire, discussing the 'tendance essentiellement démoniaque' of modern art, draws the contrast between Banville's poetry and that of his contemporaries:

Mais Théodore de Banville refuse de se pencher sur ces marécages de sang, sur ces abîmes de boue. Comme l'art antique, il n'exprime que ce qui est beau, joyeux, noble, grand, rythmique. Aussi, dans ses œuvres, vous n'entendrez pas les dissonances, les discordances des musiques du sabbat, non plus que les glapissements de l'ironie, cette vengeance du vaincu. (II, 168)

Irony, dissonance, discordance – these are the weapons of revenge against 'ce qui est beau, joyeux, noble, grand, rythmique'. Between them they go a long way towards explaining the 'lapses' in Baudelaire's poetry; the anguish felt by the poet in the act of creation turns into a need for revenge against the aesthetic of the ideal which has caused his suffering. Who wants the ideal anyway? As I have suggested in an earlier chapter, Baudelaire prefers his 'pauvre *moi*', his 'ligne brisée'. The authentic Baudelaire is the poet who, while accepting the ideal as an absurd working hypothesis, nevertheless clings to an essential *im*perfection as a source of fertile tension. Given such tension, it is almost inevitable that the resulting poetry will display a certain oscillation between the melodious and the disruptive, between *poésie pure* and the prosaic, between obedience to the ideal 'convenances' of art and experimentation that refuses, subverts or goes beyond the limits of those 'convenances'. The next two chapters push deeper into the experimental ambition of Baudelaire's poetry.

8

EXPERIMENTATION AND URBAN POETICS, I: THE LIMITS OF POETRY

Since one rarely finds Baudelaire commenting very specifically on one of his own poems, those remarks he does make are to be particularly valued. And this chapter will take as its starting-point a well-known fragment from a letter to Jean Morel, the editor of the *Revue française*, accompanying a manuscript version of 'Les Sept Vieillards':[1]

> ... c'est le premier numéro d'une nouvelle série que je veux tenter, et je crains bien d'avoir simplement réussi à dépasser les limites assignées à la Poésie.
>
> (*Corres.*, I, 583)

The mixture of ambition ('que je veux tenter'), feigned timidity ('je crains bien') and ironic self-congratulation ('avoir simplement réussi') reveals an artist pondering over the problem of *dépassement*, wavering between adherence to a classical aesthetic and exploration of new territory. It is a hesitation which has often been seen as characteristic of Baudelaire, a hesitation, to use Claude Pichois's terms, between 'audace et prudence, respect de la tradition et recherche de la novation' (I, 1295). The letter to Morel, written in June 1859, comes at a critical period in Baudelaire's dilemma between order and adventure (strictly not a dilemma – which implies choice – but rather a problem of reconciliation); it is the years separating the first two editions of *Les Fleurs du Mal* (1857 and 1861) that see Baudelaire consistently exploiting Paris as a new source of poetic inspiration and, at the same time, moving towards the experimental prose-poems which, after 1860, were to demand the greater part of his creative energy. But the hesitation itself dates from much earlier in Baudelaire's career, and reflects itself interestingly in his theoretical writings on art and literature as well as in his practice. What the first part of this chapter sets out briefly to examine is the uncertainty in Baudelaire's aesthetic position concerning the limits of a particular medium and their *dépassement*, a central issue in the letter to Morel. What I should like to trace in the second part is Baudelaire's hesitant transgression of the boundary between verse and prose. The central focus will be on form. I realize that, when Baudelaire says of 'Les Sept Vieillards' that he has simply succeeded in going beyond 'les limites assignées à la Poésie', he had other things in mind besides versification: the syntax, vocabulary, the very subject of the poem all put poetry at risk. But versification often serves as a sensitive gauge which can measure experiments taking place at other levels, whether of content, theme or imagery.

The feature of versification on which I shall now concentrate is the rhymed couplet in classical Alexandrines, and more particularly the use of enjambement in this metre. My immediate justification, which runs the risk of appearing frivolous, is that enjambement can be seen as the idea of *dépassement* carried into the realm of verse-technique. The large analogy within which I wish the argument to operate is that between aesthetic *dépassement* (of the limits of poetry) and technical *dépassement* (of the limits of the Alexandrine). A second, more practical, justification is that, in this most basic of metres, rhythmical innovation is particularly conspicuous and any infringement is easily measured against a long-established norm. Analysis of Baudelaire's more complex metres would raise correspondingly more complex problems. One of the purposes of the present argument will be to show how Baudelaire endows his couplet-verse with a greater flexibility as he experiments with new subject-matter, namely that Parisian material which will eventually take him into prose. Evidence is gathered from a range of Baudelaire's poetry, in prose and in verse, but I should like to propose as a highly significant text his contribution to the *Hommage à C. F. Denecourt*, a *Festschrift* published by Hachette in 1855 to honour the self-appointed 'keeper' of the forest of Fontainebleau and including within its covers pieces by Lamartine, Hugo, George Sand, Musset, Béranger, Gautier, Murger, Banville, Janin and Nerval.[2]

The discussion which follows restricts itself to Baudelaire's views on the limits of a medium (for example, colour and line in art, prose and verse in literature) and thereby avoids the extremely complex question of the limits of a particular art-form (art, literature, music). The restriction simplifies matters but also lends pertinence to an investigation of Baudelaire's own practice, which is concerned above all with different media rather than different art-forms (even though he sought to introduce musical and pictorial qualities into his verse, it remains essentially literary). The boundary which particularly exercises Baudelaire as a poet is that between the realm of verse and the realm of prose: the important question is how far this division corresponds to that which separates the poetic and the prosaic. Nevertheless, a glance at his comments on the media of another art-form (colour and line in art), even if they are not directly relevant to his own practice and even if

146

colour and line provide very imperfect analogies for verse and prose, will reveal general attitudes which apply to literature as well as art.

An unequivocal early statement by Baudelaire on the division of media comes in Chapter 12 of the *Salon de 1846*, 'De l'éclectisme et du doute':

Dans le siècle présent comme dans les anciens, aujourd'hui comme autrefois, les hommes forts et bien portants se partagent, chacun suivant son goût et son tempérament, les divers territoires de l'art, et s'y exercent en pleine liberté suivant la loi fatale du travail attrayant. Les uns vendangent facilement et à pleines mains dans les vignes dorées et automnales de la couleur; les autres labourent avec patience et creusent péniblement le sillon profond du dessin. Chacun de ses hommes a compris que sa royauté était un sacrifice, et qu'à cette condition seule il pouvait régner avec sécurité jusqu'aux frontières qui la limitent. Chacun d'eux a une enseigne à sa couronne; et les mots écrits sur l'enseigne sont lisibles pour tout le monde. Nul d'entre eux ne doute de sa royauté, et c'est dans cette imperturbable conviction qu'est leur gloire et leur sérénité.   (II, 472)

This passage is essentially classical. The artist chooses his territory according to his temperament (an important rider which reveals the writer's Romanticism), sacrificing his claim to all others and enjoying total freedom and security within the frontiers of his style. Baudelaire's tactical reason for introducing this eulogy of specialization is to attack eclectics, whom he judges to be devoid of passion and faith and guilty of artistic dissipation. Eclecticism pervades all levels of art: disparate styles can jostle side by side within a single work of art ('Il [l'éclectique] mêle quatre procédés différents qui ne produisent qu'un effet noir, une négation': II, 473), within the corpus of a single artist ('Il y en a qui changent en un jour du blanc au noir: hier, coloristes de *chic*, coloristes sans amour ni originalité; demain, imitateurs sacrilèges de M. Ingres, sans y trouver plus de goût ni de foi': II, 492) or within a single Salon ('turbulence, tohu-bohu de styles et de couleurs, cacophonie de tons, trivialités énormes, prosaïsme de gestes et d'attitudes, noblesse de convention, *poncifs* de toutes sortes': II, 490). The antidote to the first two examples of dispersion is single-minded confidence in one's chosen realm; the antidote to the third lies in the cultivation of the 'école' and the 'grande tradition' rather than variegated individuality. It is important to judge Baudelaire's argument in its context. He has in his sights a procession of mediocre artists whose works are of insufficient calibre to challenge the authority of a powerful theory. The unbending rigour with which he here pursues his argument for a classical aesthetic leads, however, to an extreme position. Single-mindedness, he himself realizes, cannot be an infallible criterion for a great artist; if it were, the

detested Horace Vernet should be classed amongst his *phares*. It is
clearly better to argue that specialization is necessary but not sufficient
and that additional criteria must be used to judge greatness – for
instance, that artists must be 'hommes forts et bien portants' (II, 472),
'hommes complets' (II, 473) with 'une individualité bien constituée' (II,
477).

But what happens when an artist recognized as great and individual-
istic in an admirable way shows a desire to move out of his territory?
Such is the case of Ingres. Might it be that specialization is neither
sufficient nor necessary? The difference between Baudelaire's comments on the eclectics and those on Ingres (in an earlier chapter of the
Salon de 1846) offers an interesting contrast:

Un dessinateur est un coloriste manqué.
 Cela est si vrai que M. INGRES, le représentant le plus illustre de l'école
naturaliste dans le dessin, est toujours au pourchas de la couleur. Admirable et
malheureuse opiniâtreté! C'est l'éternelle histoire des gens qui vendraient la
réputation qu'ils méritent pour celle qu'ils ne peuvent obtenir. M. Ingres adore
la couleur, comme une marchande de modes. C'est peine et plaisir à la fois que
de contempler les efforts qu'il fait pour choisir et accoupler ses tons. Le
résultat, non pas toujours discordant, mais amer et violent, plaît souvent aux
poètes corrompus; encore quand leur esprit fatigué s'est longtemps réjoui dans
ces luttes dangereuses, il veut absolument se reposer sur un Velasquez ou un
Lawrence.   (II, 458–9)

Ingres is not content with his kingdom and sacrifices his serenity in
his quest for colour. The transgression is condemned, but by no means
absolutely. The artist's stubbornness is to be admired; in the creative
process, his efforts demand a will-power which Baudelaire himself
advocated; the result is 'non pas toujours discordant'. Indeed the
'dualité fatigante' of Ingres's method procures a somewhat perverse
pleasure for certain 'poètes corrompus' amongst whom Baudelaire
might well include himself.[3] There is the excitement of danger in both
the conception and the contemplation of Ingres's work, but, as so often
in Baudelaire, the traveller into perilous, unknown seas cherishes the
return to port (here to Velasquez or Lawrence). As early as 1846,
Baudelaire thus had in Ingres a model of *dépassement* whom he was
forced to admire in spite of a theoretical heresy in the artist's approach.

Eleven years later, Baudelaire published his *Notes nouvelles sur Edgar
Poe*, in which he returns to the division of media, but now in literature.
At the end of a discussion on the merits and qualities of the short story,
he considers the validity of 'contes purement poétiques':

. . . l'auteur qui poursuit dans une nouvelle un simple but de beauté ne travaille
qu'à son grand désavantage, privé qu'il est de l'instrument le plus utile, le

rythme. Je sais que dans toutes les littératures des efforts ont été faits, souvent heureux, pour créer des contes purement poétiques; Edgar Poe lui-même en a fait de très beaux. Mais ce sont des luttes et des efforts qui ne servent qu'à démontrer la force des vrais moyens adaptés aux buts correspondants, et je ne serais pas éloigné de croire que, chez quelques auteurs, les plus grands qu'on puisse choisir, ces tentations héroïques vinssent d'un désespoir.   (II, 330)

The similarities to the Ingres passage are striking: the reaffirmation of accepted doctrine '('la force des vrais moyens . . .'); the admission of partial success ('souvent heureux'; *cf.* the earlier 'non pas toujours discordant'); the recognition of creative effort; the tone of admiration elicited by a heresy bordering on heroism; finally (given the fact that we know that Baudelaire was already experimenting with prose-poetry at the time of writing this passage on Poe), a possible disguised reference to himself ('chez quelques auteurs'; *cf.* the 'poètes corrompus' cited above). The differences of context are important, however. Firstly, the fact that Baudelaire is now treating matters of literature makes his remarks more relevant to his own creative practice. Secondly, he is faced with a model of *dépassement*, Edgar Poe, with whom he felt an extraordinary affinity (Baudelaire never claims an affinity with Ingres – although some of his comments on the painter suggest, discreetly and perhaps unconsciously, the existence of common characteristics). Both these differences lend extra irony to the passage and increase the suspicion one has that Baudelaire, whilst condemning, is himself tempted to transgress. In a way which shows the consistency of Baudelaire's self-divided temperament, the simultaneous attractiveness of aesthetic vice and virtue can be seen as analogous to his attitude towards theological sin.

Nevertheless, behind the discernible hesitations, Baudelaire still adheres to his belief in the purity of function of a given medium – or so it may appear at first. How, one might ask, can Baudelaire reconcile this belief with his own practice of writing 'poèmes en prose'? One has to read the texts carefully to realize that he never quite falls into self-contradiction. By using extreme examples of transgression, he does not actually proscribe lesser infractions; for instance, in the Poe passage, he specifically singles out 'contes *purement* poétiques' and an author 'qui poursuit dans une nouvelle un *simple* but de beauté' (my italics). The error committed by such an author is thus in misusing his genre ('conte', 'nouvelle') rather than in misusing his medium (prose); and the error might simply be one of degree ('purement', 'simple'). Baudelaire, then, does not rule out poetic prose, but he does dismiss totally poetic short stories. He uses a similar tactic in the *Salon de 1859*, when he attacks the miniature, sculptured scenes produced by Butté, which, although imaginative and ingenious,

servent à constater, importantes en cela seulement, l'un des plus grands vices de l'esprit, qui est la désobéissance opiniâtre aux règles constitutives de l'art. Quelles sont les qualités, si belles qu'on les suppose, qui pourraient contrebalancer une si défectueuse énormité? Quel cerveau bien portant peut concevoir sans horreur une peinture en relief, une sculpture agitée par la mécanique, une ode sans rimes, un roman versifié, etc? (II, 674)

One might note first of all the recurrence of a vocabulary which enshrines consistently held ideas: the notion of the usefulness of error in pointing to the rule ('servent à constater', *cf.* 'ne servent qu'à démontrer' in the Poe passage), the stubbornness of a wayward aesthetic (*cf.* 'opiniâtre' with 'opiniâtreté', used to describe Ingres) and the natural healthiness of the correct aesthetic (*cf.* 'cerveau bien portant' with the 'hommes bien portants' of 1846). But the reassertion of a conservative viewpoint (adopted, as in the *Salon de 1846*, most vehemently when the poet is taking lesser talents to task) implies rejection of only the more exaggerated searches for innovation. The 'ode sans rimes' and the 'roman versifié' are as extreme as (or more extreme than) 'contes purement poétiques'. Both the experimental ode and novel offend by combining a well-characterized genre with an unsuitable medium. Thus an 'ode sans rimes' is an aberration because an indispensable part of the French ode is that it is in rhymed verse (Claudel was not to agree). It is by no means synonymous with a 'poème sans rimes', since the definition of 'poème' is much more flexible, enjoying the advantage of not being coterminous with that of 'vers'. Baudelaire, we know, benefits from this fact in his title *Petits poèmes en prose*. The tactic of selecting as targets extreme innovations saves Baudelaire from self-contradiction; he can justifiably attack an excessive audacity while tempering his own audacity with a typical measure of prudence. In fact, however, Baudelaire does not argue the case for more moderate transgressions, but preserves a stern traditional expression – broken, it is true, by an apparently reluctant acknowledgement of the success of Ingres and Poe. The strict conservatism of the critic in this matter masks the cautiously subversive genius of the poet – albeit not for long.

The final passage, which represents the culminating point in the poet's theoretical debate on the division of media, is the famous one from his *lettre–préface* to Arsène Houssaye which preceded the twenty *Petits poèmes en prose* published in *La Presse* on 26 and 27 August and 24 September 1862:

Quel est celui de nous qui n'a pas, dans ses jours d'ambition, rêvé le miracle d'une prose poétique, musicale sans rythme et sans rime, assez souple et assez heurtée pour s'adapter aux mouvements lyriques de l'âme, aux ondulations de la rêverie, aux soubresauts de la conscience?

C'est surtout de la fréquentation des villes énormes, c'est du croisement de leurs innombrables rapports que naît cet idéal obsédant. (I, 275–6)

It is clear that by 'poétique' Baudelaire here intends not poetic vocabulary, still less poetic subject-matter, but poetic effects of musicality and expressivity, precisely those effects which are conventionally associated with the potential of verse. The barrier which Baudelaire dreams of breaching is thus the 'technical' one between prose and verse rather than the 'thematic' one between the prosaic and the poetic. His attitude towards this breach differs significantly from the attitude towards the adventures of Ingres, Poe and Butté (it could hardly be otherwise, given the context). What in their case had been infraction is now 'le miracle', 'cet idéal obsédant'; heresy has become heroism; what with Poe was the result of despair is now more positively seen as the result of ambition and dream. The half-suppressed desire to seek the new, to 'dépasser les limites', swells to the surface, in a manner reminiscent of the final quatrains of 'Le Voyage'.

The passages I have given indicate a certain, if superficial, consistency as well as development in Baudelaire's feelings towards the idea of crossing artistic frontiers. In the *Salon de 1846*, the classical theoretical position is adopted vigorously in order to demonstrate the diluted, dispersed effort of unimpressive contemporaries, but when faced with the example of Ingres's audacity Baudelaire has to recognize the courage of an unconventional talent. The same problem of a clash between espoused theory and admired infraction is later presented by Poe in the realm of literature. It seems that individual genius is not necessarily content to cultivate a chosen field and may long to appropriate neighbouring territory – not through eclecticism, but through despair, ambition or exploratory zeal. It may be that in Ingres and Poe, more than in Delacroix or any French poet, Baudelaire found his models of *dépassement*. To suppose that, as a practising writer, he remained unaware of the general relevance of their heroism to his own aesthetic explorations would be to forget that in Baudelaire the critic and poet are one. Critical writing and poetic creation, both relying on the analytical and synthetical properties of the imagination, do not occupy separate compartments of his mind. In conclusion – if one can say justifiably that Baudelaire's belief in the limits of a particular medium acts as a guiding force in his criticism (of both art and literature), one has to admit that limits also act as provocations,

151

irresistible to the artist or poet of genius. The following paragraph from *L'Art philosophique* summarizes his position perfectly:

> Tout esprit profondément sensible et bien doué pour les arts (il ne faut pas confondre la sensibilité de l'imagination avec celle du cœur) sentira comme moi que tout art doit se suffire à lui-même et en même temps rester dans les limites providentielles; cependant l'homme garde ce privilège de pouvoir toujours développer de grands talents dans un genre faux ou en violant la constitution naturelle de l'art.   (II, 604)

The second part of this chapter will examine a series of texts to illustrate an important phase in the development of Baudelaire's own art which moved hesitatingly from classical poetic form to the acknowledged modernity of the later Parisian verse and prose-poems.

When Baudelaire began to write, the rhymed couplet in classical Alexandrines was the most hallowed form of French verse, and his early poetry is dominated by this conventional metre.[4] The syntax trims itself neatly to fit the mould of hemistich and line; propositions advance the poem in clusters of couplets. Formal boundaries are there to be observed, not to be transgressed (which is not to say that infractions never occurred, even in the most classical of poets). A comparatively minor misdemeanour consists of end-stopping the first line of a couplet, so that the presentation of argument threatens to break the 'even-number rule'. Let us take as examples the second and third couplets in these six lines from 'Châtiment de l'orgueil':

> Tout le chaos roula dans cette intelligence,
> Temple autrefois vivant, plein d'ordre et d'opulence,
> Sous les plafonds duquel tant de pompe avait lui.
> Le silence et la nuit s'installèrent en lui,
> Comme dans un caveau dont la clef est perdue.
> Dès lors il fut semblable aux bêtes de la rue   (lines 17–22)

The degree of such an irregularity (which I shall designate Type A) is minimal, since metre (the line) and syntax still cohere. More adventurous and more conspicuous are couplets which overflow their limits in a flagrant enjambement (Type B):

> A l'œil limpide et clair ainsi qu'une eau courante,
> Et qui va répandant sur tout, insouciante
> Comme l'azur du ciel, les oiseaux et les fleurs,
> Ses parfums, ses chansons et ses douces chaleurs!
> ('J'aime le souvenir . . .', lines 37–40)

What I would like to establish (however rapidly) is that in his early couplet-poems Baudelaire admits such irregularities only infrequently. Neither Type A or Type B is found at all in 'A une Malabaraise' (written before 1843; 28 lines), 'Allégorie' (written before 1843; 20 lines); 'Je t'adore à l'égal ...' (written before 1843; ten lines), 'Tu mettrais l'univers ...' (written between 1840 and 1846, probably 1840–2; eighteen lines), or 'Les Métamorphoses du vampire' (written in or before 1851; 28 lines). 'La servante au grand cœur ...' (1841–2; 22 lines), 'La Béatrice' (probably 1842–8; 30 lines) and 'Paysage' (1841–5?; 26 lines) each contain only one minor infraction (of type A); 'J'aime le souvenir ...' (1841–5?; 40 lines) contains two infractions (one A and one B). There are three (3A) in 'Le Vin des chiffonniers' (before 1843; 32 lines) and three (2A, 1B) in 'Le Crépuscule du matin' (1841–3; 28 lines); four (3A, 1B) in 'Je n'ai pas pour maîtresse ...' (1840–4; 48 lines); five (4A, 1B) in 'Châtiment de l'orgueil' (1848–50; 26 lines); and six (3A, 3B) in 'Tous imberbes alors ...' (1843–5; 78 lines). It is possible, of course, that the early texts of all these poems did contain more infractions, removed during a process of revision, but to suppose this is to come close to arguing a systematic eradication of irregularities by the poet during the preparation of the *Fleurs du Mal* manuscript (with the exception of 'A une Malabaraise', the first ten poems named in this paragraph have as their earliest extant texts the proofs of the 1857 *Fleurs du Mal*). It appears to me unlikely that Baudelaire should undertake such a traditionalist's purge, especially at a time when he was becoming more experimental in his technique. One piece of firm evidence which supports the idea of a conformist Baudelaire in the 1840s is the poem 'A une Malabaraise', which was published in 1846 (under the title 'A une Indienne') in a form free from both types of irregularity.[5] The cumulative evidence of early couplet-poems, even if one allows for possible later corrections of some irregularities, still suggests that in the 1840s Baudelaire largely conformed to the syntax/metre parallel which characterizes Classical verse.

My purpose in stressing the conventionality of the poet's early couplets is to throw into relief the originality, within Baudelaire's development, of the poem now known as 'Le Crépuscule du soir', a poem of which a manuscript version was already circulating in 1851, and which may well have been composed several years before that. The text which I give below is that published in the *Hommage à C. F. Denecourt*. In fact this is the fourth extant version, the previous three being the manuscript belonging to the *Douze poèmes* (1851–2), the text published in *La Semaine théâtrale* (1 February 1852) and the manuscript sent to Fernand Desnoyers for publication in the Denecourt *Festschrift*. Although there are numerous, fairly minor, changes made by Baudelaire at each of these stages, not one affects the validity of the stylistic comments offered below. Here then is the 1855 published text:

Voici venir le Soir, ami du criminel;
Il vient comme un complice, à pas de loup; – le ciel
Se ferme lentement comme une grande alcôve,
Et l'homme impatient se change en bête fauve.
Oui, voilà bien le Soir, le Soir cher à celui   5
Dont les bras sans mentir peuvent dire: Aujourd'hui
Nous avons travaillé. – C'est le Soir qui soulage
Les Esprits que dévore une douleur sauvage,
Le savant obstiné dont le front s'alourdit,
Et l'ouvrier courbé qui regagne son lit.   10
Cependant des Démons malsains dans l'atmosphère
S'éveillent lourdement comme des gens d'affaire,
Et cognent en volant les volets et l'auvent;
A travers les lueurs que tourmente le vent,
La Prostitution s'allume dans les rues;   15
Comme une fourmilière elle ouvre ses issues;
Partout elle se fraye un occulte chemin,
Ainsi que l'ennemi qui tente un coup de main;
Elle remue au sein de la cité de fange,
Comme un Ver qui dérobe à l'Homme ce qu'il mange.   20
On entend çà et là les cuisines siffler
Les théâtres glapir, les orchestres ronfler;
Les tables d'hôte dont le Jeu fait les délices
S'emplissent de catins et d'escrocs, leurs complices,
Et les voleurs qui n'ont ni trêve ni merci   25
Vont bientôt commencer leur travail, eux aussi,
Et forcer doucement les portes et les caisses,
Pour vivre quelques jours et vêtir leurs maîtresses.

Recueille-toi, mon Ame, en ce grave moment,
Et ferme ton oreille à ce bourdonnement;   30
C'est l'heure où les douleurs des malades s'aigrissent;
La sombre Nuit les prend à la gorge, ils finissent
Leur destinée, et vont vers le Gouffre commun;
L'hôpital se remplit de leurs soupirs; plus d'un
Ne viendra plus chercher la soupe parfumée   35
Au coin du feu, – le soir, – auprès d'une Ame aimée.

Encore la plupart n'ont-ils jamais connu
La douceur du foyer, et n'ont jamais vécu!

Couplets are broken by the end-stopping of lines 1, 13, 15, 31 and 33; couplets step over their frontiers conspicuously at the end of lines 2, 6, 32 and 34. The enjambements are marked by *contre-rejets* ('– le ciel', 'Aujourd'hui', 'ils finissent', 'plus d'un') rather than *rejets* (the two examples amongst those I am discussing, 'Nous avons travaillé' and 'leur destinée', are themselves preceded by *contre-rejets*). The use of *contrerejets* at the end of a couplet signals a desire to dislocate more effectively than the use of *rejets*, partly because the isolated phrase or word will always rhyme and therefore advertise itself, and partly because the isolation often looks visually precarious, the words hanging over the abyss of the line-end. There are indications that Baudelaire was aware of this visual effect, since in the 1855 version he accentuates it by inserting a dash before 'le ciel' in line 2 and by capitalizing 'Aujourd'hui' in line 6; the same awareness of typography is witnessed in later variants when, in the 1857 version, he inserts a dash before 'ils finissent' (line 32), and in 1861, before 'plus d'un' (line 34), at the same time full-stopping after 'soupirs' and capitalizing 'plus'. The unique frequency of enjambement already makes us conscious that we are facing a very original poem, at least from the viewpoint of its versification; but as well as this distinction, there are two more points of technique worth noting in 'Le Crépuscule du soir'. Firstly, the sixth syllable loses almost all its privileges in both

> Les tables d'hôte dont le Jeu fait les délices

and

> Et les voleurs qui n'ont ni trêve ni merci

where the stress on the verb is subordinate to that given to the three nouns. Secondly, there is an unusually high incidence of weak rhymes (at a period when the general trend in French verse was towards rich rhymes): 'celui'/'Aujourd'hui', 's'alourdit'/'lit', 'rues'/'issues', 'commun'/'d'un', 'connu'/'vécu'. Indeed the richest rhyme in the whole poem is internal:

> Les tables d'hôte dont le Jeu fait les délices
> S'em*plissent* de catins et d'escrocs, leurs com*plices*,

where the nasal vowels [ɑ̃, ɔ̃] support the rhyming phonemes. Confronted with such an accumulation of unusual rhythmic devices, one has inevitably to recognize the poet's attempt to disrupt the symmetry of his earlier Classical model and to break the syntax/metre parallel.

But what drove Baudelaire to this experimentation? The answer perhaps lies in the sentence from the Houssaye dedication which links 'cet idéal obsédant' (poetic prose) to the vitality of Paris: 'C'est surtout de la fréquentation des villes énormes, c'est du croisement de leurs innombrables rapports que naît cet idéal obsédant.' It has to be said that earlier Parisian poems, 'Le Crépuscule du matin' and 'Le Vin des chiffonniers' (both written in their first versions before 1843), are relatively free from experimentation, probably because Baudelaire had not yet attained sufficient maturity as a poet to risk the conspicuously irregular. Interestingly, the second of these poems (together with 'L'Ame du vin') is 'translated' into prose in *Du vin et du hachish* (1851), as if the lure of prose and a faint premonition of the verse-prose doublets of later years already exist in the poet's mind. If the correlation between Parisian inspiration and new forms of expression stated in the Houssaye dedication seems not to obtain for these two early poems, the same cannot be said for 'Le Crépuscule du soir', in which the problem of handling city themes appears to have had its effect on the verse-form. The enjambements, the weak rhymes, the occasional demotion of the medial stress, the elevation of the trivial and the semantically banal to rhyming positions ('celui', 'Aujourd'hui', 'eux aussi', 'un'): all point to a type of verse which questions its classical symmetry and leans, however slightly, towards the rhythms, the unpredictability and the irregularity of prose. Paradoxically, verse which moves towards prosaic rhythm defines at the same time its own regularity; the intrusion of the irregular sharpens one's awareness of a lost parallelism. Nevertheless, 'irregular' verse can ease the mixture of the poetic and the prosaic, as Hugo points out: 'du moment où le naturel s'est fait jour dans le langage théâtral, il lui a fallu un vers qui pût se parler. Le vers brisé est admirablement fait pour recevoir la dose de prose que la poésie dramatique doit admettre. De là, l'introduction de l'enjambement . . .'[6] In 'Le Crépuscule du soir', Baudelaire presents himself as a poet working with new material, dissatisfied with the old dispensation and venturing into formal dislocation in order to evoke, through the play of rhythm and a certain gaucherie, the poignant disharmony of Parisian life. The inspiration of the city will eventually draw him across the boundary between verse and prose; and the audacities that he risks even in the first versions of 'Le Crépuscule du soir' (the first extant versions date from 1851–2) represent an early step in this direction.

The formal bizarreness of 'Le Crépuscule du soir' takes on even greater significance when we consider it in the context of the Denecourt *Festschrift*. In reply to an invitation from Desnoyers, one of the editors of the volume, to contribute 'des vers sur la *Nature*' (I, 1024), Baudelaire sent his already-published 'Deux crépuscules' (now 'subtitled' 'Le Soir' and 'Le Matin' and presented in that order) and two prose-poems, the first 'Le Crépuscule du soir', the second 'La Solitude', written, one suspects, especially for the *Festschrift*. The perversity of sending two specifically urban verse-poems instead of something 'sur la Nature' has been noted as typical; and I suppose that it is in some way perverse to send prose-poems when one has been asked for 'des vers'. But the choice and collocation made by Baudelaire are important to the study of his development, for the years preceding the publication in 1855 mark 'a decided reorientation of his aesthetic, moral and political ideas' (Leakey 1968, 192). Leakey explains that 'the invitation gave to Baudelaire a welcome opportunity of formally rationalizing his new attitude [towards Nature], and of assimilating to it his increasing consciousness of his role as a poet of Paris' (Leakey 1968, 192). It is not difficult to imagine that the poet was particularly aware of his context, his specific talent and the fact that he had a ready-made audience of celebrated poets and writers. What better opportunity therefore to demonstrate not only his changing view of Nature but also his experiments with his own style? The formal significance of the poet's contribution can be swiftly gauged if one realizes its double uniqueness: (a) the two prose-poems are the very first that Baudelaire published, and (b) it was to be the *only* occasion on which he published verse-poems and prose-poems side by side. These facts, together with the odd similarity of titles (and themes) within the four poems, underline the unusualness of the context in which Baudelaire chose to place his already unusual verse on a Parisian twilight. It is as if he were now arguing by implication that an urban aesthetic carries as its consequence a necessary experimentation with poetic form.

The close juxtaposition of the two poems, one in verse and one in prose, with clearly cognate titles, is an invitation to compare. Here then is the prose-poem, 'Le Crépuscule du soir' as it appeared in 1855:

La tombée de la nuit a toujours été pour moi le signal d'une fête intérieure et comme la délivrance d'une angoisse. Dans les bois comme dans les rues d'une grande ville, l'assombrissement du jour et le pointillement des étoiles ou des lanternes éclairent mon esprit.

Mais j'ai eu deux amis que le crépuscule rendait malades. L'un méconnaissait alors tous les rapports d'amitié et de politesse, et brutalisait sauvagement le premier venu. Je l'ai vu jeter un excellent poulet à la tête d'un maître d'hôtel. La venue du soir gâtait les meilleures choses.

L'autre, à mesure que le jour baissait, devenait plus aigre, plus sombre, plus taquin. Indulgent pendant la journée, il était impitoyable le soir; – et ce n'était pas seulement sur autrui, mais sur lui-même que s'exerçait abondamment sa manie crépusculaire.

Le premier est mort fou, incapable de reconnaître sa maîtresse et son fils; le second porte en lui l'inquiétude d'une insatisfaction perpétuelle. L'ombre qui fait la lumière dans mon esprit fait la nuit dans le leur. – Et, bien qu'il ne soit pas rare de voir la même cause engendrer deux effets contraires, cela m'intrigue et m'étonne toujours.

Even though the verse is much more Parisian in its inspiration than the prose, there is an obvious similarity of theme (the contrasting effects of evening twilight). Marcel Ruff comments:

Le sujet est donc apparemment lié à celui du premier poème en vers, mais le même point de départ ... conduit à deux méditations ou rêveries très différentes. Il est visible que Baudelaire se livre là à une sorte d'expérience: il cherche quelles variations l'artiste doit tirer du même thème selon qu'il le traite au moyen du vers ou de la prose.   (Ruff 1967, 120)

The experiment, however, is not simply performed at a thematic level (as Ruff seems to suggest) and does not leave unchanged the accepted boundary between verse and prose; the formal characteristics of each medium are called into question. I have already said that the rough-edged verse-poem infiltrates the territory of prose (to the extent that in the manuscript version sent to Desnoyers Baudelaire – very exceptionally – went so far as to 'paragraph' his verse divisions by indenting their first line). The prose-poem, on the other hand, annexes some of the qualities of verse: the paragraphs studiously maintain a stanzaic consistency of length, individual sentences have the predictability of poetic metre (*e.g.* the ternary rhythm of 'plus aigre, plus sombre, plus taquin', or the antithetical balance of 'Indulgent pendant la journée, il était impitoyable le soir'); a rudimentary symmetry is evoked throughout by the use of binary constructions; the whole *enchaînement* has the Pythagorean inevitability of a sonnet. The passage is still prose of course (indeed it is not easy to conceive of a lyrical verse-poem containing a chicken-throwing incident). Baudelaire cultivates the 'ton raisonneur' which he was to see as one of the specific registers open to the short-story writer;[7] but even the ratiocination – to use Poe's term – is turned to paradoxical and poetic ends in the synthesizing image of exterior darkness shedding interior light: 'L'ombre qui fait la lumière dans mon esprit fait la nuit dans le leur.' The juxtaposition of the two poems naturally provokes debate, and rather than strengthening the correctness of the belief that poetry and prose must be kept separate, it raises, on the contrary, the question of their interpenetrability.

With this same question in mind, we could consider the verse-prose doublets, 'La Chevelure'/'Un hémisphère dans une chevelure' (originally titled 'La Chevelure' and changed only in 1862 when it appeared in *La Presse*) and 'L'Invitation au voyage' (the same title for both verse and prose). These doublets resemble the *Festschrift* pair in that they are evidence of the poet's attempt either to define the distinctiveness of each medium or to judge how far they can be allowed to overlap. But there is an important difference: in the dusk poems verse and prose infiltrate each other's territory, whereas in the above doublets verse-techniques (stanzaic paragraphs, refrains, rhythmic repetitions, alliteration and assonance) invade the prose without any counter-movement of prose into the verse (in fact, 'La Chevelure' and the verse 'L'Invitation au voyage' are as far from prosaicness as any poems in *Les Fleurs du Mal*). For Baudelaire, the dusk poems are doubly innovatory, in a way that the other pairs are not. It is only in the Parisian pieces that one finds this two-way experimentation.

The relevance of Baudelaire's own statement in the Houssaye dedication about Paris and poetic form goes beyond its context and reaches back into the poet's career. I hope to have shown the significance of the fact that the earliest text in which Baudelaire displays great freedom in the use of enjambement (in particular) has a Parisian theme, that his next (and more radical) experiment in the extension of the limits of poetry, *i.e.* the writing of prose-poems, also occurs, only a few years later, within a specifically Parisian context; and finally I would suggest that, in choosing to group – as his contribution to the Denecourt *Festschrift* – two verse-poems and two prose-poems treating in varying degrees the theme of twilight in Paris, he may well be demonstrating his own awareness of the relationship between the two forms of experimentation (rhythmical unpredictability in verse, prose-poetry), as well as the relationship between experimentation and urban theme.

The same urban pressures can be seen at work on the versification of the famous 1859 trilogy of Parisian poems dedicated to Victor Hugo, 'Le Cygne', 'Les Petites Vieilles' and 'Les Sept Vieillards', the latter bringing us back to the letter to Morel. These three pieces, the originality of their conception, and the way in which they do gloriously succeed in passing beyond the limits traditionally assigned to poetry, have been justly admired. Their dramatic energy strains the limits of verse.[8] The compelling advance of theme, event, thought or image is reflected in one oddity of versification which the poems have in common, namely a very noticeable use of stanzaic enjambement.[9] Stanzas 4–7 of 'Les Sept Vieillards' provide one obvious example. Here, the visually conspicuous 'M'apparut', a *rejet* belonging syntactically to the preceding stanza, serves an expressive function; the dislocation of the expected rhythm caused by the second example ('Lui donnait la tournure et le pas maladroit/(new stanza) D'un quadrupède infirme ou d'un juif à trois pattes') supports the notion of unsteady infirmity. Not a single one of these quatrains is the normal self-contained unit; propositions spill over the bounds of the stanza, and the form cracks as it did in 'Le Crépuscule du soir', except that here the unit is the quatrain rather than the couplet. The same happens in 'Le Cygne' between stanzas 1 and 2, 4 and 5, 5 and 6, 6 and 7. The use of the device in 'Les Petites Vieilles' (between stanzas 2 and 3, and particularly between 4 and 5) has already been examined (see p. 111).

These examples of stanzaic enjambement are not the only ones in Baudelaire, but there are very few others[10] and these are certainly amongst the most remarkable – together with the ultimate *dépassement* from octet to sestet found in 'Recueillement', yet another city poem. It is conversely significant that there is an almost complete *absence* of stanzaic enjambement in quatrain poems which are more or less contemporary with the 1859 Hugo trilogy but which do not treat Parisian material. For example, between the 36 verses of 'Le Voyage', written in the early months of 1859, there is only one conspicuous stanzaic enjambement (lines 128–9), occurring in a passage (lines 113–32) where the quatrain/proposition parallel struggles to maintain itself against the surging anticipation of the final voyage 'sur la mer des Ténèbres'. There are no examples of the device in 'Danse macabre' (December 1858), 'Chant d'automne' (September–October 1859), 'Chanson d'après-midi' (1859–60), 'L'Amour du mensonge' (probably 1860) or 'Rêve parisien' (1859–60?; not strictly a Parisian poem despite its title).

The occasional disintegration of a formal unity such as the line, the couplet or the quatrain, is indicative of the structural freedom which Baudelaire allows himself in his Parisian poems. Here, above all, one recognizes Baudelaire's mature ability to appropriate style to subject-matter ('l'adaptation du style au sujet', I, 182, was one of the important lessons he initially thought to expound in his preface to *Les Fleurs du Mal*). It is as if the impatient, convulsive forces of a modern city were offering themselves, in their diversity, as a challenge to the power of that poetic imagination which Baudelaire elevates so royally in the *Salon de 1859*. Although the possibility that verse might scarcely be able to contain such forces had perhaps been suspected as early as the first 'Crépuscule du soir', it was well and truly confirmed by the decisive switch to prose-poems made in 1859–60, and to prose-poems of a kind very different from those earlier efforts published in 1855 and 1857 (in *Le Présent*), as Suzanne Bernard has pointed out (Bernard 1959, 112–19). Again, the 1855 *Festschrift* provides the best material to illustrate Baudelaire's development: 'Le Crépuscule du soir' and 'La Solitude', both originally consisting of four short paragraphs, are 'modernized' in 1861 (or 1862) so that the first becomes four times and the second three times longer. No other prose-poems, as far as is known, were revised and lengthened to the same degree. I shall pursue the analysis of the transformation of 'Le Crépuscule du soir' in the next chapter.

The broad stages of Baudelaire's hesitant progress from classically moulded verse to freely rhapsodic prose could be seen in clear outline if we were to study in greater detail all versions of the four poems presented as homage to C. F. Denecourt. Of the 'Deux Crépuscules', 'Le Matin' is largely respectful of syntax/metre parallels, although there are two broken couplets and one tentative overspill (lines 22–3); 'Le Soir', on the other hand, is boldly exploratory and a prelude to the versification (and subject-matter) of the 1859 Hugo trilogy. The two prose-poems show a perhaps excessive neatness, which disappears in 1861–2 in favour of a freer, dynamic composition, more typical of the Parisian prose-poem.

The first part of this chapter discussed Baudelaire's attitude towards the limits of artistic territories; the rest based much of its argument on the overstepping of metrical limits. Can the single device of enjambement be linked with the larger theoretical heresies which Baudelaire both condemned and admired? That a point of technique can draw to itself ideological value had been proved by the 'bataille d'*Hernani*', where the blatant enjambement of lines 1–2 was seen as a deliberate flouting of the classical model and a symbolic act expressive of Hugo's desire to pass beyond accepted convention. While I am not suggesting that Baudelaire intended any such provocation (that battle had already been won), I would argue that the transgression of verse-frontiers was for him an important, if minor, act of liberation in his progress as a poet (and especially as a poet of Paris); it is the notion of artistic *dépassement* carried on to the level of versification. *Dépassement* and enjambement do not relate to each other merely by verbal accident, or through some arbitrary trick of metaphor; their relationship is rather one of clear metonymy, the apparently insignificant detail of versification being contiguous with, and reflective of, the whole spirit of Baudelaire's sometimes apprehensive aesthetic adventure.

9

EXPERIMENTATION AND URBAN POETICS, II: THE TRANSFORMATION OF A PROSE-POEM

Of all Baudelaire's prose-poems, 'Le Crépuscule du soir' is, apart from being his first in print, also remarkable for the *number* of times it was published or prepared for publication in the poet's lifetime.[1] Its only rivals in this respect are 'La Solitude' and 'Les Projets', poems with which Baudelaire clearly associates it.[2] Almost seven years after its first appearance, during the last months of 1861 or the first months of 1862, Baudelaire refashioned his poem, surrounding a modified original with three new paragraphs at the beginning and two more at the end. In a letter (8 October 1862) to Arsène Houssaye, editor of *La Presse*, he speaks of several 'morceaux' which have been 'remaniés et même *transformés*' (*Corres.*, II, 263) between their publication in the *Revue fantaisiste* (1 November 1861) and their submission to *La Presse* in 1862. 'Le Crépuscule du soir' is certainly one of these 'morceaux transformés'[3] in which Houssaye was invited to study 'la proportion entre le vieux, le neuf, et le rajeuni' (*Corres.*, II, 264). Why, when Baudelaire was suffering ill-health, faced with one financial crisis after another, ensnared in the exhausting ritual of the Académie application and laden with other creative projects, did he undertake this radical transformation of a prose-poem? The original version, after all, had served him well on three occasions already. The deliberateness of the decision to rework, emphasized by the scarcely conducive circumstances, encourages us to seek in this poem evidence of a conscious development in the poetics of Baudelaire's prose-poetry. Suzanne Bernard, judging it 'indispensable . . . de bien considérer les dates', has already attempted to 'suivre de l'intérieur l'évolution de la pensée créatrice chez Baudelaire entre 1857 et 1866' (Bernard 1959, 113–14), but several of her conclusions have since been invalidated by the discovery of an 1862 proof containing versions of poems (including 'Le Crépuscule du soir') the reworking of which she had presumed to be later and to have suffered from Baudelaire's worsening health. Of the additional paragraphs which conclude the later 'Crépuscule du soir' she says: 'lorsque Baudelaire les ajouta au texte primitif, purement anecdotique . . .

162

comment n'a-t-il pas senti qu'il greffait un second poème sur le premier, différent de caractère et d'inspiration?' The reworking is considered 'curieux' and 'fâcheux' and evidence of 'un essoufflement, un tarissement de l'imagination créatrice'; it gives the impression that 'Baudelaire n'a plus la force créatrice nécessaire pour imposer à sa matière une ordonnance artistique, et qu'il se borne à "copier le dictionnaire"' (for this last group of quotations, see Bernard 1959, 118–19). Harsh words, no matter what the date of composition, and based on an oddly restricted notion of 'ordonnance artistique'. This chapter will aim to demonstrate the experimental aesthetic which underlies 'Le Crépuscule du soir' and which, far from proving Baudelaire's artistic decay, shows his tenacious spirit of adventure.

The text which I shall use is that found in the fourth *feuilleton* of proofs for *La Presse*, due for publication in September–October 1862 but in fact never published. In order to give some idea of the 'le vieux, le neuf, et le rajeuni', I have adopted the following method, admittedly rudimentary: the italicized words indicate additions to the immediately preceding version published in the *Revue fantaisiste* (1 November 1861), while words in bold print indicate major alterations to that text. The substance of lines 35–9, it is important to note, *begins* the poem in the *Revue fantaisiste*.[4] For the first version of the prose-poem, see Chapter 8, p. 157.

> *Le jour tombe. Un grand apaisement se fait dans les pauvres esprits fatigués du labeur de la journée, et leurs pensées prennent maintenant les couleurs tendres et indécises du crépuscule.*
>
> 5   *Cependant, du haut de la montagne, arrive à mon balcon, à travers les nuées transparentes du soir, un grand hurlement composé d'une foule de cris discordants que l'espace transforme en une lugubre harmonie, comme celle de la marée qui monte ou d'une tempête qui s'éveille.*
>
> 10   *Quels sont les infortunés que le soir ne calme pas, et qui prennent, comme les hiboux, la venue de la nuit pour un signal de sabbat? Cette sinistre ululation nous arrive du noir hospice des Antiquailles, et le soir en fumant et en contemplant le repos de l'immense vallée, hérissée de maisons dont chaque fenêtre illuminée dit: 'C'est ici la paix maintenant, c'est ici la joie de la famille!' je puis, quand le vent souffle de Fourvières, bercer ma pensée étonnée à ce redoutable écho de l'Enfer.*
>
> 15   *Le crépuscule excite les fous. Bizarre! Bizarre!* J'ai eu deux amis que le crépuscule **rendait** tout malades. L'un méconnaissait alors tous les rapports d'amitié et de politesse, et maltraitait comme un sauvage le premier venu. Je l'ai vu jeter à la tête d'un maître d'hôtel un excellent poulet *dans lequel il croyait voir je ne sais quel insultant hiéroglyphe.* Le
> 20   soir, précurseur des voluptés *profondes*, lui gâtait les choses les plus succulentes.

L'autre, *un ambitieux blessé*, devenait, à mesure que le jour baissait, plus aigre, plus sombre, plus taquin. Indulgent *et sociable encore* pendant la journée, il était impitoyable le soir, et ce n'était pas
25   seulement sur autrui, mais sur lui-même, que s'exerçait rageusement sa manie crépusculeuse.

Le premier est mort fou, incapable de reconnaître sa **femme** et son **enfant**; le second porte en lui l'inquiétude d'un malaise perpétuel, *et, fût-il gratifié de tous les honneurs que peuvent conférer les républiques et les*
30   *princes, je crois que le crépuscule allumerait encore en lui la brûlante envie de distinctions imaginaires.* **La nuit qui mettait ses ténèbres dans leur esprit fait la lumière dans le mien**; et bien qu'il ne soit pas rare de voir la même cause engendrer deux effets contraires, **j'en suis toujours comme intrigué et alarmé.**
35   **O nuit, ô rafraîchissantes ténèbres, vous êtes** pour moi le signal d'une fête intérieure, **vous êtes** la délivrance d'une angoisse*!* Dans la solitude *des plaines*, dans les **labyrinthes pierreux** d'une capitale, scintillement des étoiles, *explosion* des lanternes, **vous êtes le feu d'artifice de la déesse Liberté!**
40   *Crépuscule, comme vous êtes doux, et tendre et brillant! Les lueurs roses qui traînent encore à l'horizon comme l'agonie du jour sous l'oppression victorieuse de la nuit, les feux des lampes qui font des taches d'un rouge opaque sur les dernières gloires du couchant, les lourdes draperies qu'une main invisible attire des profondeurs de l'Orient, imitent tous les sentiments*
45   *compliqués qui luttent dans le cœur de l'homme.*

On dirait encore d'une de ces robes étranges de danseuses, où une gaze transparente et sombre laisse entrevoir les splendeurs amorties d'une jupe éclatante, comme sous le noir présent transperce le délicieux passé, et les étoiles vacillantes, d'or et d'argent, dont elle est semée, représentent ces feux de
50   *la fantaisie qui ne s'allument bien que sous le deuil profond de la nuit.*

The transformation is undoubtedly drastic. What is the effect of the additions? In what way do they alter the import of the original? What is the significance of the alterations made within the original? How well is it integrated into its new context? It is with these questions in mind that the present study of the text is undertaken.

After a typically curt opening,[5] in which the brevity of expression tries – rather melodramatically – to capture the awesome and elemental simplicity of a cosmic event, the omniscient voice makes the first of many comments which seek to establish a reciprocity between inner and outer worlds. The 'esprits fatigués' reflect the uncertain hues of twilight, offering a satisfying *correspondance* easily readable by the poetic observer. But the 'Cependant' disturbs the interpretative innocence of lines 1–3 and introduces a movement much heavier in poetic charge. The detection of a contrast is reminiscent of lines 5–12 of the verse 'Crépuscule du soir', where the relief of having finished a hard day's work,

O soir, aimable soir, désiré par celui
Dont les bras, sans mentir, peuvent dire: Aujourd'hui
Nous avons travaillé!

is opposed to the anticipation of the night's evil:

Cependant des démons malsains dans l'atmosphère
S'éveillent lourdement.

As in the verse-poem the good-hearted workers are considerably less interesting than the 'démons malsains'; and whereas the 'grand apaisement' enters the poem with no ceremony, the 'grand hurlement' is ushered in expectantly by a procession of adverbial phrases which locate its trajectory long before it is identified. This trajectory is important and the adjectival phrase beginning 'composé d'une foule de cris' superimposes upon it a musical development: the three-stage movement from mountain through 'les nuées transparentes' to the narrator's balcony corresponds to the movement from discord through space to harmony. As if to strengthen the antithesis between these first two paragraphs, the similes of the tide and storm contradict through their verbs the initial suggestions of descent and repose ('tombe'/ 'monte', 'fatigués'/'s'éveille'), and confirm through their use of opposition the narrator's balcony as the privileged mid-point between the 'grand apaisement' and the 'grand hurlement', between valley and mountain. The balcony, besides being here a possible indicator of urban scene (the only one in lines 1–7), is in itself a poetic site, balanced at the edge of exterior and interior, a symbolic place of choice between two modes of poetry. This second paragraph infuses tension into the poem and creates a spatial design, situating the narrator at an intersection, a 'croisement' of one of those 'innombrables rapports' (I, 276) which Baudelaire saw as characteristic of large cities.

A question heads the third paragraph: the narrator is able to read without difficulty the scene he contemplates and to construct its *légende* ('chaque fenêtre illuminée dit: "C'est ici la paix maintenant . . ."'); but what he hears is more resistant to interpretation and, consequently, more evocative ('je puis . . . bercer ma pensée'). There is conspicuous recourse to metaphor and syntactic patterning ('lugubre harmonie', 'sinistre ululation', 'redoutable écho') in an attempt to capture the mysterious in the web of language. Almost coincident with this switch from confident knowledge to poetic conjecture is a switch in modes. Until the question-mark in line 9, the passage belongs to a narrative-descriptive mode, relating with some immediacy a specific set of 'events' (although it is possible, on first reading, to see some iterative force in the first paragraph). But the 'nous' of line 10, the habitual 'le soir' and the plural implications of the restrictive 'quand le vent souffle' dispel the expectations of a pure narrative and promise a piece of general reflection based on *repeated* experience.[6] This subtle transition eases the modulation which integrates the old and the new (*'Le crépuscule excite les fous. Bizarre! Bizarre!* J'ai eu deux amis'); the poet simply moves from reflection based on observation (including present observation) to reflection based on memory and substantiated by anecdote.

The poet's friends provide a third reaction to twilight, sharing a bizarreness with 'les fous' but replacing excitation with chronic irritability. Whereas these two examples dominated the original poem, here they become in a sense digressive, not in their thematic substance but rather in their tone. The chicken-throwing incident always risked appearing comic, but the 1862 addition of 'dans lequel il croyait voir je ne sais quel insultant hiéroglyphe' renders it painfully burlesque. It is as if twilight induces in the friend a state perversely akin to 'cet état mystérieux et temporaire de l'esprit, où la profondeur de la vie, hérissée de ses problèmes multiples, se révèle tout entière dans le spectacle, si naturel et si trivial qu'il soit, qu'on a sous les yeux – où le premier objet venu devient symbole parlant' (I, 430). It is possible of course that the irony of this dubiously privileged moment is self-directed; Baudelaire's 'mauvais vitrier', like the 'maître d'hôtel', is victim of a satanic irritability provoked by an apparently trivial object. In 1862 the second friend becomes transformed into an 'ambitieux blessé' incapable of finding satisfaction (a modification which is particularly interesting in view of Baudelaire's own application for a seat in the Académie). But he too is treated ironically, in the contrast between noble syntax on the one hand and familiar tone and unpleasant-sounding neologism on the other in 'que s'exerçait rageusement sa manie crépusculeuse'. The major function of both examples, here and in the original, is to throw into relief the poet's own reaction. In the 1855 text the contrast led simply to the general comment that 'bien qu'il ne soit pas rare de voir la même cause engendrer deux effets contraires, cela m'intrigue et m'étonne toujours', a restrained conclusion which seems a deliberate suppression of the lyrical impulse, curbed by the search for a sonnet-like precision. The 1862 text offers no such closure; the introduction of the slightly tentative 'comme', made possible by the passive construction ('j'en suis toujours comme intrigué et alarmé'), adds subtlety and inconclusiveness to the mood. The way is left open for the lyrical surge of lines 35–9, which, whilst having the force of an explosion, is not a gratuitous or unprepared addition. The transformation of 'l'ombre qui fait la lumière dans mon esprit fait la nuit dans le leur' into 'la nuit qui mettait ses ténèbres dans leur esprit fait la lumière dans le mien' is beautifully purposeful, in that the effect on the poet is now promoted to the main clause, producing a carefully ordered sequence the elements of which are systematically retuned in a lyrical register in lines 35–6, where 'nuit' and 'ténèbres' are apostrophized and 'la lumière' becomes 'une fête intérieure'. This high lyricism is very different from the *Revue fantaisiste* version of this paragraph, which there opened the poem:

La tombée de la nuit a toujours été pour moi le signal d'une fête intérieure et comme la délivrance d'une angoisse. Dans les solitudes comme dans les rues d'une capitale, l'assombrissement du jour et le scintillement des étoiles et des lanternes éclairent mon esprit.

The flat closing sentence contains no excitement and, with its repeated 'et' and long-winded double subject, might even be thought cumbersome. The repositioning of the paragraph in 1862, drawing it closer to 'la nuit . . . fait la lumière dans le mien', allows Baudelaire to drop 'l'assombrissement du jour . . . éclaire[nt] mon esprit' which expresses the same idea. This emendation is part of a general tautening. The phrase 'des plaines', for instance, seeks to balance with 'd'une capitale' and to stiffen the antithesis between rural space and urban compression (the change from 'rues' to 'labyrinthes pierreux' has the same effect); the insertion of 'explosion' allows the syntax to support the ABAB structure (rural/urban/rural/urban) perfectly. As his climax Baudelaire takes the combination 'fête'/'délivrance' and, keeping major phonetic elements, expands them into the dazzling allegory: 'le feu d'artifice de la déesse Liberté'. The poeticization of these lines succeeds so admirably that Georges Blin goes so far as to suggest that with suitable typographical disposition they could stand as verse (Blin 1948, 158). It is indeed instructive to see how Baudelaire takes uninspired prose and flexes it into 'une prose poétique' nicely adapted to the 'mouvements lyriques de l'âme' (I, 275–6). Since this paragraph belongs both to the original material (in its substance) and to the new material (in its mood), it is a key transitional passage, emblematic of the change wrought by the poet. One further achievement of these lines is that the 'signal d'une fête intérieure' supplies a unifying, contrastive echo of the earlier 'signal de sabbat'; the poet's reaction to evening is set against that of the 'infortunés' as well as against that of the 'deux amis'.

What can one conclude about the modifications brought to the original four paragraphs? The most striking tactic adopted by Baudelaire is his conscious widening of the gap between different tones: the addition of 'je ne sais quel insultant hiéroglyphe' pushes towards the burlesque, while the reworking seen in lines 35–9 draws the reader into lyricism. It is scarcely apppropriate to ask, as Suzanne Bernard does, 'comment [Baudelaire] n'a-t-il pas senti qu'il greffait un second poème sur le premier, différent de caractère et d'inspiration?' (Bernard 1959, 118). Scarcely appropriate, since the clash and clamour of tones is to be sought, not smoothed away. Baudelaire not only establishes a difference between first and second poem (to use Bernard's terms) but exaggerates a difference *within* the original poem. The polarization of burlesque and lyricism fashions a 'soubresaut de la conscience' with quite deliberate intent. The modifications to the original material show Baudelaire mastering the art of that 'prose poétique' capable of capturing the unpredictable acrobatics of the mind, an 'idéal obsédant' confessed to in his 1862 *lettre–préface* (I, 275–6).

As the poem draws to its close, the text, returning to the immediacy of lines 1–9, becomes a duel between the descriptive voice and the elusive intricacy of its material. The opening paragraphs rested on the contrast between 'les pauvres esprits fatigués' and 'les infortunés que le soir ne calme pas', a contrast which excluded the narrator as observer; the central paragraphs proposed a further contrast, now including the narrator and indeed throwing into prominence his own reaction to twilight. The final paragraphs narrow the focus to concentrate on the narrator's personal struggle with his interpretative task. Contrastive groups disappear. Construction by antithesis is abandoned in favour of a technique of determined accumulation which fights to appropriate the increasing complexity of this special hour. The interpretative weapon is the same as in lines 1–3: analogy. But whereas there the thoughts of the 'esprits fatigués' passively took on the 'couleurs tendres et indécises du crépuscule', here the roles are reversed: the details of the outer scene ('les lueurs roses', 'les feux des lampes', 'les lourdes draperies') are obliged to imitate the drama of the human soul. This firmly homo-centric vision (reinforced later by the way in which the stars are made to represent the workings of the human imagination) indicates already a creative victory in which the meaninglessness or hostility of things is overcome; it allows the poet to shrug off the 'oppression victorieuse de la nuit'. And the simplicity of the earlier equation ('pensées'/'couleurs') is now replaced by a vastly more complex algebra: qualifying clauses accompany each of the three subjects, layers of comparison ('comme l'agonie du jour . . .') and metaphor ('les lourdes draperies') serve to complicate the major analogy generated by the verb 'imitent', so that the very syntax mimes the 'sentiments compliqués' which are the true centre of attention.[7]

As if these analogies are insufficient, Baudelaire launches another description, making no attempt to conceal the nature of his effort ('On

168

dirait encore d'une . . .'). The carefully proposed metaphor of the dress (linked by some to the 'robes surannées' of 'Recueillement'), so urban in its connotations, belongs to a set of metaphors which go to the heart of Baudelairean poetics, what might be called, at the risk of sounding pretentious, his poetics of the glimpse. On a simple erotic level, we find it in 'A une mendiante rousse':

> Blanche fille aux cheveux roux,
> Dont la robe par ses trous
> Laisse voir la pauvreté
> Et la beauté.

The images of eyes behind tears, of 'soleils mouillés/De ces ciels brouillés' in 'L'Invitation au voyage' are further examples of beauty glimpsed through a veil. But the essential matrix for such images is that found in *Notes nouvelles sur Edgar Poe*:

C'est à la fois par la poésie et *à travers* la poésie, par et *à travers* la musique que l'âme entrevoit les splendeurs situées derrière le tombeau.

(II, 334; the italics are Baudelaire's)

Poetry is the gauze through which paradise is perceived.[8] The marvellous dress, which in its various parts is at once 'éclatante' and 'transparente et sombre', hints at a whole poetics and metaphysics. To its spatial dimension is added that of time, in a simile boxed so typically within a comparison ('comme sous le noir présent transperce le délicieux passé'). The two dimensions are of course closely intertwined in Baudelaire's universe, but this particular *rapprochement* is a fine illustration of the poet's comment: 'profondeur de l'espace, allégorie de la profondeur du temps' (I, 430–1). With such imaginative leaps, Baudelaire multiplies the suggestivity of his conclusion, demanding an effort from the reader altogether different from that demanded by the anecdotes of lines 15–34.

Ironically it is the beauty of these closing paragraphs that has caused unease: such fine expansive poetry deserves more impressive harbingers. But this is to fail to see that the beauty gains precisely by being in the context of what is largely analytical commentary, in the same way as the 'feux de la fantaisie' shine more brightly set in a sky of deepest black. The powerful effect to be had from relief, the juxtaposition of the intense and the neutral, is one that Baudelaire cultivates with growing confidence. 'Recueillement', with its much-admired opening and closing lines which in Valéry's view render the rest 'nul et inexistant' (Valéry 1957–60, I, 610), audaciously demonstrates (as we have seen above, pp. 135–8) in sonnet form the aesthetics of relief, and indeed provides a model for this prose-poem in its tripartite division; both poems sandwich prosaic lines of little resonance between a poetic introduction and an even richer conclusion. There is little doubt that Baudelaire recognized this use of relief as a technique, a fact confirmed by the Asselineau anecdote cited earlier (p. 136).

It is important to reflect, although rather obvious, that the 'art de la gradation' implied in that anecdote can take place only in time. The 'weak' lines are redeemed and given their function retrospectively by the success of the strong lines. In 'Le Crépuscule du soir' the clash of tones has been noted; but it is the ordering of the tones that is crucial, their passage through time. (Try, for instance, to imagine the poem with the anecdotal and lyrical passages reversed.) The moving lyricism of the conclusion resolves all dissonances and persuades the reader to accept the switches of direction. The space crossed by the poem ultimately transforms the discordances into harmony, just as the 'foule de cris' blended musically as they moved through 'les nuées transparentes' to the narrator's balcony. This musical recuperation is one of the lessons given by the poem in its transformed state.

The reworking has created an experimental poem, odd as Baudelaire intended his prose-poems to be, and provocatively so. The 'ordonnance artistique' may not be as convention would wish but it does exist. In the *Notes nouvelles sur Edgar Poe* (1857), Baudelaire, talking of the idea of unity in a work of art, insists on an important distinction: 'la condition vitale de toute œuvre d'art, l'Unité; – je ne veux pas parler de l'unité dans la conception, mais de l'unité dans l'impression, de la *totalité* de l'effet' (II, 332). The distinction between the two types of unity, in a passage largely plagiarized from Poe, is significantly Baudelaire's own. The poet implies that a work may be born of different ideas and different sparks of inspiration, but that this disparateness need not be detrimental provided that the effect on the reader is eventually one of unity. Baudelaire underlines the word '*totalité*', since the vital 'unité dans l'impression' is achieved through a cumulative reading in which everything, whether indirectly or directly, leads to the conclusion: 'Tout pour le dénoûment!' (II, 331). The transformation of 'Le Crépuscule du soir' shows these artistic notions being put into practice in a way that would have surprised Poe. From what we know of the poem's history the 'unité dans la conception' is evidently absent, but Baudelaire's skill in integrating his material and particularly the irresistible power of his conclusion ensure that the 'unité dans l'impression' is singularly preserved.

NOTES

1 The poetics of craft

1 See Benjamin (1973) *passim*.
2 For a consistently sensitive discussion of those images of the poet to be found in Baudelaire's literary criticism (and sometimes elsewhere), see Lloyd (1981).

2 A singular clarity of timbre, I: sound repetition and conventional form

1 Much of the material in Chapters 2 and 3 is a remodelling and an abridgement of the arguments proposed in my earlier monograph, *Some Functions of Sound-Repetition in 'Les Fleurs du Mal'* (1975).
2 Repetition naturally refers to repetition of identical phonemes. But I occasionally feel justified in including in a pattern non-identical but similar sounds, *i.e.* pairs of voiced and unvoiced consonants ([b/p, g/k, z/s, v/f, d/t, ʒ/ʃ]), nasal vowels ([ɑ̃, ɛ̃, ɔ̃, œ̃]), the semi-vowels [w] and [ɥ] and certain pairs of vowels ([ɛ/e, y/u, œ/ø, a/ɑ]).
3 Roy Lewis (1982), 133–7, uses the term 'amplified rhymes'. His whole chapter on rhyme (126–48) is required reading.
4 For a more detailed discussion of how Baudelaire succeeds in merging and translating his sources, see Chesters (1984).

4 Sound patterns and the secrets of composition

1 Much valuable work has already been done in this field. The most exhaustive commentary has been given by Nuiten (1979) in an excellent, readable book. Shorter studies have also been illuminating, particularly Alison Fairlie's essay, 'Mène-t-on la foule dans les ateliers?' (1981, 228–49). This essay, as well as being a pleasure to read, contains a useful bibliography of relevant works (246–7, notes 5 and 6). Of these one might cite Séguin (1938, 164–95); Doucet (1957); Noyer-Weidner (1964; 1976, 180–212); and Pommier (1968, 150–69). One could also add the article by F. W. Leakey and Claude Pichois on the different versions of 'Les Sept Vieillards' (1973) and another essay by Alison Fairlie on 'Une gravure fantastique' (1981, 216–27). Most general studies on Baudelaire contain some pages devoted to variants.

2 For other examples of this uncontroversial point, see the variants of 'A celle qui est trop gaie', lines 10–11 and particularly lines 33–4 where the more intense 'vertigineuse' took the place of 'délicieuse' in the final stanzas:

> Pour châtier ta chair joyeuse,
> Pour meurtrir ton sein pardonné,
> Et faire à ton flanc étonné
> Une blessure large et creuse,
>
> Et, vertigineuse douceur!
> A travers ces lèvres nouvelles,
> Plus éclatantes et plus belles,
> T'infuser mon venin, ma sœur!

The [d-s-ø/d-sœ] of 'délicieuse douceur' is sacrificed, the internal rhyme, 'joyeuse'/'creuse', is preserved and enhanced by the [ʒ] (to give [ʒwajøz/ -ʒekrøz/-ʒinøz]), and the [vɛrt] of the new adjective launches the dominant pattern of the following lines, the [tr-vɛr/ɛvr/vɛ] of 'travers'/'lèvres'/ 'nouvelles'.

3 I am adopting the chronological order followed by Leakey and Pichois (1973).

4 This virtuoso performance rather overshadows the following similar but less impressive change (in 'Les Sept Vieillards') from:

> Les fantômes le jour raccrochent le passant;
> Les mystères partout coulent comme des sèves

to

> Où le spectre en plein jour raccroche le passant!
> Les mystères partout coulent comme des sèves.

The tiny introduction of 'Où le' [ul] prepares the ground for its much more important, metaphorically rich, internal rhyme, 'coulent', so forceful that it displaces the main caesural stress.

5 Rhymes

1 The phrase 'seul générateur du vers français' is taken from Ténint (1844, 101).

2 See *Corres.*, I, 376–7 for Baudelaire's request for a rhyming dictionary (made to Poulet-Malassis) and his clear statement that he had never owned one. For a brief but illuminating account of the relationship between a poet and such a dictionary, see 'Nerval et Richelet', Fairlie (1981), 304–7.

3 Cited by D. H. T. Scott (1977, 20).

4 See Clive Scott (1980, 104–27) for a persuasive and informative presentation of rhyme viewed with the same stress on context.

5 For a more developed reflection on this 'juxtaposition', see Chesters (1985b).

6 Banville's words are nicely appropriate, even though he is talking of end-rhymes: 'Mais surtout ne faites jamais rimer ensemble deux adverbes, si ce n'est par farce et ironie' (Banville 1872, 75).

7 See his article in *Le Boulevard*, 26 January 1862.

8 Prévost (1953) has some excellent pages (322–4) on the influence of rhyme in the creative process.

9 See Roy Lewis (1982, 141–2), for the hypothesis that the nineteenth century still found it acceptable to give both endings the pronunciation [ɛr].

10 It is not possible to move away from the subject of rhyme-schemes and stanza forms without mentioning the sonnet, the most frequent form of poem found in *Les Fleurs du Mal*. The sonnet, after all, is commonly defined as a fourteen-line poem divided into four stanzas (two quatrains and two tercets) and displaying an interlocking rhyme-scheme in the tercets. Baudelaire's exploitation and violation of the sonnet's characteristic features have been investigated by several critics. The reader is referred to Cassagne (1906), Prévost (1953), Schofer (1970), Gendre (1976), D.H.T. Scott (1977), Rachel Killick (1980) and Claude Pichois (1982).

6 Pattern, expectation, surprise

1 Banville's advice reads: 'Tâchez d'accoupler le moins possible un substantif avec un substantif, un verbe avec un verbe, un adjectif avec un adjectif' (Banville 1872, 75).

2 Valéry, for example, declines to supply a partner for the B-rhyme 'menteur' in the last stanza of 'L'Insinuant'; instead, he offers the reader a third A-rhyme.

3 Much of what follows has been fertilized by Barbara Smith's *Poetic Closure* (1968).

7 'Lapse' and recuperation

1 The key critical text to read on Baudelaire's creative difficulty is Pichois 1967, 242–61.

2 For a longer defence of 'Recueillement', see Riffaterre (1971, 184–9).

3 For a detailed examination of this rule and Baudelaire's treatment of it, see Chesters (1985a).

4 See Chesters (1985b).

8 Experimentation and urban poetics, I: the limits of poetry

1 For the circumstances and precise transcription of the manuscript (of both poem and letter), see Leakey and Pichois (1973).

2 For a thorough and interesting account of this exceptional *Festschrift*, see Leakey (1968).

3 Disguised reference to himself is not uncommon in Baudelaire: *cf.* the anonymous poet to whom he attributes a stanza from 'Les Phares' in his

Exposition universelle, 1855 (II, 595), and the 'poète ... qu'un vers de Malherbe ... jette dans de longues extases' alluded to in *L'Œuvre et la vie d'Eugène Delacroix* (II, 754).

4 I define Baudelaire's early poetry as that written in or before 1851, the latest possible date of composition of 'Le Crépuscule du soir' – the reason for this seemingly arbitrary definition will become apparent. Argument based on the chronology of Baudelaire's verse always needs to be accompanied by an important caveat. The date of composition of his early poems (in particular) only rarely coincides with the date of the first extant texts of these poems. Although we may be fairly certain that 'Je t'adore à l'égal ...', for example, was written in its first version before 1843, that first version will almost certainly have differed, in some stylistic details, from its first extant text (in this case, the proofs of the 1857 *Fleurs du Mal*). It is considerably less likely that the verse-form will have changed. Thus, for those early couplet-poems of which we have no version earlier than 1857 but of which we are more or less sure that pre-1851 versions existed, I am presuming that the verse-form remained unaltered. These poems are: 'Allégorie', 'La Béatrice', 'La servante au grand cœur ...', 'Je n'ai pas oublié ...', 'J'aime le souvenir ...', 'Je t'adore à l'égal ...', 'Tu mettrais l'univers ...', 'Paysage' and 'Les Métamorphoses du vampire'. 'Le Crépuscule du matin', first published in 1852 but thought to have existed in an earlier version, also qualifies as an early poem. Five couplet-poems have first extant texts which pre-date 1851: 'A une Malabaraise', 'Je n'ai pas pour maîtresse ...' (AABB quatrains), 'Tous imberbes alors ...' (first texts: 1841–6), 'Le Vin des chiffonniers' (first text: 1848–51) and 'Châtiment de l'orgueil' (first text: 1850). Evidence regarding the existence of early versions of certain poems is found in Ernest Prarond's letter to Eugène Crépet written in 1886; see the full text and Claude Pichois's annotations in Pichois 1967, 11–36. Throughout the preparation of this chapter I have relied heavily on F. W. Leakey's investigations into the chronology of Baudelaire's texts (see Leakey 1967, 343–6, and Leakey 1969, xiii–xiv and particularly 341–73).

5 It is true that 'Tous imberbes alors ...', another early extant text, contained six infractions in its 78 lines. I would argue that this piece is quite untypical in its convoluted syntax (which affects the verse-form) and that its style is partly in imitation of Sainte-Beuve, to whom the poem is addressed and whose poetic manner is characterized, according to Baudelaire, by 'les longs enlacements des phrases symboliques' (see pp. 79–80 above.) Such 'enlacements' as are to be found in the poem are perhaps intended to be more typical of Sainte-Beuve than Baudelaire. Both this poem and the slightly later 'Châtiment de l'orgueil' (a fable-like poem, rare in Baudelaire, in which the narrator skilfully manipulates the verse for dramatic effect) show the poet to be capable of flexibility in his use of the couplet. The decision not to exploit it more often is all the more significant.

6 *Lettre–préface* written for Ténint, 1844.

7 For thought-provoking reflections on the tone and other aspects of

Baudelaire's prose-poetry, see Alison Fairlie's two seminal articles in Fairlie 1981, 150–63 and 164–75.

8 Taking up the vocabulary of the poet's letter to Morel, R. Kopp and Claude Pichois affirm that 'ces poèmes, évoquant sur un ton volontairement prosaïque le fantastique de la capitale, marquent la limite extrême atteinte par Baudelaire dans les poèmes en vers' (Kopp and Pichois 1969, 83).

9 Occasionally the result of 'une de ces longues phrases, s'étendant sur plusieurs strophes, qu'affectionne Baudelaire dans les poèmes de sa dernière manière' (Leakey and Pichois 1973, 270).

10 Other notable examples are to be found in 'Le Vampire', 'Un fantôme', 'L'Amour et le crâne' and 'La Fin de la journée' (all poems written in lines shorter than the Alexandrine). A less conspicuous 'run-on' effect between tercets is found in several Baudelaire sonnets (*e.g.* 'Le Mort joyeux' or 'Spleen: Pluviôse . . .') but rarely gives the impression of dislocation.

9 Experimentation and urban poetics, II: the transformation of a prose-poem

1 It was published in *Fontainebleau. Hommage à C. F. Denecourt* (1855), *Le Présent* (1857), *Revue fantaisiste* (1861) and *Le Figaro* (1864); although prepared for publication in *La Presse* in the autumn of 1862, it never progressed beyond proofs. This chapter appeared in Bowie 1982, 24–37. I am grateful for the advice given during the preparation for this earlier publication, particularly by Alison Fairlie.

2 The three poems were grouped together in *Le Présent, Revue fantaisiste*, proofs corrected for *La Presse* and in Baudelaire's list of 50 poems drawn up in preparation for the publication of the *Petits poëmes en prose* (1869) and eventually overseen by Asselineau and Banville after the poet's death in 1867.

3 'La Solitude' and 'Les Projets' are in the same category. The 'morceaux remaniés' are 'L'Horloge', 'La Chevelure' and 'L'Invitation au voyage', poems in which a few details have been changed.

4 For a complete presentation of variants, see Kopp 1969, 63–6; the present text has been established from this editor.

5 See, for example, the openings of 'Le Fou et la Vénus' ('Quelle admirable journée!'), 'A une heure du matin' ('Enfin! seul!'), 'Le Gâteau' ('Je voyageais'), 'Les Yeux des pauvres' ('Ah! vous voulez savoir pourquoi je vous haïs aujourd'hui'), 'Un cheval de race' ('Elle est bien laide') or 'Perte d'auréole' (' "Eh! quoi! vous ici, mon cher?" ').

6 The mention of two proper names connected with Lyons (the 'hospice des Antiquailles' and 'Fourvières' [sic]) has been seen as a 'curieuse résurgence d'un souvenir lyonnais' (Kopp 1969, 272). It also suggests that Baudelaire, at the time of reworking 'Le Crépuscule du soir', was prepared to see his prose-poetry as urban rather than specifically Parisian. He does speak of 'la fréquentation *des grandes villes*' in his *lettre–préface* to the prose-poems published in *La Presse*; and in the second of the 'Notes diverses sur *L'Art philosophique*', he records 'le vertige senti dans *les grandes villes*' and the

'sensations d'un homme sensible en visitant *une grande ville inconnue*' (II, 607; the italics in the last three quotations are mine).

7 In order to set into a wider context the description of night contained in lines 35–50, see the thorough and illuminating article by Gérald Antoine (1967).

8 Inhabiting this same bright, rarely-glimpsed paradise is the redemptive 'Etre aux ailes de *gaze*', whose theatrical analogue in 'L'Irréparable', the 'être, qui n'était que lumière, or et *gaze*', lays low 'l'énorme Satan' (the italics are mine).

BIBLIOGRAPHY

Antoine, Gérald 1967, 'La Nuit chez Baudelaire', *Revue d'Histoire littéraire de la France*, 67, 375–401.

Aragon, Louis 1975, *Les Yeux d'Elsa* (Paris: Seghers).

Austin, L. J. 1956, *L'Univers poétique de Baudelaire: Symbolisme et Symbolique* (Paris: Mercure de France).

Bandy, W. T. 1972, *Index des rimes des 'Fleurs du Mal'* (Nashville: Vanderbilt University).

Banville, Théodore de 1872, *Petit Traité de poésie française* (Paris: Charpentier).

1886, *Dames et Demoiselles* (Paris: Charpentier).

1972, *Œuvres*, 5 vols (Geneva: Slatkine Reprint).

Barthes, Roland 1972, *Le Degré zéro de l'écriture, suivi de Nouveaux Essais critiques* (Paris: Seuil).

Benjamin, Walter 1973, *Charles Baudelaire: A Lyric Poet in the Era of High Capitalism* (London: New Left Books).

Bernard, Suzanne 1959, *Le Poème en prose de Baudelaire jusqu'à nos jours* (Paris: Nizet).

Black, Michael 1975, 'Why it is so, and not otherwise', *New Literary History*, 6, 477–89.

Blin, Georges 1948, *Le Sadisme de Baudelaire* (Paris: Corti).

Bonnefoy, Yves 1969, 'Baudelaire contre Rubens', *L'Ephémère*, 9, 72–112.

Bowie, Malcolm, Alison Fairlie and Alison Finch, eds. 1982, *Baudelaire, Mallarmé, Valéry: New Essays in Honour of Lloyd Austin* (Cambridge: Cambridge University Press).

Brûlat, P. 1892, 'Une Statue à Baudelaire. Chez M. Leconte de Lisle', *Le Journal*, 30 September.

Brunetière, F. 1887, 'Baudelaire', *Revue des Deux Mondes*, 1 June.

1894, *L'Evolution de la poésie lyrique en France* (Paris: Hachette).

Carter, A. E. 1963, *Baudelaire et la critique française, 1868–1917* (Columbia: University of South Carolina Press).

Cassagne, A. 1906, *Versification et métrique de Ch. Baudelaire* (Paris: Hachette; Slatkine reprint, 1973).

Chambers, Ross 1971a, 'The Artist as Performing Dog', *Comparative Literature*, 23, 312–24.

1971b, ' "L'art du comédien" ou le regardant et le regardé. Autour d'un mythe baudelairien', *Saggi e ricerche di letteratura francese*, 11, 189–260.

Bibliography

1978, 'Baudelaire et l'espace poétique: à propos du "Soleil"' in *Le Lieu et la Formule: Hommage à Marc Eigeldinger*, 111–20 (Neuchâtel: La Baconnière).

Chesters, Graham 1975, *Some Functions of Sound-Repetition in 'Les Fleurs du Mal'*. Occasional Papers in Modern Languages, 11 (Hull: Hull University Press).

1978, 'Baudelaire and the Limits of Poetry', *French Studies*, 32, 420–34.

1982, 'The Transformation of a Prose-Poem: Baudelaire's "Crépuscule du soir"', in *Baudelaire, Mallarmé, Valéry: New Essays in Honour of Lloyd Austin*, eds. Malcolm Bowie, Alison Fairlie and Alison Finch, 24–37 (Cambridge: Cambridge University Press).

1984, 'A Political Reading of Baudelaire's "L'Artiste inconnu" ("Le Guignon")', *Modern Language Review*, 79, 64–76.

1985a, 'Baudelaire et un problème de versification: voyelle + e atone', *Bulletin des études parnassiennes*, 7, 15–26.

1985b, 'Baudelaire and Zeugma', *Parnasse*, 2, 54–68.

Desprez, Louis 1884, *L'Evolution naturaliste* (Paris).

Doucet, J. 1957, 'Quelques variantes de Baudelaire', *Les Etudes classiques*, 25, 327–43.

Ducondut, A. 1863, *Examen critique de la versification française, classique et romantique* (Paris: Dupray de la Mahérie).

Empson, William 1961, *Seven Types of Ambiguity* (London: Penguin Reprint).

Faguet, E. 1910, 'Baudelaire', *La Revue*, 1 September.

Fairlie, Alison 1981, *Imagination and Language: Collected Essays on Constant, Baudelaire, Nerval and Flaubert* (Cambridge: Cambridge University Press).

Fongaro, A. 1973, 'Aux Sources du "Recueillement"', *Etudes baudelairiennes*, 3, 158–77.

Gendre, A. 1976, 'Examen syntaxique et stylistique de quelques sonnets baudelairiens', *Etudes baudelairiennes*, 8, 46–96.

Huret, J. 1891, *Enquête sur l'évolution littéraire* (Paris: Charpentier).

Jakobson, R. 1960 'Linguistics and Poetics', in *Style in Language*, ed. T. Sebeok (New York: Technology Press of M.I.T.).

Killick, Rachel 1980, 'The Sonnet in *Les Fleurs du Mal*', *Dalhousie French Studies*, 2, 21–39.

Kopp, Robert 1969, *Charles Baudelaire. Petits Poëmes en prose* (Paris: Corti).

and Pichois, Claude 1969, *Les Années Baudelaire. Etudes baudelairiennes*, 1 (Neuchâtel: La Baconnière).

La Drière, C. 1965, 'Prosody', in *Encyclopedia of Poetry and Poetics*, ed. A. S. Preminger (Princeton: Princeton University Press).

Landais, N. and Barré, L. 1853, *Dictionnaire des rimes françaises* (Paris: Didier).

Leakey, F. W. 1967, 'Pour une étude chronologique des *Fleurs du Mal*: "Harmonie du soir"', *Revue d'Histoire littéraire de la France*, 67, 343–56.

1968, 'A Festschrift of 1855: Baudelaire and the *Hommage à C. F. Denecourt*', in *Studies in French Literature presented to H. W. Lawton*, eds. J. C. Ireson, I. D. McFarlane and Garnet Rees, 175–202 (Manchester: Manchester University Press).

1969, *Baudelaire and Nature* (Manchester: Manchester University Press).

and Pichois, Claude 1973, 'Les sept versions des "Sept Vieillards"', *Etudes baudelairiennes*, 3, 262–89.

Lewis, R. A. 1970, 'The Rhythmical Creation of Beauty', *Forum for Modern Language Studies*, 6, 103–26.

1976, "La Cloche fêlée": an Essay in the Analysis of a Poem', *Zambezia*, 4, suppl., 1–27.

1982, *On Reading French Verse: A Study of Poetic Form* (Oxford: Clarendon Press).

Lloyd, Rosemary 1981, *Baudelaire's Literary Criticism* (Cambridge: Cambridge University Press).

Mallarmé, S. 1945, *Œuvres complètes*, eds. H. Mondor, G. Jean Aubry, Bibliothèque de la Pléiade (Paris: NRF, Gallimard).

Maurras, Charles 1902, 'La Maladie de Baudelaire', *La Gazette de France*, 20 October.

Meschonnic, Henri 1973, *Pour la poétique III.* (Paris: Gallimard).

Noyer-Weidner, A. 1964, 'Stilempfinden und Stilentwicklung Baudelaires im Spiegel seiner Varianten', in *Linguistics and Literary Studies in Honor of Helmut A. Hatzfeld*, ed. A. S. Crisafulli, 302–27 (Washington: The Catholic University Press of America; reprinted in Noyer-Weidner, 1976, 180–212).

1976 (ed.), *Baudelaire* (Darmstadt: Wissenschaftliche Buchgesellschaft).

Nuiten, Henk 1979, *Les Variantes des 'Fleurs du Mal' et des 'Epaves' de Charles Baudelaire* (Amsterdam: APA-Holland University Press).

Olovsson, H. 1924, *Les Rimes de trois poètes romantiques: Musset, Gautier, Baudelaire* (Lund: C. Bloms Boktryckeri).

Pichois, Claude 1967, *Baudelaire: études et témoignages* (Neuchâtel: La Baconnière).

1973 (ed.), *Lettres à Baudelaire, Etudes baudelairiennes*, 4–5 (Neuchâtel: La Baconnière).

1982, 'Nerval, Baudelaire et les formes littéraires', in *Baudelaire, Mallarmé, Valéry: New Essays in Honour of Lloyd Austin*, eds. Malcolm Bowie, Alison Fairlie and Alison Finch, 95–104 (Cambridge: Cambridge University Press).

Poe, E. A. 1951, *Œuvres en prose*, trans. Charles Baudelaire, ed. Y.-G. Le Dantec, Bibliothèque de la Pléiade (Paris: NRF, Gallimard).

Pommier, J. 1968, *Autour de l'édition originale des 'Fleurs du Mal'* (Geneva: Slatkine Reprint).

Prévost, J. 1953, *Baudelaire: essai sur l'inspiration et la création poétique* (Paris: Mercure de France).

Quicherat, L. 1850, *Traité de versification française*, second edition (Paris: Hachette).

Richards, I. A. 1936, *The Philosophy of Rhetoric* (London, New York: Oxford University Press).

Riffaterre, M. 1971, *Essais de stylistique structurale* (Paris: Flammarion).

Ruff, M. 1967, 'Baudelaire et le poème en prose', *Zeitschrift für französische Sprache und Literatur*, 77, 116–23.

Bibliography

Schaettel, M. 1976, 'Schèmes sensoriels et dynamiques dans "Parfum exotique" de Baudelaire', *Etudes baudelairiennes*, 8, 97–118.

Schofer, K. 1970, *Baudelaire the Sonneteer* (unpublished Ph.D. dissertation, University of Princeton).

Scott, Clive 1980, *French Verse-Art: A Study* (Cambridge: Cambridge University Press).

Scott, D. H. T. 1977, *Sonnet Theory and Practice in Nineteenth-Century France: Sonnets on the Sonnet*, Occasional Papers in Modern Languages, 12 (Hull: Hull University Press).

Séguin, M. 1938, *Aux Sources vivantes du symbolisme: Génie des 'Fleurs du Mal'* (Paris: Messein).

Smith, B. H. 1968, *Poetic Closure* (Chicago: University of Chicago Press).

Starobinski, J. 1970, *Portrait de l'artiste en saltimbanque* (Geneva: Skira).

1975, 'Les Rimes du vide', *Nouvelle Revue de psychanalyse*, 11, 133–43.

Ténint, W. 1844, *Prosodie de l'école moderne* (Paris: Didier).

Valéry, P. 1957–60, *Œuvres*, 2 vols, ed. J. Hytier, Bibliothèque de la Pléiade (Paris: NRF, Gallimard).

Verlaine, P. 1972, *Œuvres en prose*, ed. J. Borel, Bibliothèque de la Pléiade (Paris: NRF, Gallimard).

INDEX

Index

Index

183

Index